...probably won't have heard of ...

arguably he has done more to protect nature than David
Attenborough. We have plenty of environmental warriors
keen to face down the engineers who would destroy our
natural world. But what we also need in the Anthropocene are
environmental arbitrators and conciliators to bridge the divide.
Purseglove is one such unsung hero ... and he writes beautifully.'
Fred Pearce, *New Scientist*

'An engrossing and eye-opening book, epic in scope,
surprisingly enjoyable, astute, wise and profoundly important.'
Richard Smyth, *Geographical*

'Purseglove will have you poring over food labels in a bid to
save natural landscapes and the animals that rely on them.'
Liz Kalaugher, *BBC Wildlife*

'Purseglove offers hope. Never underestimating the damage we
have done, nor the difficulty of repair, his is a positive message.'
Lord Deben, *Country Life*

'*Working with Nature* is part-memoir, part-blueprint,
part manifesto ... Purseglove's world is tangible,
sensual and beautifully described.'
The Planner

This updated paperback edition published in 2020

First published in Great Britain in 2019 by
Profile Books:
29 Cloth Fair
London EC1A 7JQ
www.profilebooks.com

Typeset in Sina to a design by Henry Iles.

ISBN 978-1788161602
e-ISBN 978-1782834960

Working with Nature

Saving and using the world's wild places

Jeremy Purseglove

PROFILE BOOKS

For Sue Taylor,
Laura Purseglove and
Eleanor Purseglove

Contents

Gardening the globe

I am in Central Asia, standing on the banks of a mighty river, famous in history as the Oxus, which flows down a gorge where wild tulips glow like fire coals among the rocks. From the almond and walnut forests of this Eden, flower bulbs were carried along the Silk Road to Europe. Emerging from the cliffs, the river fans out to create an immense inland delta of glittering channels, islands and silvery scrub. Eagles soar over this great wilderness and above them, seeming to float in the smoke-blue air, rise the snow-capped peaks of the majestic Pamirs.

Below me dredgers are mending a bank broken by floods which have obliterated farms and apricot orchards under a waste of river cobbles. Against the scale and elemental force of this river, the great machines seem like children's toys and the massive cubes of concrete shoring the bank appear no more than tumbled dice. As the project environmentalist I debate with the engineers whether to set back the banks to allow the river full rein or reclaim more land as the local people would prefer. But as a warming world melts the mountain snows to threaten unprecedented floods, our old certainties about cultivating nature are challenged as never before.

Surveying this embattled scene I realise that it is over thirty years since rivers took over my life and I entered a world where stone and steel are pitted against mere flowers, but where the seemingly fragile forces of nature seem increasingly able to fight back.

River engineering in Tajikistan with the mountains of Afghanistan beyond.
Against the might of nature the concrete blocks seem like tumbled dice.

My father was a botanist and, for as long as I can remember, plants and flowers have been at the centre of my life. An initial interest in flora soon widened to a fascination with landscapes, gardens and wild habitats and into a working life looking for practical ways to protect them, first as an ecologist in the water industry and then as an environmentalist worldwide.

What I do for a living is like gardening on a global scale. Working with engineers and developers, I make decisions that set aesthetics and ecology alongside the need to make the engineering stand up and the balance sheets work. I am not against development. Early in my professional life I came to realise that there is often a creative way of managing landscapes which can bring us their practical benefits without destroying their beauty and biodiversity. We *can* consume resources, provided we do so carefully and do not consume all of them. What I've learned of this approach to development is the subject of this book: asking and trying to answer the question as I survey threatened areas of forest and wetland, 'How can this landscape earn its keep and so secure its future?'

My initiation into the complexities and urgency of this question came in the 1970s, when I visited the Biesbosch delta of the Rhine in the Netherlands. This is one of Europe's great wetlands and it is now a National Park. At the time, the warden took me into his office and showed me two things: the encyclopedic book of regulations, which had been drawn up to defend the reserve, and an X-ray of his broken ribs. Even in civilised modern Holland, without an army of police to enforce the rules, he had been beaten up when he tried to persuade the local people who lived off the place to leave it alone for the wild birds. This was a lesson I never forgot. There are very few habitats, especially in the developing world, which you can protect by putting a fence around them. The real power over them lies in the hands of the person holding the chainsaw. So, if they are to survive, they need some kind of economic base which is self-policing. As the environmental sound bite goes: 'Use it or lose it.'

In 1977, as the first environmentalist in the British water industry, I was called out by a river engineer to untie a woman from a willow tree. She had warned the engineer that, if he chopped down the tree, he would have to take her with it. I didn't know about river engineers. I didn't then know that rivers had to be engineered. But the engineer explained his dilemma. Left untouched the tree would block the river, which would then inundate the nearby houses, including that of the protester. So would I persuade her to go home and leave him to get on with the job? She made it clear, however, that along with other ratepayers who paid the engineer's salary, she valued the river at the bottom of her garden not as a concrete drain but for its willows and dragonflies. Here was a seemingly irreconcilable conflict. But eventually the engineer and I designed a scheme which reduced the floods and still protected the trees.

My subsequent working life has been as a broker for nature conservation with civil engineers, those supremely practical professionals who build roads, supply water and facilitate agriculture. Like the attendants of apocalypse, they are the first on the scene to repair damage after flood, drought or even war. Theirs is a world of concrete, steel, specifications and mathematical certainties. Mine is a world of interesting insects, unusual weeds and the indefinable ways we value beautiful places. On the face of it these worlds are mutually exclusive; indeed, often on a collision course. But it didn't turn out like that during my time in the water industry. We found we could work together – that we could both control floods and conserve river habitats.

Engineers are excellent problem-solvers. Once they are presented with a course of action, they set to work. They can use the machines that had previously canalised rivers to create ponds – even put the bends back in rivers they had previously straightened. Mighty dredgers can be used to transplant delicate forget-me-nots and create a niche for nesting moorhens. They can do gardening on a heroic scale, and which is no mere prettification. Nature conservation is now a mainstream activity of the Environment Agency and trees are seen as a practical ways of reinforcing river banks, while adjacent wetlands are valued as a safety valve for floodwater. Working with nature is now understood as the most effective way to control flooding. This approach is no longer confined to Britain. It is practised by American engineers working throughout the USA and in 2007 I worked with a local community in Tajikistan to plant a new forest to prevent the banks of the mighty River Oxus from eroding and to help control the floods.

This work has taken me all over Britain and around the world: to Ghana, Bulgaria, China, Burundi, Rwanda, Mozambique, Iraq, India, Turkey, Albania, Tajikistan, Dubai, Kalimantan, Kazakhstan, Belize, Bangladesh, Papua New Guinea, the Bahamas, Pakistan and

Creative digger – a machine that was previously a destroyer of habitat now transplants waterside plants as part of creative river management.

Trinidad. I have carried out assessments for such major projects as a new bridge over the Zambezi between Zimbabwe and Zambia and for a bridge over the Nile at Aswan in Egypt. In 2010 I set off for many months in a small pickup, camping with a couple of local biologists to map a proposed 1,000-kilometre-long power line corridor in Mozambique.

These journeys have also taken me back to the countries where I had spent my childhood. I was born in Africa and spent many childhood years in the Far East and the Caribbean, where my father worked as an agriculturalist in the now vanished British Empire. What I learned in all those places and the adventures I had there have provided the basic material for this book, which is a voyage round the world and through a lifetime's work. As reportage from the front line of nature conservation it represents a snapshot of twenty-five years of environmental history at a time of unprecedented damage to the planet.

During those years I have witnessed many of the problems, and much of the damage – including some very inappropriate engineering. In Pakistan I was sent out to assess irrigation engineering designed to grow cotton. What I found was that, with best intentions but also with a lack of understanding of the full impacts of what they were doing, the engineers had created a saline desert incapable of growing any crops at all. On another occasion I worked on floodbanks beside the River Mekong in Vientiane in Laos. The banks had been insensitively located too close to the river and, instead of preserving the charming riverside teahouses and embankment avenues, these were swept away and the banks were surmounted by a motorway.

However, time and again I have found that the engineers can turn things around and use their skill and ingenuity not only to create fine landscapes and habitats but also to reverse the damage of previous thoughtless engineering. In 2005 I led the environmental team on a project to replace a major road in Hindhead in Surrey with a tunnel. This had long severed and damaged the outstanding landscape and habitat of the Devil's Punch Bowl but, only a decade on, peace and beauty are restored. In 2006 I was involved with the building of a small dam in Kazakhstan which, instead of destroying habitat, as is so often the case, restored part of the cruelly drained and exploited Aral Sea.

As with engineering, so with land use. A river should mean more than just a drain. A farm should be more than just a place that produces food. But all over the world, technology and money have led to single-crop monocultures which employ very few people and create impoverished landscapes, often with terrible side effects. This is something that I have often observed, whether employed to carry out audits on tropical plantations or working with British farmers to promote conservation on their land. Intensive cereal farming in England has all too often created a sterile habitat without birds or flowers and also worsens floods. The palm oil plantations of the Far East have destroyed the rainforest. In Turkey major dams have starved the downstream countries of water and the resulting droughts have exacerbated war. In Florida and the Caribbean intensive rice cultivation has destroyed mangrove swamps, which are wonderful for birdlife as well as providing a crucial defence against storms and rising seas. But here again the land can be managed much more creatively. In Bangladesh I carried out an audit on rice growing in the delta, where mixed cultivation of fish, vegetables and bamboo alongside the rice created a wonderfully diverse and sustainable landscape. Even the notorious monocultures of palm oil in Indonesia can be improved by setting aside sizeable nature reserves within the plantations, creating lagoons to reduce pollution from the palm oil mills and maintaining responsible policies in relation to the workforce.

We must grow food and other crops to survive, but there are plenty of decent alternatives to those grim industrialised monocultures. Following one model we can take a typical intensive modern farm and modify it, setting aside a proportion of land for habitats and building in a wider brief for the social and cultural assets, which it affects. And if we are lucky there are elegant, often traditional models which intrinsically create their own beauty and productivity. The bluebells in an English wood benefit from some woodland clearance for timber and firewood. The cocoa tree thrives best in the rainforest shade, so chocolate farmers will defend the forest to protect their livelihood. These are habitats that may be utilised in order to justify their existence. What is more, the sustainable commodities they produce can then be certified and marketed as environmentally friendly, which is good for business.

If abused, nature can take revenge on us, but it is also wonderfully forgiving. That redeeming relationship lies at the heart of this book. After all the arguments have been made, there is something else that keeps pulling me back to the eccentric and often uncomfortable boundary between ecology and heavy engineering. It is the places themselves. Landscapes are often their own best advocates. Many are the planning committees I have observed setting out on an inspection to decide a site's fate and then returning, rain-soaked and mud-spattered, but with a fresh determination in their eyes to save some meadow or copse which never seemed worthwhile in the abstract debate of the committee room. I will always remember haggling with a farmer to retain a riverside meander on his land as part of a river engineering scheme. Suddenly, as we looked at the site, the blue spark of a kingfisher shot down over the water like a low firework. 'You win,' he said. That bird sealed our bargain.

CHAPTER 1

The Orchid Gardens

Saving and using the forests of Indonesia

When we first arrived at the great house it rained for a week. My parents and I perched in its unfamiliar shadows, which smelled of bats and tropical damp. Only one room was free from leaks. Fungus and the fingers of fern sprouted on steps and windowsills, as if seeping out of the very seams of the neglected building. Outside the storm fell upon the garden and the encircling city like a World War. The sky flashed green. Heart-stopping thunder claps sent flocks of parrots screaming from the wind-lashed bamboos and then faded away over the trees with the rumble of retreating aircraft. Veils of warm rain, humming as they came, swarmed across the garden, consuming and dissolving everything they overtook. So unlike the timid patter of English rain, the downpour epitomised everything about this awesome place. It was absolute and immense.

It was my first experience of Asia. The year was 1954, I was five and my father had been appointed as director of Singapore's Botanic Gardens. Of course, as a child, everything seemed to me enormous from my lookout on the high verandah, where I could fit my head neatly beneath the house's polished timber handrails. But

Outside the Director's House in the Botanic Gardens in 1956, aged seven. Then as now the gardens were a world apart from the rest of Singapore.

returning, sixty years on, the house, now a museum, still seemed vast. Built on a hill in the 1860s, it has the scale and confidence of a Victorian railway station, with its soaring pillars supporting a lofty verandah, designed like all the living quarters to be upstairs to catch any available breeze which might alleviate the notoriously humid Singapore climate, cloying as a steam bath, reverberating with the hiss of cicadas by day and the piping of frogs by night.

The verandah projects like the prow of a ship, commanding panoramic views over a foaming ocean of tropical vegetation, culminating in the forest reserve, which is the heart of the Botanic Gardens. This forest is the last survivor of the dark jungles which had shadowed the whole of Singapore Island before the foundation of the city by Stamford Raffles. A shrunken relic, meticulously managed and exhaustively studied, there still clings to this little patch of trees a sense of the oldest Singapore: older than the seedy steaming colonial city of my childhood, now almost completely obliterated beneath the modern metropolis; and older than the first settlement. A neutral world of spiny rattans and stilt-rooted *Pandanus,* it is the last retreat of a rotting implacable greenness, long-banished from a city which, now more than any other in the world, epitomises control.

Nature has not been entirely exiled from the new Singapore. Far from it. The city is famous for its landscaping, a tradition partly inherited from the Botanic Gardens. However, the lush greenery, which creates such a successful foil to the freeways and tower blocks, is a highly manipulated tableau. The illusion of tropical luxuriance is created by the bedding out of thousands of flowering pot plants into a framework of punctiliously sprayed and weeded groundcover. The new Singapore is a computer capital of steel and glass, where all deviancy is outlawed, litter is unknown and police have the power to enter your property and empty the paddling pool or even a flower vase in case they are breeding mosquitoes. The old house and its gardens stand aloof from the tides of change, which lap up to its perimeters. This isolation, as I was to discover, has a long and dramatic history.

After we arrived and the rain finally stopped, we began to notice that we were sharing our home with a large company of fellow tenants and visitors. The most obvious were the monkeys, which seemed to regard us as rival occupants. They entered the house, stole the food, jumped on the dog and were only driven off by the catapults of our cook's six children. Our other companions belonged to the hours of darkness. At dusk, the flying foxes, most satanic-looking of the bat-tribe, would gather in chattering hordes to roost in the great tembusu tree. As the lights came on it was the turn of the stag beetles and geckos, which fought life-and-death battles in the suspended translucent bowls of the light shades, casting vast puppet-like shadows across the ceiling. Later still there was the occasional appearance of an eight foot python, which, after regular raids on the chicken run, was finally smoked out of its hollow tree and stuffed for the benefit of the Singapore Natural History Museum.

But by far the most entrenched and all-intrusive possessors of the house were the orchids. On the stairs, in the bathroom, lined up in serried ranks around the building, these unnatural-looking pot plants, their rigid fanlike growth tied to a cane and mulched with charcoal, were the true spirits of the place. *Dendrobiums* like flutings of shell-pink porcelain or coils of yellow-green pasta; freckled spidery *Arachnis;* succulent sunset-coloured *Vandas; Trichoglottis* like snippings of maroon flock wall paper and *Cattleyas* fit for a soprano's décolletage. Their sinister glamour was not enhanced by the whiff of dilute urine, with which they were watered as a primitive substitute for liquid fertiliser. My mother firmly announced that they had to go or she would. The orchids are flower made flesh and as far from the purity and fragility of a primrose as it is possible to be. Evolved by nature to survive the drilling rain and further hybridised to last in a bowl of water for up to a month, the cell tissue of their petals has the consistency of plastic. The only really convincing artificial flowers are imitation orchids. This is because the waxy originals don't look all that real either. Yet they encapsulate the contradictions which lie at the heart of all gardens and sum up our ambivalent relationship with the natural world, deeply rooted both in love and exploitation.

Orchids are status symbols, design accessories and the ultimate possession. They are stolen and smuggled. They make money. They have been the subject of bestselling books, notably *Orchid Fever*, which links the allure of their glistening orifices and rosy labial folds with sex. Their own highly evolved sex life, which encompasses pseudo-copulation with insects and symbiosis with rare invertebrates, trapped in elaborate nets and tumbled down chutes, suggests that Darwinian evolution, as with the plant breeding which further hybridises them, is ultimately self-destructive. The orchid is the modern version of the tulip, for which the seventeenth-century Dutch invested, gambled and lost fortunes. In Bangkok and Singapore it is now the basis of a multi-million-dollar cut-flower industry, which owes its entire existence to the research a quiet unworldly botanist carried out in the Singapore Botanic Gardens. However, the circumstances in which he carried out his research make for one of the most dramatic untold stories of twentieth-century science.

War and Eden

In February 1942 the tranquil Eden of the Botanic Gardens lay beneath a pall of oily smoke as Singapore burned on the eve of the Japanese invasion. Until the eleventh hour waltzes and gavottes had floated out from the Gardens' bandstand, just as the daily tea-dance continued at the Raffles Hotel. Fatally the massive military defences of the island only pointed seawards and there was nothing to stop the Japanese once they had swept down the Malay Peninsula. A complacent colonial society with an obsessive reliance on 'face' was actually facing the wrong way and fled down to the port to struggle onto the last overloaded ships.

As the enemy closed on the city, 'the Final Perimeter' included the Gardens, where the Director's House received a direct hit from a shell and doomed defensive trenches were excavated in the lawns. When Singapore fell, more than 120,000 soldiers and civilians were marched off to the infamous Changi Prison and the even more terrible Burma Railway. They included fifty staff from the Gardens, twenty-three of whom were to lose their lives. But, as the smoke cleared and Singapore was renamed Syonan-to – 'Light of the South' – by the victorious Japanese, some curious developments took place in the Botanic Gardens.

On 17 February a British botanist peeped from a locked upper room at the long straggling column of his countrymen trudging towards Changi. He was John Corner, assistant director of the Botanic Gardens. The following day, his boss, the Gardens' director Eric Holttum, cycled down from the Director's House to join Corner and Professor Tanakadate, the Japanese geologist given control of the Gardens – which remained in many ways a world apart from the war. According to Corner's account, Holttum was apparently unaware of the general internment order. It is probable that neither were aware of the *sook ching* ('purification through purge') taking place that week, in which up to 25,000 Chinese were herded into the sea and machine-gunned to death.

For the next three years, Corner and Holttum, two of the greatest tropical ecologists of their generation, would pursue their botanical researches under house arrest within the Gardens, under a succession of sympathetic Japanese scientists, all united by a love of flowers and a reverence for scholarship. Their pre-occupation with the finer details of natural history contrasted with the horrors of war around them. Corner was a world authority on fungi and Holttum on ferns – both among the first life forms to move in as the works of man decay in the tropics. Corner observed with professional detachment 'a delicate little toadstool, a species of *Coprinus*' flourish in the sodden matting of his room. They supplemented their rations with the scrapings of fish bags, which, as Corner recorded, included the 'disarticulated ends of crabs' legs and the ossicles of starfish'. In 1942, Corner was ordered to collect marine molluscs for no less than the Emperor Hirohito, himself an enthusiastic biologist and fellow of the Linnean Society, with a particular interest in slime moulds and sea slugs. The fishing party had to scoop up their specimens from a sea strewn with the floating corpses of the Emperor's victims.

If the relationship between the scientific community in the Gardens and the rest of the world was strange, the relationship between the English botanists was stranger still. Two more ill-assorted personalities could not have been singled out to share a downstairs room in the Director's House, with infinite leisure to explore the intricacies of orchid nomenclature but under the permanent threat of a revolver kept ready and loaded on the commanding officer's desk. Eric Holttum, the Gardens' director before the war, was an unassuming Quaker, mild and straight-laced, and celebrated for his kindness. John Corner, his junior, was a flamboyant figure, a brilliant lecturer, and notoriously confrontational. The two men detested one another.

Before the war, Corner used to ride a horse around the Gardens and trained monkeys to collect inaccessible orchids and other plants for him from the tops of trees. To get through the tropics, he insisted, you needed strong drink, strong women and strong music. During the war he raided alcohol from the bottled specimens in the Raffles Museum in order to concoct his own wartime version of Singapore Sling. He liked to paint the teetotal Holttum as an Attlee to his Churchill: a modest man with a lot to be modest about. In fact, Holttum, who had been awarded the Croix de Guerre in the Great War and, much to Corner's annoyance, refused to salute the Japanese flag, had more than a streak of bravery. Corner, on the other hand, had a highly developed sense of how to save his own skin. In 1945, it was Holttum who stood on the steps of the herbarium to defend the most precious botanical archive in South East Asia, which, after three years of meticulous conservation by the Japanese, was threatened with torching by liberating Australian troops.

Holttum and Corner agreed on one thing, however. They both paid subsequent tribute to the Japanese scientists who helped them preserve the Gardens' scientific collection, which held the key as they saw it to the understanding and preservation of the ecosystems of South East Asia.

Like all technology, botanical science in South East Asia has proven to be double-edged. Henry Ridley, the greatest of the Botanic Gardens' directors, introduced rubber from Brazil and so opened up the forests, which he so loved and studied, to their first major clearance in the early 1900s. A century later I was grappling with the environmental consequences of oil palm, to find that, a generation before, my own father had actually introduced this crop to the Solomon Islands, whence it came back to haunt me.

Nonetheless, Corner found a way of elevating natural science as a neat solution to the difficult choice between a patriotic prison sentence and the comfortable status of resident botanist. He wrote of those who refused to stay and help him tend the Gardens for the Japanese: 'I asked if anyone would accompany me, but in vain: I saw that at heart they were not scientists.' He was doing it for the orchids.

As for the orchids, they never looked back. Holttum's studies were to lay the foundations for Singapore's lucrative orchid industry and what were rare luxuries in the West thirty years ago are now standard fare in every flower stall or cornershop. In 2006, Singapore exported more than $14 million of orchid flowers across the world. This in turn is part of a far larger global orchid industry, with major exports from Thailand, Taiwan and the Philippines. Such a seemingly innocent pleasure as a bunch of flowers carries its own environmental cost. The cut flower industry, which was worth more than £2 billion in the UK in 2007, carries a heavy carbon footprint whether the flowers are grown under glass in Germany or the Netherlands or flown in from the tropics. In Kenya and Colombia, where most of the UK's cut flowers come from, local communities suffer health problems from the use of pesticides and, above all, from pressure on water used up for flower irrigation.

In 1957 my father staged a stand of orchids at the Chelsea Flower Show with cut flowers flown in from the Singapore Botanic Gardens. They were a novel sensation and won prizes. In the same year in the Singapore Flower Show he entered a flower quite unheard of in the Far East: a dandelion. It won first prize. One of the lessons that commodities tell us about our unsustainable lifestyles is that they supply far more than the basic necessities. They feed on our dreams.

Fire in the forest

When I returned to Singapore in 2001, after nearly half a century, it seemed like a glorious coincidence. But in fact the wheel had come full circle. Growing up in this place had helped make me an

The luxuriant vegetation of lianes, palms and ferns typical of the tropical rainforest.

environmentalist and now the nature of my work was drawing me back – to the wider challenges of Indonesia. It was a journey that soon dispelled any illusions of childhood nostalgia.

The island of Singapore, which has the Gardens at its heart, is the same size and shape as the Isle of Wight and linked by a causeway to the tip of the Malay Peninsula. From there John Corner once heard the roar of tigers across the straits at Johor Bahru. To imagine them now in such a place is like recalling the dodo.

Singapore lies at the economic epicentre of a far greater pattern of islands: the fabulous Malaysian archipelago. The Victorian naturalist, Alfred Russel Wallace, like all subsequent travellers, used Singapore as his base, and in the decade when the Gardens were founded, went island hopping around the region he called the Malay Archipelago, now including Malaysia and Indonesia. His journey, like Darwin's voyage of the *Beagle*, helped to lay the foundations of our understanding of natural selection. It also gives us a window into a tropical Arcadia which until very recently remained largely intact. For eight years he travelled among the forested islands, whose diversity, second only to South America, is legendary for its orang-utans, tigers, birds of paradise, birdwing butterflies and that fetid parasite of the forest floor, *Rafflesia*, the largest flower in the plant kingdom.

But the special place in that remarkable list is reserved for the extraordinary variety of orchids. Magnificent though garden orchids are, to see them in the wild is to appreciate the difference between a moulting macaw in a pet shop and a whole clamorous flock of them flying towards you over the tree tops in the early morning light. In their native habitat, wild orchids hang like delicately fragrant candelabra from the great forest boughs which are scaled with their overlapping leaves like the crested ridge along a lizard's spine. Suddenly you see them for what they really are – the most extravagant yet subtle flowers in the world. But to see them like this is becoming ever more difficult. Over past decades in South East Asia, they have become rarer and rarer in the wild and in some cases extinct entirely. As I progressed on my journey into Indonesia, I was to find out why.

In 1997 smoke hung over Singapore for the second time in a century. Planes crashed in the smog and the airport was closed. But this was not a world war and the smoke was not only in Singapore. The choking haze extended from Thailand to the Philippines and finally drifted as far north as Hong Kong. Schools closed and people were issued with masks. It was like an old London smog, but far more lethal, since each floating particle in fog is coated with a protective skin of water. In this case the toxic atmosphere was breathed in raw. The huge islands of Borneo and Sumatra were on fire.

Rainforest burned and felled to grow palm oil.

Since then 'the haze', a reeking white mist which blankets South East Asia, has become a regular event between July and October every year. In just two years, between 2009 and 2011, Indonesia lost 1.24 million hectares of forest. And then came the terrible fires of 2015, the worst to date, when members of parliament in Kalimantan had to wear face masks during debates and warships cruised the coast to pick up refugees fleeing the flames. Indonesia had become a 'carbon bomb' and in just three weeks it released more carbon into the atmosphere than Germany's total carbon output for the year.

The perpetrators of these fires are never precisely identified. Rainforests, swathed in their moist cocoon of ferns and orchids, are difficult places to ignite. But once fires have begun to desiccate this juicy veil of epiphytes, the trees become progressively easier to burn. Then they can be opened up for the loggers, who can also claim that, since the forests have been destroyed by these unfortunate fires, they can default on the loans they obtained for their logging concessions and spend the money on something else. By this process, accelerated by the ease with which logs can be floated out down the wide lowland rivers, the forests of the East Indies have been and continue to be destroyed.

Four years after the great burning of 1997 I made my way across the remote hinterland of southern Borneo, now known as Kalimantan. I travelled for two days by light aircraft, in Land Rovers along roads of gluey mud, and upriver by speedboat. Everything I saw was burned and felled to the horizon. A ragged fringe of trees still leaned out over the river's edge. Behind them extended mile upon mile of scorched stumps and sprawling vines, all that is left of the great forests of Borneo, the third largest island in the world. On the occasional blackened spear there survived the mossy cushion of an orchid triggered by stress into a last futile flowering. The only colour came from a few giveaway blue tarpaulins, the temporary shelter from the downpour for loggers intent on collecting the last saleable splinters of tropical hardwood.

Our final landing place felt like the end of the world, a wilderness frontier with nothing wild left in it. The wharf oozed slime and slippery ladders ascended a jetty, supporting a single hut, which acted as store and transit station. A dank black cockerel with blank reptilian eyes perched on the shop counter. The reek of tobacco was a welcome mask to the fouler smells of rotting fruit and sewage. On the door was a poster of David Beckham. Beyond the stacks of timber awaiting collection, the grey river with its thin green fringe wound away into the empty hinterland. A solitary canoe headed upstream in the pelting rain.

FSC – saving the forest by using the timber

Logging in Borneo started in 1967 but only got into its stride in the 1990s. Of its component regions – Kalimantan, Sarawak, Brunei and Sabah – around 60 per cent of forest has now gone and 90 per cent is anticipated to go in the next few years. Only little Brunei retains a majority of swamp forest cover, since the Sultan is able to concentrate on the more lucrative business of oil and natural gas. Elsewhere in Indonesia, Sumatra is largely cleared and the small islands of special importance for their endemic species, found nowhere else, are largely a write-off. All that remains are little islanded national parks and nature reserves similar to those we have in Western Europe, and even these are being relentlessly nibbled away. With the fall of Suharto in 1998, the logging business fell out of the relatively restricted control of the dictator's cronies and a few rich families. There has since been a frantic free-for-all scramble to mop up the last of it. Further afield the forests of the Philippines, with their jade vines and monkey-eating eagles, are largely gone and the Malay Peninsula is intensively cultivated from shore to shore except for some isolated reserves. Thailand is now a net importer of wood.

Where does all the timber go? Much of it ends up in Jakarta for internal use within Indonesia. But a great deal goes directly to the central hub and financial engine of the region, Singapore. From there it will feed the insatiable appetite of cities such as Bangkok and Tokyo, but the UK also imports on average £800 million of tropical hardwoods a year, a fair proportion of which was illegally logged. It reaches you as elegant artefacts, furniture, paper, and most commonly converted to plywood in your local hardware store. Sometimes it doesn't even look like wood and turns up as thin sheets of boarding, known to DIY suppliers as medium density fibreboard (MDF) or oriented strand board (OSB). This often contains tropical hardwood and some very toxic, possibly cancerous, glues into the bargain.

Although architects sometimes specify sustainably grown timber, the way this is obtained, even on large contracts, is through the builders going along to the local store. Like the rest of us, when they get there, they will often as not have no means of knowing exactly what they are buying. The British construction industry also uses quantities of plywood as shuttering to contain concrete when it is poured for foundations. After the concrete sets, the timber shuttering, which has been obtained at such a terrible environmental cost from the rainforest, either rots or is thrown away.

The remains of the great forests of Indonesia have also been recruited for a more sinister purpose. To understand this you have to delve into the confusing world of timber terminology. When I was a child we used to buy tins of Rock Salmon, though no such thing as a rock salmon ever swam in the sea. This was a generic term for dogfish but it really meant any old thing that was left in the bottom of the net. The wood from the giant trees of the South East Asian dipterocarp forests such as *Shorea* and *Hopea* is similarly lumped together under the generic trade term 'balau'. This is commonly used in garden furniture and decking. There were large stores of it in the timber yards of the UK until the wet spring of 2001 when the foot-and-mouth epidemic began to get out of control. The piled carcasses of sheep and cattle would not burn and when the authorities found that the creosoted railway sleepers previously used to ignite them were creating air pollution, they turned in desperation to the British supply of balau. As we know from the destruction of Borneo, this burns well and much of the UK supplies of this most endangered of tropical hardwoods were consumed to feed the pyres. The profligacy of this is especially shocking, but I find it hard to accept that rainforests should be destroyed even for the most beautiful artefact or the main support beam of a public building.

But there is a clever way of turning this problem on its head by recognising the blindingly obvious. Rainforests can and should provide us with what they fundamentally consist of – sustainably grown wood. We can save the forest by using its timber, providing we don't take all of it and we use it carefully. In this way the forest should provide its own salvation. Wood is a constantly renewable commodity, since in theory there are always more trees drawing daily energy from the sun and converting it into timber. For this reason it is regarded as a more sustainable material than alternatives such as plastic, which are oil-based and so use up fossil fuel as well as polluting the seas. In addition, very high energy levels are needed to manufacture plastic or steel. Wood just has to be cut down and, when no longer needed, it can rot away, enriching the soil and providing a habitat for insects as it does so. By contrast a piece of plastic is a curse forever. Landfill sites are bursting at the seams with metal and plastic and, even if plastic is burned, the elements remain, polluting the atmosphere. Greenpeace recommend that it is always better to use wood than plastic. What they don't do is help us with the dilemma of choosing between a piece of plastic and a lump of wood cut down from the rainforest. This is where *Certification*, which is taken from the Latin *certificare,* meaning 'to make sure', comes in.

In Anna Jenkins' Welsh kitchen hangs a wooden spatula. Perhaps one day it will hang in a museum and be recognised for what it is: a small object, which has helped to change the world. In 1995, this was the first commodity which, as a result of a rigorous checking system, could be confidently marketed as a sustainably grown wooden object. It was produced by the Forest Stewardship Council, an independent organisation established in 1994 and known in the trade as FSC, for which Anna worked. Look in most books (including this one) and you will find the FSC logo relating to the source of its paper. The FSC subscribes to ten guiding principles for the production of timber, including conservation of biological diversity, respect for indigenous peoples' rights, a proper forest management plan and long-term monitoring. It operates a *Chain of Custody*, whereby FSC-certified wood can be reliably tracked through every agent that handled it from the the forest, where an independent certifier has vetted the method of production, to the store where it was bought. In the twenty-five years since that first certified kitchen spatula was sold, more than 200 million hectares of sustainably managed forest or plantation have achieved FSC certification. The FSC also certifies non-timber forest products such as cork, bamboo and latex as well as pulp for paper and clothing.

Among the multitude of practical problems concerning the FSC's pioneering heroism are two outstanding questions: *What does it mean, and How do you know?* The honest answer to the first question is that sustainable timber harvesting on the ground is often something of a fudge: a combination of best guess and the precautionary principle. Above all, sympathetic forest management means largely avoiding clear felling. The best idea is to mimic the natural fall of an old tree, which then lets in light for *Potential Crop Trees* (PCTs) or seedlings waiting for their chance to provide the next generation of timber. The speed with which many tropical hardwoods grow makes this a practical proposition. A careful plan would then retain some pristine forest and ensure that felling and hauling timber does minimum damage.

Now comes the question that keeps the suppliers of sustainable timber awake at night. How do you really know, when the hand-over of every load in a succession of remote logging stations is subject to the infinite deviousness of the locals, whether you are ending up with the genuine article, regardless of the paperwork and stamp it comes with? Nobody could question the probity of the FSC, but could it be that they are occasionally duped along the line? You can't always be sure. But we have to start somewhere. And the trained auditors know that their credibility is all they have to sell, a major motivation for vigilance.

A risk remains that the certifiers will opt out of the challenges of supply and credibility posed by the developing world and concentrate on easier sources such as wood from Europe and North America. The eco-friendly panelling proudly displayed in Cornwall's Eden Project, for example, comes from the huge quantities of softwood blown down in the great storm, which swept through Les Landes in southern France in the winter of 2000. This is legitimate and we need all the wood we can get to avoid eating into our last forests. But ultimately the only way to save the rainforests is to use them sustainably and then market them. Otherwise, the world's richest and most spectacular habitats will simply be left in the hands of the cowboys.

The forests of Russia

There is even more at stake in this issue of certified timber than the tropical rainforest. All over the world, our forests contain the timber we need, which can be sustainably used if we certify it properly. In 1992, I worked in Russia during the heady days of Gorbachev's regime. Broken statues of Lenin, gazing heavenwards and smeared in yellow paint, lay piled like rockeries in the parks. I worked with a team of brave young students who had walked unarmed up to the tanks when they rolled into the streets of Moscow in the previous summer. We were there to set up a protected area in the forests south east of Moscow.

Our base was a workers' holiday camp where waltz music crackled out from the speakers over a deserted dance floor but was soon lost in the immensity of the surrounding woods. An old lady in a mushroom hat shuffled a little dance to herself under the trees. Beyond, the great Russian forest of fairy tales extends over a land surface comprising one sixth of the globe. In the clearings deep bronze bells boom out from onion-domed churches, and wooden houses, tricked out in white and green paint like iced ginger bread, throbbed with New York rap from the radio. Everywhere the good things from the forest were turned to use and beauty. The pine was tapped for resin for musical instruments and carved and painted for wooden spoons and the famous Russian dolls. Even the neat way they split their winter logs and stacked them herringbone fashion in carved timber shelters seemed more like folk art than any ordinary woodshed.

This mighty forest of spruce and birch, full of wolves, little black snakes, all-consuming mosquitoes and a continuous carpet of lily of the valley with its swooning fragrance, poisonous berries and flowers like tiny white teeth, rolls away largely unbroken to the Pacific. In a few places in the furthest east, the wolves are replaced by Siberian tigers padding through the snow.

The great woods of the Russian Federation account for 25 per cent of the world's pristine forest and contain the greatest area of old growth of any forest in the world. With the break-up of the USSR and the collapse of communism, which for all its social evils and disregarded pollution, maintained huge natural systems wrapped in a nineteenth-century sleep, the Russian forest has been up for grabs. By 2002, some 30 per cent of its timber had been illegally logged and it was estimated that 2–3 million hectares of forest were on fire every year. The role of the FSC is therefore critical and now Russia is second only to Canada in having the largest area of FSC-certified forest in the world. However, in 2014, Greenpeace published the results of its satellite imagery-based analysis of an area of north-west Russia where it claimed that loggers had been working under cover of the FSC seal of approval to remove unsustainable quantities of timber from large intact forest landscapes. Without the presence of FSC or equivalent organisations in these great wildernesses, the situation would surely be worse, but there is clearly a permanent need for vigilance: *What does it mean, and How do you know?*

Shampoo from the rainforest: the perils of palm oil

There is yet another by-product of rainforest destruction, which is likely to be a regular part of our typical day and was the reason why I was first paid to visit Indonesia. As you fly over many cleared areas of South East Asia, you often look down on a dark green quilt of tree cover set out on a geometrical grid. These are plantations of oil palms, the Sitka spruce of the tropics.

Palm oil is obtained from the fat orange fruits of a tree resembling a date palm, which is native to the forests of Central Africa. The fruits are crushed in a mill, yielding one of the most versatile of all vegetable oils, partly because it has an especially long polymer chain. It is a staple of margarine, cooking oil, shampoo, suntan lotion and washing-up liquid. The multitude of products that often contain palm oil include toothpaste, lipstick, vitamin pills, biscuits, crisps, coffee creamer and salad cream. It has even been used to run cars. Look on the label for *palmic acid* and you may establish whether you are using it. The main alternative comes from the soya bean but this too has its own catalogue of environmental costs, including genetic modification.

If you drive the six-hour journey from Singapore to Kuala Lumpur, the capital of Malaysia, you travel through unmitigated oil palm, the neat colonnades marching to the horizon above a planted groundcover of tropical vines. Ferns grow on the tree trunks, wild pigs scavenge for oil fruit and rats live under the vines. Otherwise the plantations don't provide much of a habitat. Oil palm requires

A palm oil plantation in Indonesia. The serried ranks of palms march to the horizon.

lowland with high rainfall and is set to expand in the Far East, West Africa, and Central and South America.

A major problem with palm oil is the murky relationship between plantation owners and loggers. There are many examples where oil palm has moved into the vacuum created by forest clearance or into declining rubber estates. At other times loggers can be seen using the road infrastructure of the palm plantations to penetrate ever deeper into the forest. And in many cases the loggers and the planters are the same people. These may include companies belonging to generals, the families of presidents, and Malaysian Chinese who dominate so much business in South East Asia.

Until the birth of a fledgling democracy in Indonesia in 1998, environmental pressure groups were powerless, and the situation is little better today. In some cases, operators use the excuse of proposed oil palm as a justification to go in and log. In the worst cases, many of the great fires of Indonesia were actually started as a means to secure the ultimate prize of palm oil, which is far more valuable than timber. Added bonuses are the opportunity to write off loans on logging concessions and claim substantial insurance since the forest had been mysteriously damaged.

This is the most unacceptable price we pay for palm oil products. But there are three other main categories of destruction that arise on a badly run palm plantation: pollution, social deprivation and loss of biodiversity due to unrelieved monoculture. On most oil palm plantations the fruit is taken to a mill on the site, where it is crushed and heated to extract the oil. The mill chimneys produce black smoke, which pollutes the air, and from the mill drains there issues an evil-smelling purple sludge, which resembles the worst silage effluent you can imagine and kills all life in the rivers.

Social deprivation resulting from oil palm can affect both the plantation workers and the previous forest dwellers. Many workers are housed in the same rickety shacks originally put up for the mill construction workers, with sewage dribbling down the gullies between the buildings into malarial pools of palm sludge. Those who lost their homes when the forest was cleared for palm oil may sometimes be compensated and given work on the estate but all too often are simply evicted.

Palm oil plantations do not need to be like this. Like all engineering operations they can be done badly or perfectly well. Codes of good practice exist for treating the sludge with settlement lagoons and reducing smoke emissions from the stacks. The spent husks of the fruit, which will poison a stream if they are left beside it, can be used as a mulch for the trees, thereby reducing both waste and the need for herbicides. On a well-managed estate, the operator will provide decent housing and take on the responsibility of providing schools, playing fields, churches and mosques. Given the large size and isolation of the plantations, they often become the chief employer for miles around and also the main social basis for the plantation workers. A well-run palm oil operation often has a huge community spirit and regular raucous parties are attended by the entire workforce. This I discovered to my dismay when I returned exhausted to my rest-house after a long day canoeing up rivers and inching along slippery log bridges to survey an estate. A reception committee awaited me with all the kit required for karaoke. 'Mr Jeremy, Mr Jeremy,' they chorused, 'Will you sing "Delilah"?' There was no escape.

Proper planning of a palm oil estate can turn a sterile monoculture into a relatively diverse system for wildlife. The golden rule is to avoid clearing virgin forest in the first place and then to set aside a substantial proportion of the estate (a minimum of 10 per cent but it can be much more) for forest and swamp habitat. These can form a system of corridors along all the rivers and streams, which are linked in turn to pockets of forest if any have survived. This is the classic model of keeping to a modern commercial monoculture but gently modifying it to create a better balance between wild habitat and agriculture, and is known as 'offsetting'. The forest corridors often help to support people as well as wildlife, since they may contain cocoa, jackfruit and rubber trees, which are harvested to supplement local incomes. Such is the huge size of a typical palm oil estate that the proportional forest land which is set aside can have real impact. A well-run estate may be better protected than many state nature reserves which are often poorly resourced and defended.

In 2004, the Roundtable on Sustainable Palm Oil (RSPO) was formed to promote the sustainable production and use of palm oil. This is a certification scheme which sets out to do for palm oil what the FSC is doing for timber. Membership includes growers, traders, retailers and investors in the palm oil business, together with major environmental bodies. It undertakes practical projects and develops codes of practice involving good ecological, social and pollution management principles. In this way it should be possible to produce our shampoo and margarine in a far less damaging way and then, subject to a properly transparent checking system, market them as sustainable products.

The way to change the world is to produce convincing examples of good practice and then promote them as standard practice. These may then be tied to an eco-labelling system, which producers can be persuaded to sign up to on account of the edge they might gain in the market, and the reverse scenario of bad publicity, resulting in lack of confidence from shareholders and a consumer switch to alternative products. In time it might be hoped that these high standards will become the legally accepted norm rather than just the exception subscribed to by an environmentally conscious minority. The dilemma for conservationists is whether to oppose all palm oil, since clearly even fairly degraded rainforests are more exciting places than the most ecologically integrated plantation. The right strategy is surely to oppose bad practice and also promote best standards. Otherwise, if the palm oil industry is bypassed, it will simply be left in the hands of organisations which regard environmental concerns as laughably irrelevant.

The author surveying riverside rainforest in Kalimantan in order to retain it within a proposed palm oil plantation..

PNG: butterflies and palm plantations

One of my first palm oil projects was in Papua New Guinea. Affectionately known as PNG, this is the eastern half of New Guinea, the second largest island in the world and the wildest card in the colourful pack that comprise Wallace's Malay Archipelago. Down the centre of PNG and its Indonesian neighbour, Irian Jaya, rises a formidable mountain range, which has preserved until recent times a remarkable Stone Age culture within its inaccessible valleys. This also continues to help protect some of the finest rainforests in the Far East, which echo with the shrieks of saffron plumed birds of paradise as they swoop tantalisingly through the upper canopy. The ice-cold torrents which surge down through the mist-cooled forests of the mountain flank are very different from the wide green waterways of Borneo. If you tried to float timber down them, it would end up as matchwood on the jagged river rocks. However, communal land tenure in PNG, whereby it is illegal to privately own land except as part of the tribe, is less of a barrier to development than it might at first seem. While it is impossible to purchase land to set up a nature reserve, it seems that there is nothing to prevent loggers being able to bribe their way past community leaders and get their hands on the timber.

My reason for visiting this remote part of the world was that I had been called to the rescue of a very remarkable insect.

The Queen Alexandra birdwing butterfly was discovered for science in 1906 in eastern New Guinea, when it was 'brought down with a blast from a shotgun'. It is the largest butterfly in the world and such a high flier that it disappears like a lark into the firmament. The butterflies are so huge that they look like Chinese paper kites, sailing down out of the blue. On late afternoons, as the light softens, the great birdwings float into the sunlit village clearings to feast on the garden hibiscus blossoms. With them glide the lime-green Priam's birdwing and the peacock-blue Ulysses butterflies; insects of a silken magnificence, which relegate the local birdlife to a mere sideshow.

The Queen Alexandra, as befits an aristocrat, is fastidious in its habits, its caterpillars choosing only to nibble the leaves of one species of vine, known as Dutchman's pipe. Partly as a result, the butterfly is of very restricted range and, as luck would have it, this coincided with one of the palm oil plantations where I was working. As a result the integration of plantations with habitat was of paramount importance. Vines were propagated and grown up the palm trees. But they were soon damaged by the workers harvesting the palm fruit, and anyway the butterflies took one look at their food plant in these uncongenial surroundings and drifted away.

The Queen Alexandra birdwing butterfly. It is the largest butterfly in the world and is so huge that when first discovered it was brought down by a shotgun.

A better strategy was to mimic the forest edge habitat with enclaves and corridor strips along the rivers. All butterflies are sun lovers and so prefer glades of secondary bush to dense blocks of primary forest. As a result the master plan for maintenance and expansion of habitat corridors enriched with vine planting, based on proper survey of insect populations and a satellite image of the estate, is starting to reverse the trend of butterfly decline. In so remote an area, proactive support from the main local employer is also the only hope to prevent cumulative forest destruction by passing immigrants practising slash and burn. It can also help to police the predations of rich collectors who (amazingly) still send agents out to look for this rare species for their private collections.

If you have butterflies at the bottom of your plantation, the conservation strategy is challenging but not impossible. If tigers come out at night to hunt pigs down your palm oil avenues and they in turn are hunted by the local indigenous tribe surviving in your enclaves, as well as by powerful entrepreneurs, then the situation becomes more difficult. In 1999, the palm oil operation for which I was working acquired existing plantations in Sumatra and Kalimantan as a consequence of its decision not to start afresh with any virgin forest sites in New Guinea. This has to be the right approach, but given the standards of most other operators, it is inevitable that they would also inherit an environmental can of worms.

Sumatra: tiger penis soup

The Sumatran tiger, which is a separate subspecies, has suffered a 95 per cent decline this century and is now reduced to around 100 animals. The insatiable Chinese market for tiger penis soup, based on the false premise that the tiger's performance will be passed on to boost the flagging libidos of those who drink this nasty liquid, remains a major threat.

Despite these problems, the palm oil planters I was working with discovered that their newly acquired Sumatran plantation had quite a healthy population of tigers, which came in from the neighbouring and far from protected forest. The previous owner announced, nonchalantly, 'I have shot five. Would you like a skin?' when the new company took possession. Other cultures' enthusiasm for slaughtering or capturing wildlife is perhaps especially shocking to the British. Birdwatchers recently went to an Indonesian forest in order to witness the final mating display of a threatened species. Having spent a fruitless day sweating through the bush, they returned to find their driver had purchased a pair at the local market complete with chicks, all expiring in a cage on the back seat of the boiling car. I remember carrying out an ecological survey in southern Turkey with a guide, whose urban outfit of baggy trousers, spinsterish cardigan and what appeared to be bedroom slippers led me to doubt his preparation for fieldwork. I was wrong. A roller, which is a magnificent kind of turquoise and chestnut crow, flew by. Fatally I expressed my admiration. Instantly, he pulled a revolver from his cardigan pocket and took aim. The roller uttered a ghastly croak and plummeted earthwards. Beaming toothlessly in anticipation of my gratitude, my guide went off to retrieve the lifeless bird. Its destruction was the first direct negative environmental impact of the Environmental Impact Assessment.

This pervasive approach to wildlife, not to mention the tiger penis soup, is enough to make you feel that agonising over the relatively respectable contents of your supermarket trolley is a matter of fiddling while Borneo burns. But even more serious for the tigers and other creatures is the loss of habitat as a result of clearance for goods such as palm oil and plywood, leaving the isolated populations in increasingly non-viable islands of habitat. On their Sumatran estate, the planters immediately initiated tiger patrols to control hunting by outsiders and began to persuade the local tribesmen to cease the practice of trapping. For the proposed new palm planting, we carried out a detailed survey of existing forests within their ownership in order to retain these and tie them into a linked system of habitat. As with the butterflies, the cover favoured by tigers is easy to create: dusty thickets of bamboo and clumps of ginger, splashed with sunshine and stripy with shadows.

In addition the planters began to explore land swaps in order to obtain the core tiger territory and save it from almost certain destruction by the adjacent owner. A girdle of plantation around the edge of an entire system is the only practical way to save forest from random incursion. It may be argued that the already shrunken tiger populations are doomed, but if this is the case the forest pockets still contain tapir, gibbon, argus pheasant and some fine orchids. Anything saved now from the wholesale clearance will be tomorrow's nature reserves.

A modern definition of environmental good practice must include people as well as wildlife. In the developing world the lives of people and especially the culture of indigenous forest people are inextricably bound up with the ecosystem, while the social dominance of any major economic enterprise is hard to grasp from the perspective of centralised urban Europe. The manager of a remote palm estate is like a feudal baron of the Middle Ages or a colonial administrator from the days of empire. 'Road he bugger up,' remarked a local Papuan, as we watched the lorries wallowing to their axles in mud on the so-called road to a plantation site. The blockage had lasted a fortnight and already trees had been felled, makeshift shelters erected and a local market set up. This is how villages are born. With such isolation, the operator at the end of the road is king of his own domain and, depending on the style of the operation, is the major local force for good or evil. The palm oil planter has the power to create a major new nature reserve as part of the plantation or to wipe out everything in sight.

For the same reason, law and order is a major social issue. In PNG, the grandchildren of the Stone Age people, who were first discovered by the outside world in the 1930s, now put on their warpaint for the TV cameras with the aid of a vanity compact. But in reality, bows and arrows have been replaced by machine guns. Daylight hold-ups are the norm and every property in the capital, Port Moresby, is ringed with razor wire. More often than not you will survive, though Papuans take a humorous delight in stealing all your clothes. In the days when Japanese tourists ventured into these wild parts, an entire party was left to walk home stark naked. But there is a less amusing side. In 1997, one plantation had to withstand an armed siege following a strike, and the manager of another one was stabbed to death. In these circumstances the stabilising influences of a well-run estate, both for society and the ecosystem, have to be weighed against the disruption that any kind of development can create in the wilderness. Ponder these dilemmas as you shampoo your hair or stir-fry your vegetables with cooking oil.

The Dayaks of Kalimantan

In 2001, I went to Kalimantan to carry out an environmental audit of the palm oil estate of Harapan Sawit Lestari, which is Indonesian for 'Our Eternal Hope is Oil Palm'. A few months earlier, on a drizzly night in February 2001, 118 men, women and children were taken by truck to a playing field in the nearby town of Sampit and hacked to death by Dayak headhunters under the headlights of the vehicle. On the estate there were rumours that the Dayaks, whose forests have been drastically cleared for palm oil, were massing on the far side of the river. The estate workers hung banners out of their windows to indicate they were not Madurese, unpopular immigrants from an overpopulated island settled on Kalimantan by central Indonesian government and to date the exclusive target of the Dayaks' fury. The Dayaks are a sympathetic and largely peaceable people, but violence is never far away.

When I arrived in Kalimantan I found the displacement of Dayak forest-based livelihood by oil palm a hot political issue, especially among environmentalists in Jakarta. I met the local environmental pressure group. They appeared charming and sincere in their concern for the Dayaks. 'The forest is their life,' they explained. To replace the Dayaks' centuries' old sustainable lifestyle with a compensation package and a job in the mill was to miss the point. I agreed entirely. On the environmentalists' urging I went to meet the Dayaks themselves, whom I found equally charming. But they were certainly not tree-huggers. Most Dayaks shoulder chainsaws and the leader of opposition to plantation development could not meet me because he was out logging. It would have been patronising and naive to expect otherwise. The Dayaks I met were understandably after every last material benefit they could obtain from the estate for themselves and all their families.

However, the widespread claim by some palm oil developers that it was the Dayaks who started the great burning of Indonesia is unjust. Dayaks have survived forever on the system of slash and burn, especially on the lowland areas. What has kept the forest system in balance has been the lack of technology, such as machinery for forest clearance. The West has now supplied this technology, together with a market for timber and palm oil which pays for it. In this way small-scale clearance by the forest people has expanded into wholesale destruction. To remedy this situation, some plantation operators are now starting a programme to do everything they can for their local indigenous people in PNG, Sumatra and Borneo. Although they have inherited estates where the original forest dwellers have been treated scandalously, they are continuing consultation through independent facilitators, initiating community development programmes and extending the smallholder systems to include as many local people as possible, and this in turn is reflected in the certification of their product. Owing to such international concern, some Dayaks of Sarawak, for example, are said now to be seriously rich and able to aspire to the kind of lives that you and I take for granted.

Taking stock of palm oil

In all these ways we have started to mitigate the negative impacts of the palm oil monocultures in South East Asia, but we still have a long way to go. Over a decade since the formation of the RSPO roundtable certification system in 2004, Indonesia still goes up in smoke every autumn and some fires have been identified on roundtable-certified plantations. In 2013, certified sustainable production only accounted for 15 per cent of global production and much palm oil that reaches you is a mix of both responsibly and irresponsibly produced oil.

Nonetheless the RSPO has to be a good starting point for driving the transformation of the industry. In December 2014, it became mandatory in the EU for all food products containing palm oil to have the word 'palm oil' spelled out on the packaging, so it can no longer be hidden under the generic term 'vegetable oil'. However, while some products state that their palm oil is sustainably certified, others do not. To help the bemused shopper through this minefield, Chester Zoo is developing an online shopping list to show which chocolate biscuits and margarine brands contain 100 per cent RSPO-certified sustainable palm oil, together with a list of manufacturers committed to using certified palm oil. Between 2000 and 2014, consumption of certified sustainable palm oil has quadrupled in the UK and a target of 100 per cent is planned for Europe for 2020.

Meanwhile the FSC has nearly 3 million hectares of certified forest in Indonesia, which equates to 2 per cent of the total forest area. With such initiatives the wild orchids might just start to return to their beleaguered habitats.

Back to the Garden

In Singapore the city horizons are ringed with cranes and the air is loud with the sound of jackhammers. It is said that the average life of a building between refurbishments is seven years. Nobody has calculated the quantities of construction plywood that this involves and few people know whether the private parts of tigers are being traded in one of the elegant restaurants. The collapse of the tiger economy back in 1998 seems a long-distant memory. There are, though, a few small cracks in this perfectly manicured metropolis. Cobras occasionally emerge from the drains in the deluxe housing condominiums. In some of the landscaped piazzas between the stylish tower blocks, whole sections of paving have subsided a few inches, reminding you as you stumble that most of Singapore is built on a low-lying swampy island, vulnerable to sea-level rise.

In the heart of the city, the Botanic Gardens have been cherished and exquisitely restored. In 2015, they were declared a World

Heritage Site. The monkeys and the flying foxes are banished. But the pythons are still there. 'Plenty. Plenty', say the gardeners. Pythons in Singapore and Bangkok, like foxes in Birmingham and jaguars in Belize, are urban opportunists, snaffling chickens and scavenging around dustbins. The old dirt track behind the Director's House is now a tarmac road and the stream beside it, where we used to fish for guppies, is a concrete storm drain. But the house itself is impeccable, right down to the ceiling lamps, except for the room where Corner and Holttum were interned, which now dispenses Pepsi-Cola. The dried plants in the Herbarium, which they fought so hard to preserve, are still there, comprising our major record of a world lost beyond recovery. The house is the centrepiece for the new Orchid Gardens, where joggers pause to listen to their mobiles and nature is worshipped with a proper, if blinkered, deference. Back lit with the phosphorescence of tourists' flash cameras, the orchids rise triumphant, wave upon wave of coral, salmon and violet, reclaiming the place once and for all. In the middle of the house, at the very centre of the whole flamboyant display, is a golden orchid in a glass case.

Within many exploited landscapes we still cherish enchanted gardens. As we shall see, nowhere is this more so than in the Garden of England.

CHAPTER 2

The green cliffs of Dover

Conserving the Kentish countryside

Steep roads, a tunnel through chalk downs are the approaches;
A ruined pharos overlooks a constructed bay;
The seafront is almost elegant; all the show
Has inland somewhere, a vague and dirty root:
Nothing is made in this town.

Dover, W.H. Auden, 1937

The white cliffs of Dover are turning green: they are actually growing grass. For a cliff to remain a cliff, it must be inherently unstable. The sea nibbles at the base and the cliff comes crashing down, exposing a clean vertical face. But nowadays, railways, car parks, the neatly landscaped spoil from the Channel Tunnel, and even a flyover at the bottom of the cliff, interfere with this natural process. The slopes have started to erode to a gentler angle of repose and the cliffs of Dover begin to assume the bland uniform green of the rest of the county of Kent.

The tunnel that Auden observed in his poem now extends beneath the sea. Unless you take the boat, the sense of arrival through a historic port from France into England is largely obliterated. If you take your car on the train, you sit in a sealed carriage, containing some photographs of Kentish orchards and oast houses, before emerging into a world of concrete walls and steel gantries. In minutes you are whisked onto a motorway, which creates its own linear desert of ugliness and boredom, sealing the hapless traveller from any sense of England's once greatest quality: its vivid and varied character. As you continue your journey further across the country, you will look out on the sameness and dullness of the modern British countryside.

The eastern counties, the Midlands and much of the south of England are similarly bland, dominated by huge featureless arable fields. Where fifty years ago every little valley bottom had a sinuous tree-lined brook, these have often as not been reduced to straightened ditches fledged with a mean strip of stinging nettles.

The face of modern British farming: immense ploughed fields of agribusiness.

Most of us would assume they were always ditches. In the middle of the immense fields you may notice a few isolated large trees, often stag-headed and muffled in ivy. These were never planted deliberately in the middle of the crop. No landowner would create such an obstacle to be cultivated around. The trees are sole survivors of vanished hedges which were simply too large to remove easily when the rest of the hedge was bulldozed. Similarly, country lanes sometimes zigzag aimlessly across huge empty spaces, providing the only clue to the line of a long-lost hedge and an even more ancient parish boundary. If you travel to the west of England, cattle replace the cereals and sheep become dominant on the hills, with barbed-wire stock fences replacing the hedges.

There is no need for England to be like this and this chapter sets out many ways in which we can preserve a diverse yet productive landscape through a moderate approach to land use. But instead, throughout much of the country, we have the same basic monotony of agribusiness and intensive monoculture until we reach the indistinguishable suburbs and industrial estates of the nearest town. Any place. Anywhere. No one remarks on this, since we all know that is what much of England looks like. When something is gone you don't miss it – especially the generation that never saw what came before. But I remember it. I even revisit it when I return in dreams to the enchanted gardens of my childhood.

The Weald of Kent

In 1957, my parents, returning from Singapore, bought a house in Sissinghurst in the Weald of Kent. The previous owner had kept it as a shrine to her first husband, an admiral. Much of the furniture was sold with the house on the understanding that as little as possible should be changed. The admiral's tree, which he had planted, was never to be felled. The admiral's log, which he had lopped off it the day he died, was not to be burned. It was darkly implied that the admiral, or at least his ashes, lay beneath his tree.

We all loved the place with the enthusiasm of returning exiles, but for my mother, from the moment she first set eyes on it, this house was to remain the abiding passion of her life. A crooked Tudor chimney rose from among spires of cottage garden flowers. Dark low-beamed rooms smelled of wood smoke and furniture polish. The door opened onto mornings filled with the apple-green light of an orchard and beyond, the hillside tilted down and away to a beckoning world of meadows, water and woodland. Before me now is the 1950 Ordnance Survey for our parish: *'Scale – Six Inches to One Statute Mile or 880 Feet to One Inch'*. I have only to unroll this wrinkled sheet of paper and I can walk into the map: Bull Wood, The Wilderness, Spencer's Shaw, Great Swifts and Little Swallows.

The Kentish Weald is made of clay, wood and iron, but especially wood. The clay, which laid down the ridges unfolding into the blue distance, bakes hard in the summer cornfields, where the warm air is ripe with the silage smell of pineapple weed. But in the dimpled tracks running into the woods, the mud is always cool and soft, with puddles in hoof prints and the toothpaste sweetness of the water mint. The woods survive from the great forest of Andred's Wald, as in the German *Wald* for 'wood', which shadowed the Weald into Saxon times, long after most English forest had been cleared. In April the unfurling coppices of hornbeam and hazel ring with the cuckoos answering one another and fill with a bluebell aquarium light. In July, when the light thins after a night's rain to a high-summer mellowness, bringing with it a premonition of autumn, the woods go dark. Hung with the papery-green lanterns of the hornbeam seed and smelling foxily of stinkhorn fungus, they are possessed by the throaty crooning of the wood pigeons. Through them seep dark streams, stained with the ore for which the Romans came and which made the Wealden ironmasters rich.

Traditional buildings, which are always a hallmark of the most distinctive places, are here built directly out of the landscape, in this case wood, iron and clay. Doors and windows are silvered oak, studded with iron or fixed with iron hasps. Timber-framed buildings, infilled with the clay and straw known as wattle and daub, are a great glory of the Weald. Bricks and tiles, made from the fired Wealden clay are a signature tune of this landscape. Paths, chimneys and many houses are built of brick, ranging from rust red to pink and grey, dusted with lemon-green lichen and splashed white with the droppings of house martins, nesting under the eaves. The walls of my favourite Wealden vernacular buildings are hung with tiles, below which they are lapped with white-painted weather boarding. To describe the extraordinary marriage of opposites in these two materials, imagine the snowy coolness of pleated white linen meeting the subtly dented texture and glowing vermilion of cooked crabs' backs. The rows of tiles, which tilt out from the walls where they overlap each other, seem to come out to meet the sun whose warmth they absorb and reflect in an astonishing range of fiery russets. But the best thing about them is how they were made. The hornbeam, which thrives best in the stiff Wealden clays and so dominates the woods, burns with the hottest flame of any English tree. It is traditionally used to fire the tiles, creating, as no other timber can, a recipe from wood and clay which is literally the essence of the Weald.

If you look at the tiles, they are never perfect rectangles, and this failed attempt at symmetry is a characteristic of the whole delightfully crooked landscape of the Weald. The shadow line beneath each row of tiles and each strip of weatherboarding is always slightly crinkled. The houses and the wonky brick paths, which lead up to them, seldom achieve a true right angle. The dark holly trees, which Kentish farmers considered bad luck to remove from the hedges, corkscrew up to the light. The fields and the switch-back lanes, which follow their quirky boundaries, show clearly that, unlike a grid of Midland enclosure hedges, this was never a laid-out landscape. It was actually cut out of the forests, which suddenly swallow the veering lanes in a tunnel of green and spill their wood anemones and dog's mercury out from under the bulging hedges. The forest is always fighting back.

But for many years a long shadow hung over my family's Kentish idyll. In 1967, my sister Erica, then aged ten, was injured in a car accident on a twisty Kentish lane. Repeated resuscitation ensured her survival, although she was permanently brain-damaged. Summer after summer, she was pushed out in her wheelchair, dressed by my mother in impeccable flowered smocks, the centrepiece of our perfect garden. She never spoke but gurgled and seemed to smile at the stimulation of music or laughter. She existed in this way for twenty years. Among many things, this left me with a permanent sense of our inability to handle the sophisticated technologies we have invented, a dilemma which lies at the heart of most of our current environmental problems.

Gardens of the Weald

Kent is perhaps most famous for its gardens, which more than anything else display this tension of a formal structure gently blurred and softened by the natural exuberance of vegetation. Traditional Kentish gardens, from village patches to the great set pieces, rarely attempt to emulate a curve. If they did, they would not be nearly so interesting. Fruit and flowers tumble out across the main path to the front door and the topiary leans out drunkenly in a triumphant failure to achieve the geometrical shapes to which it aspires. Our home was within easy reach of two exceptional gardens. I could walk through the woods to Sissinghurst Castle or cycle over to Great Dixter beyond the Sussex border.

Great Dixter is a medieval timber-framed manor house adapted in 1911 by Edwin Lutyens for Nathaniel Lloyd, a photographic printer. Lloyd's expertise helped to create the magazine *Country Life*, which was a major showcase for the collaboration between Lutyens and Gertrude Jekyll, out of which grew the greatest English gardens of the twentieth century. In the architectural details at Dixter, Lutyens made inspirationally inventive use of the Wealden vernacular materials of wood and tiles, which perfectly complement

Great Dixter, Sussex. The timber-framed house is hung with russet tiles typical of the buildings of the Weald.

the timber in the house and are set on edge in the risers of the steps and round the arches in the garden walls. Until he died in 2006, the garden was continually reinvented by Nathaniel's son Christopher, known as Christo, within the Edwardian framework and cottage garden tradition, which he had inherited.

For many years an important part of any visit to Great Dixter was Christo's mother. Known as 'the Management', old Mrs Lloyd was a direct descendent of Oliver Cromwell, from whom she perhaps inherited her large nose, domed forehead and formidable personality. With a trug over her arm, dachshund at heel, she pottered around in a long rusty skirt and children's Start-rite sandals, shawled and scarfed like an elderly version of Little Red Riding Hood. She had a mischievous sense of humour and would delight in ensuring that Christo's dinner guests were ensconced for coffee in the upper solar, just in time for the public to be shown round. Omitting any reference to the most obvious occupants of the room, the guide would itemise each article of furniture, right down to the antique chairs upon which the family and their self-conscious guests were sitting, frozen like dummies in a Tussaud's tableau.

However, old Mrs Lloyd was not the only eccentric chatelaine of a Wealden garden.

Sissinghurst Castle is perhaps the most famous garden in England, with a box office appeal based on an irresistible combination of aristocracy, sex and gardening. Almost as many people who come to admire the flowers also come out of curiosity over the personalities who planted them. The story of Vita Sackville-West and Harold Nicolson has been told in countless books and even films: how they rescued the ruined buildings from beneath rusting scrap iron and nettles to make a great romantic garden in which they lived in separate buildings, pursuing their separate love affairs, his with men and hers with women, nonetheless devoted to each other within the horticultural framework of an amiable marriage.

My family regarded them with a mixture of awe and hilarity. Vita's appearance was striking, to say the least. She was very tall and habitually wore lace-up boots and riding trousers, from the pockets of which emerged secateurs and unravelling trails of garden twine. With the obligatory accessories of long-handled cigarette and string of pearls, she has been described as Lady Chatterley to the waist and the gamekeeper beneath. In addition her hair looked as if she had been dragged through one of her species rose bushes backwards and her face had something of the summer pudding complexion of her famous purple border. Nonetheless, with her queenly voice, she had a gracious presence and, though not reckoned by her friend Virginia Woolf to be a great writer, she was certainly a visionary for the landscape.

Occasionally seen as comical, though aristocratic to their fingertips, the Nicolsons were set off to perfection by the vistas of their own creation. At Sissinghurst there is a long green walk, leading to a moat backed by a naked marble Dionysus. Returning from London one afternoon, Harold frolicked down this avenue with their pet dog, only to disappear with a loud splash into the duckweedy water at the end of the perspective. Less authenticated is the story, widely retailed in the village, that Vita, feeling faint after one too many gins, was pushed by the gardeners up the path between her resplendent borders, her long booted legs dangling over the edge of the wheelbarrow. She was indeed the prize delphinium and the ultimate ornament of her garden. Even now that they are long dead, Vita and Harold are part of what the visitors come for.

But the visitors create their own problems. The Nicolsons always opened the garden to the public, which was often busy even in their time. But as the place has achieved the status of a heritage icon, lawns and paths wear out beneath the tramp of horticultural pilgrims, some of whom are not averse to helping themselves to shoots and roots as a small *Souvenir de Sissinghurst*. Even more difficult to prevent is the erosion of atmosphere, as an intimate romantic little garden blocks solid with admirers who destroy the very quality which they came to admire. The National Trust, which now owns Sissinghurst, is a past master of managing these problems. They build brick paths and intensively aerate the lawns to withstand the physical pressure. The car park is discretely shrouded in trees. An apparently careless rapture of tangled vines and clematis is achieved by the artfully concealed effort of very careful gardening. Above all, a combination of late opening times and a staggered ticket system, so instant entry to the garden is not guaranteed on arrival, has brought down the visitor numbers to a manageable level.

There is, however, an even greater challenge for the inheritors of Sissinghurst. Gardening, perhaps even more than music, is an art, which exists within the unfolding dimension of time. Hour by hour the light changes. The buds open. The petals fall. That is the essential beauty of a garden. More problematically, plants die and others grow to crowd out their neighbours. In this way, plant associations, which are the great fascination of this kind of garden, cannot be held immobile like a painted picture or a weave of material. To remain truly alive and dynamic, gardens must keep changing. This was vigorously asserted by Christopher Lloyd at Great Dixter, who often told me that, after he was no longer around to evolve his masterpiece, its lasting heritage should not be the garden itself but the inspiration it may have passed on to those creating future gardens. In fact, shortly before he died, Christopher set up a trust which continues to creatively evolve his garden. His ghost will nonetheless haunt any trustee who tries to fossilise it. Although the present gardeners at Sissinghurst rightly insist that most of the individual planting has been changed since Vita's day, the Trust's job is to maintain indefinitely the spirit of her garden, with its famous coloured compartments. This must therefore somehow involve putting the flowers to sleep.

If you climb the rose-red tower at Sissinghurst, you can look out over the landscape, which Vita rightly regarded as the perfect setting for her islanded jewel. Indeed the tower, built of local brick, its turrets roofed with oak shingles, is a classic expression of the surrounding Weald. I first went up there with her and I remember the conversation turned on the masonry bees which were colonising the tower. Here was a familiar dilemma. The charming wildlife was eating away at the mortar. Vita was a romantic but she was also ruthlessly practical. With a patrician sweep of her cigarette holder, she indicated their imminent destruction. Behind this practical concern there lay a general anxiety known to all gardeners: the expense and labour of upkeep. Even for the Nicolsons, the gardeners' wage bills, the delectable temptations of new plants from a nursery, not to mention the ever-crumbling buildings, presented a permanent challenge. Christopher Lloyd used to say

Sissinghurst Castle surrounded by intensive arable farmland. The National Trust is now modifying the adjacent Home Farm to restore its hedgerows and other habitats.

of his silvery oak manor house, 'Spring is announced at Dixter by the love song of the death watch beetle.' All gardeners know that the ground elder is waiting to move like a green tide back into the heart of the iris clumps when they cease to take control.

Standing on the tower again I realise that there have been two major changes to the estate farm in the sixty years that I have known it. In the 1950s and early 1960s I remember a small-scale mixed operation of cereals, cattle, orchards, hay meadows and hops, which helped to pay for the garden at its heart. This was the typical Wealden landscape celebrated by Vita in her long poem 'The Land', set in the Kentish valley of the River Eden, which helped to make her name. In that poem she describes all the hard work of the farmer's year: hedging, ditching, ploughing, spraying the orchards and the rotation of crops. However, it is the framework of 'embroidered fields', each with their local names and their loved small corners, that reinforce the sense of place and home.

> With here Lord's Meadow tilted on a hill
> And Scallops' Coppice ending in a gate
> And here the Eden passing by a mill..

Vita saw the garden at Sissinghurst as the climax and concentration of its surrounding farmland. The separate garden compartments echoed the enclosed farm fields. The local hay meadows with their crimson orchids, pale lilac cuckoo flowers, cheerful dog daisies and cranesbills the colour of thunder clouds were an almost subconscious inspiration for the melting mixtures of meadow flowers, which fill the garden borders. Sissinghurst was crafted out of its Wealden setting, as a musician might score a symphony for lawnmower and wood pigeon.

By contrast the working landscape of the countryside, which inspired the garden, was never designed by anyone. It simply arose as a consequence of farming settlement, limited by basic resources and technology, which ensured that local materials and the lie of the land were dovetailed for the practical production of grain, wool, fruit and timber.

Vita died in 1962 and soon after that the matrix of farm hedges began to unravel as the fields were enlarged to accommodate the ever-expanding cereal crops. By the 1970s the view from the tower in May was dominated by the neon-yellow oilseed rape which throbbed up luminously from the middle distance. The heavily-pruned hedges seemed to shrink under a tide of intensive arable which swept up to the very edges of the garden. This was a trend which was happening all over Kent and indeed all over the country. Artificial fertiliser made it possible to dispense with the rotation of crops and everywhere the combination of money and technology opened the way to intensive monocultures.

Then around 2005 things changed again as the National Trust set out to restore the Sissinghurst estate farm back to its former gentler character which Vita would have recognised. Now, once again the garden appears anchored to its countryside rather than marooned in it. The recovering hedges sweep down like crinolines to the field edge, glossy with blackberries and the scarlet berries of briony and guelder rose, all interlaced with self-sown hop bines which have held out in the hedge through the years of agribusiness. Where not so long ago there was just plough land and barbed wire fences, the garden nut trees lean out to the long grasses and leafy shadows of the restored old park. With the field margins left deliberately unploughed, weeds provide cover for voles which attract hawks and owls, so perhaps one magic evening Vita's vision when she was establishing her famous White Garden might yet become reality: 'I cannot help hoping that the great ghostly barn owl will sweep silently across a pale garden, next summer, in the twilight – the pale garden that I am now planting, under the first flakes of snow.'

Wool and wild fowl

But there is one huge change in the modern Kent countryside which would astonish Vita. The farm has become the garden and the garden has become the farm. Sissinghurst Castle is a seven-acre garden now, employing seven gardeners and using up considerable resources in machinery, plants and materials. Together with Highgrove and Hidcote, in Gloucestershire, it is said to be the most expensively maintained garden in England. However, its visitors not only pay for the garden's keep but go on to visit the local pubs, hotels and shops. Tourism is now the basis of 75 per cent of the rural economy, whereas farming is only 10 per cent. The increasingly beleaguered farmers survive by a combination of B&B and

farm produce such as cider and cherries, together with environmental subsidies.

If you look deep into the view from Sissinghurst tower, you may
with a little insider knowledge detect the best bits of woodland or
grassland habitat which are now protected nature reserves owned
by conservation organisations. These are managed and gardened
to the inch. The Woodland Trust carefully coppices its woodlands
to let in the right amount of light for the bluebells, and the Kent
Wildlife Trust mows its orchid meadows even though there is no
real market for the hay.

The question of what society wants of the British countryside
has become ever more open to interpretation as the farming
economics which automatically created a working landscape have
collapsed. Kent, squeezed between London and the Channel ports,
is a front-line county and perhaps begins to show us the shape of
things to come for the rest of Britain. Our vision of that future
is profoundly influenced by idealism for a past, partly mythical
landscape enshrined in art and literature but also by deep anxieties
about tidiness and decay. With ecology and aesthetics rather than
the economics of agricultural production so often in the driving
seat, this has led to some interesting conundrums.

Looking north-east from Sissinghurst Castle tower, the distant
Downs create a blue smudge on the horizon. This is traditional
sheep country and even thirty years ago the collapse of sheep
farming had led to rapid regeneration of blackthorn and gorse
thickets. With no sheep to nibble them any more, the low
grasslands, dense with scabious and wild thyme, were threatened
with extinction. However, naturalists bent on a remedy to this
problem encountered implacable opposition from an unexpected
quarter. Nature is not slow to fill a vacuum and previously
endangered Dartford warblers had started to nest in the thickets.
When the botanists arrived to clear the scrub, the birdwatchers
were waiting for them. Fierce debates still break out between
ecologists, especially since some organisations, such as Plantlife,

draw their paying membership from flower lovers, while the Royal Society for the Protection of Birds (RSPB) is funded by ornithologists. Vita, agonising over which bellflower to set against her clematis, would have sympathised.

As money began to be spent on nature conservation both to acquire reserves and protect special places from development, the conservationists had to come up with less arbitrary reasons to champion the birds and flowers that they loved. Over the years these have evolved into an elaborate set of criteria based on species but more importantly on habitats. These in turn have been used to underpin a wide range of legally protected nature reserves which include National Nature Reserves (NNRs) and Sites of Special Scientific Interest (SSSIs). The criteria to justify these include rare and endangered species and habitats, but also ones that are seen as typical and special to the UK. Thus the black-winged stilt is a rare bird on the edge of its range in Britain though abundant throughout Europe, Asia and Africa. By contrast we may take bluebell woods for granted but they are one of the special glories of England and, being dependent on a relatively frost-free Atlantic climate, not found in very many places beyond our shores. In time these criteria have further evolved into targets and these in turn become the drivers for grant aid offered to ecologists to manage their reserves.

Typical examples of such targets are wading birds, which were once a classic feature of English farmland but have become increasingly threatened by agricultural improvement. One of the best places to see target-driven nature conservation is on the coastal Kentish marshes, where wide spaces and keen winds offer a perfect antidote to the lush woodlands of the Weald. This is also the land of sheep. 'Sheppey', within the complex of the North Kent Marshes facing the Thames Estuary, means literally 'the isle of sheep', while Romney Marsh to the south on the Sussex border has been celebrated for centuries for the quality of its wool. But by the 1970s our warm clothes were made of synthetic material, so there was more money in wheat than wool. A fleece is now only worth around 70 pence, which scarcely pays for the shearing, and even the value of lamb is precarious. The bleating flocks, which had created low grass swards enticing thousands of wading birds and wild duck, increasingly gave way to cereal crops. However in the 1980s the government offered environmental grants known as stewardship to landowners to forgo ploughing and maintain their damp sheep pastures for the lapwing and the redshank.

Philip Merricks is a sheep farmer who also loves birds. Unusually for a man who manages nationally important reserves, he does not represent a nature conservation organisation. He is a hard-headed, highly commercial private farmer and this seems to me a useful model for integrating agriculture and nature conservation. On his land in Romney Marsh, where deliberate flooding to hinder invading German tanks in the Second World War had created habitat for the exotic spoonbill, all it took was Philip's enthusiasm, supported by stewardship payments and the arable revenue from the rest of his farm, to block off some ditches and put the land under sheep and cattle. Now, where in 1990 there was just a square mile of clods, you crest the old sea wall and look down on skeins of wild duck alighting on 400 acres of water and waving reed. Redshank and lapwing returned to breed and one morning the farmworker excavating a new pond reported that a large white bird with a strange beak was standing beside the digger. The spoonbill was back. 'This landscape is absolutely timeless', enthused one visitor before being gently corrected. It was four years old.

At Elmley in the North Kent Marshes, Philip farms a 3,000-acre grazing marsh following specific targets for breeding waders for which the Department for Environment, Food and Rural Affairs (DEFRA) pays him a stewardship grant. Accordingly he carries out very careful management to maximise breeding waders and ensure their chicks reach adulthood. This includes careful control of water levels and livestock grazing to create an uneven sward of hollows, pools, muddy margins and sheltering tufts of grass just right for the young birds. Another big factor is predator control. Having taken a lot of trouble and spent a lot of public money getting the birds to breed, it is a serious failure if the chicks are then all snaffled by foxes and crows. As Philip explains, without that final step he would be setting up a wader trap, having enticed the birds in and then provided a perfect breakfast invitation for all the predators for miles around. He therefore fences, traps and shoots, and explains all this to the visiting public. The high figures of surviving chicks on his land are compelling. In these ways Philip is effectively gardening lapwings and his husbandry is as complex and controlled as that of any horticulturalist working in the borders of Sissinghurst or Dixter.

This targeted approach to conservation management has become the norm for very many habitats in the UK, often modelled on the

Lapwing and Golden Plover circle over a pond at the Kent Wildlife Trust's Oare Marshes in the Thames Estuary.

traditional farmland which created such rich natural diversity in the past. In the 1950s flowery meadows were cut for hay without a thought for botanical beauty, but now cattle are fed from the silage that you see in huge black plastic bags or, most recently, that ugliest and least sustainable of cereal crops, maize. If the meadows were simply abandoned, they would soon revert to scrub and then open woodland, as, in time, would most land in the British Isles. So the few remaining flower-rich meadows have been bought by conservationists and are still mown every summer to preserve them. The hay is sold for horses but it is hardly a great earner. The real rewards are the swaying flowers and dancing butterflies – each species carefully surveyed, named and counted to achieve a scientific value which then earns the environmental grant. But just as we have refined and perfected this approach to conservation, a radically new and charismatic aspiration is gaining popularity, not just among the arcane disciplines of ecology but in the media. This refuses to focus its attention on any particular species, habitat or target but instead is driven by a simple though seldom-defined idea: rewilding.

Rewilding

To see rewilding in action you can cross the border from Kent into Sussex and visit a country estate whose approach to management lies at the opposite end of the spectrum to the Elmley Marshes. Knepp Castle is a 3,500-acre estate where, faced by falling profits on its intractable clay land, the landowner abandoned conventional farming in 2001. Instead he made gaps in the hedges and introduced deer and hardy breeds of cattle, ponies and pigs, which, like wild animals in a true wilderness, range free over the entire area. In the gently rolling Weald dotted with spreading oaks, a white windmill gleams among the trees far to the south, and beyond, on the furthest horizon, is the misty whaleback of the South Downs. The estate itself resembles the Sissinghurst Castle farm, but taken a step further in natural regeneration. The straight farm ditches have turned back to winding streams. The once-flailed blackthorn hedges now march into the fields, radiant with white blossom in spring and melodious with nightingales on summer evenings. The fields themselves are no longer cropped but waist high with flea-bane, buttercups and teazles. In damp corners, dense thickets of sallows have sprung up, providing the food plant for an exception-ally large population of purple emperor butterflies. Environmental grants, organic meat sales, campsites and the proximity of Gatwick Airport has ensured that rents from cottages and converted barns for offices have proved critical in holding the place together com-pared to previous agriculture.

This is 'process-led' land management reinstating natural processes that would have occurred in the absence of human activity, or so the theory goes. The more extreme advocates of rewilding in 1990s America saw earliest civilisation's original adoption of agriculture as an historic wrong turning, though that is surely a serious case of closing the stable door after the horse has bolted. Rewilding is the exact opposite of target-driven nature conservation, where the natural systems are elaborately manipulated to deliver very particular species or habitats. Instead, you sit back and see what turns up. Indeed the nightingales and purple emperors at Knepp were a complete surprise to everyone.

Every gradation of conservation between these two extremes of target-led and process-led management has its passionate protagonists and its textbook examples. At the National Trust's Wicken Fen in Cambridgeshire, where I have been actively involved over 25 years, we ranch ponies and cattle over a 1,000-acre wetland. We do not shoot or trap the foxes and crows, and we do not move our stock from one paddock to the next, but allow them to roam free over the entire area. They are our East Anglian equivalent of wild bison.

Above all, we do not seek to put the requirements of any one species ahead of the experimental process that we are watching unfold. In recent years, cranes have started to breed in the nearby Lakenheath Fen, an RSPB reserve run on strict target-driven principles. As the crane population expands beyond the Lakenheath site, a pair has taken to circling Wicken Fen in springtime as if they were prospecting to breed. You hear them before you see them, a fluting insistent bugling which makes the hairs stand up on the back of one's neck, gradually increasing in intensity until the birds materialise overhead. It is the true sound of wilderness – of the mighty Russian steppe. But alas, they are not for our Wicken wilderness. Cranes will not breed unless they have an area from where livestock is excluded and, sixteen years into our process experiment, that would mean breaking the rules. The Lakenheath warden comes over and watches them wistfully through his binoculars and longs for us to shut just one gate and give his birds a cattle-free corner where they might breed. Even he has his problems, however, in guaranteeing success for his neatly target-driven strategies. Marsh harriers are known to prey on baby cranes, thus one prime target species can be found actively devouring another. The natural world has an exasperating way of refusing to follow the rules.

I am sure that if the process system of management we have adopted at Wicken Fen were to only create rather boring habitat we would abandon the experiment. In fact we now have clouds of duck and golden plover in winter, breeding waders and black- necked grebe in summer and marsh harriers which patrol the fen on long dark wings. This approach is also cheaper than the elaborate management we carry out elsewhere on the fen. Our warden, who has successfully created all this and is at heart a rewilding man, mutters darkly about 'gardening', which he uses as a pejorative term to describe a high-maintenance approach that he would not countenance on the newly created parts of his reserve. We are good friends but on this matter we agree to disagree. I maintain that we are still gardening at Wicken but in a more relaxed way. We have perimeter fences. We manipulate water levels. We employ vets for

Wicken Fen, Cambridgeshire, where ponies and cattle are ranched over a thousand-acre wetland.

our livestock, and when these become too many for the reserve we will have to remove some. Theoretically we could control stock numbers by introducing wolves or lynx to create a truly natural equilibrium but on a small reserve in crowded England, with a whole constituency of neighbours and National Trust members to placate, this tactic would be a step too far.

The reintroduction of the wolf is a hardy perennial in the British press but dismissed by many rewilders as a red herring and distraction from the more achievable aims of process management. This may be because they recognise that the scale of the British landscape is too small to accommodate such a beast. It is estimated that the whole of the Cairngorms could only support two pairs of wolves before their cubs would stray beyond the park boundaries and have to be culled. But I suspect that there is actually something going on within the rewilding debate which is wider and deeper than just another scientific technique for managing nature reserves. Rewilding has a romantic, even primal, appeal in a country where 80 per cent of us live in cities. The journalist George Monbiot, the high priest of rewilding in the UK, in his book *Feral*, describes reserves such as Wicken as 'informed by the curatorial ethos'. I agree but don't feel ashamed of it. He is happy to conserve meadows which require regular mowing but 'would prefer to see these places labelled culture reserves', suggesting that nature closely involving people is not real nature at all. But he makes some very well-directed hits against the overgrazed wet deserts of the British uplands, where the subsidy is farmed rather more than the sheep. Describing sheep as the 'white plague', he has performed the useful task of making the rest of us in nature conservation seem reasonable but earned the hatred of hill farmers, who complain that he and others like him intend to turn the much-loved stone-walled pastures of the Lake District into a second rate Alaska.

Woodland coppicing

How we restore and manage woodland is another conservation controversy. Traditional ecologists have long carried out rotational clearance of woodland known as coppicing. This echoes the regular clearance carried out by previous generations for fencepoles, hop poles and firewood. The resulting sunlit glades create spectacular displays of bluebells, and in the woodlands of East Kent near Canterbury they help conserve some very special orchids and butterflies. However, the rewilders point out that if we ceased coppicing, the butterflies might reduce but many moths and beetles would thrive even more. What they would like to see are grazing animals such as wild boar creating a patchy wood pasture without human hand. They say that dazzling sheets of bluebells, however beautiful, are an indication of an impoverished ecosystem, almost a monoculture, because animals which would have eaten them in the wild wood are no longer there.

These debates over the different levels of human intervention lie at the heart and soul of modern British nature conservation. This book celebrates an alternative model to rewilding, one in which humanity actively manages and harvests the natural world as opposed to total wildernesses where people are relatively absent. However, I think there is an important place for rewilding in the English countryside, as there is also for target management and all the gradations between. To insist on a single 'correct' solution for conservation management would be to create a predictable landscape almost as monotonous as the monocultures. All the different approaches contribute to the many layered palimpsest of the English landscape, quirky and profoundly humanised by the undesigned contributions from every era since the Pleistocene to the present day: patches of ancient woodland, medieval field boundaries and even the Second World War pillboxes that perch on the convenient eminence of a Bronze Age cairn.

What I do not accept are the intensive monocultures that wipe out the palimpsest at a stroke and the case against them is one of the main drivers of this book. Few monocultures are uglier than unmitigated commercial forestry. All over Kent, and indeed all over England, there are large plantations of conifers grown for softwood, the original planting of which was often underpinned by tax breaks. As an economically questionable and environmentally damaging crop, this was the forester's equivalent of wheat. This was especially damaging where the conifers replaced that select category of habitat known as 'ancient woodland', since these deciduous woods, carefully coppiced over many centuries, had evolved the richest assemblies of birds, flowers and insects. Throughout Britain in the post-war years, as meadows and marshes were ploughed for cereals, ancient woodland was felled and planted with fast-growing American Sitka spruce, which cast an acid carpet of needles over the bluebells and a shadow of permanent darkness over the woods. In the 1970s, the Forestry Commission killed many massive oaks in Sherwood Forest to make way for the alien spruce. The old 'England of the Greenwood Tree' went into a semi-industrialised sleep.

But compared to the ploughed habitats, this was sleep rather than death. Along the narrow rides between the black and birdless plantations, the last of the primroses still held out and, even in the deepest shadows, the old hazel stools pushed up pallid springtime sprouts like potatoes in a cellar. In the late 1990s, the conservationists, now managing many areas of ancient woodland, cleared large tracts of conifers and three years later the butterflies were back. What is more, environmentalists are now buying open farmland to plant it up and so reunite the last severed parcels of woodland. A total contiguous system makes a far better habitat than the sum of the scattered parts, and in some places purchase of small but critically sited plots can quadruple the area of forest cover. The Forestry Commission has also signed up to a long-term programme of conifer removal from all its ancient woods.

When Vita Sackville-West first discovered her ruined castle beneath the briars and bedsprings, she wrote: 'I saw what might be made of it. It was Sleeping Beauty's castle.' As the landscape of Kent is brought back to life as a habitat for wildlife, this restoration has not so much involved pulling out the briars as putting them back, and the sun-filled woodland is a wakening beauty if ever there was one.

Apple orchards

The woodlands are not the only traditional elements of the Kentish landscape which are coming back to life. 'Kent, sir,' exclaims Mr Jingle in Charles Dickens' *Pickwick Papers*, 'everybody knows Kent – apples, cherries, hops and women'. Hop gardens and fruit orchards are an archetypal image of South-east England. Yet both crops were originally novel commodities, into which farmers diversified when faced with a surplus market for the main staples of grain and meat. British farmers are living through the fourth great arable supply and demand crisis in historic times.

The first came in the Middle Ages. Between 1100 and 1300, the population of England quadrupled. Cereal expansion boomed. Then came the Black Death. By 1400, the population had halved and there was no one to eat the bread. Wool, milk and rabbits were adopted as more flexible commodities. In 1656, agricultural surplus led to another collapse of farm prices, culminating in an emergency measure by Oliver Cromwell to sanction an unprecedented export of food to the continent. Hops and fruit, which were known and grown by the Saxons, had been further developed as a luxury by the Tudors, with improved varieties imported from the Low Countries. They were seized upon by the Kentish landowners, who could easily export them up the Thames to London. When grain prices crashed again in 1879, partly as a result of cheap imports from America, leading to an intermittent recession which was to last into the 1930s, the hops and the fruit enjoyed a further golden age.

You can still find apple orchards throughout Kent and Sussex, although more than a third have gone from the High Weald since the 1960s. Tucked into the angle of a wood or embowering a weatherboarded cottage, the mossed cottage trees provide nesting habitat for goldfinches, linnets and turtle doves. Green woodpeckers love orchards as, more problematically, does the beautiful bullfinch with its destructive taste for apple buds. In spring the orchard grass is moonlight pale with cow parsley, and strewn in autumn with the windfalls, bubbles of cidery juice, which lure the dancing wasps and the scrumping children. Their names evoke five centuries of apple culture: Ribston Pippin, Blenheim Orange, Peasgood Nonsuch, Egremont Russet and Worcester Pearmain. They also represent the march of fashion. Golden Delicious, which supplanted them, is now fast joining them to become yet another period fruit.

But the real heartland of commercial fruit growing in Kent was and remains the brick earth country around Sittingbourne and Faversham. Here the cherry orchards created an entire landscape of snowy blossom between the North Downs and the Thames Estuary. Sheep were driven across the county originally to act as lawnmowers beneath the tall standard trees. In the 1960s, a shepherd would typically look after 200 ewes in the orchards. The wool paid his salary and the lamb was the profit. The apple-picking was a dangerous ritual involving the masterly use of hooks, baskets known as kibseys, tied to the waist, and tall ladders of larch and ash, splayed at the bottom and oiled with linseed. If the ladder slipped, the trick was to hang on even if you swung upside down, as the ladder could only fall deeper into the heart of the tree. But there were plenty of broken bones and occasional fatalities. If the ladder making and the picking were crafts, the transport system was a tour de force of precision timing. At Teynham, where Henry VIII's fruiterer, Richard Harris, had originally pioneered commercial cherry-planting, the stationmaster in the 1950s could manipulate the rail network to convey huge quantities of perishable fruit to markets as far away as Scotland. A further revolution in transport was to change all this.

Apple and cherry farming is a romantic but risky occupation. Compared to the relative predictability of wheat, fruit lies at the mercy of hail, rain and above all a spring frost, which can wipe out 70 per cent of the year's crop. After the last war this uncertainty of production was outweighed by the safety anchor of a virtual monopoly. Apart from bananas and tangerines, Britain had little other fresh soft fruit available. With no refrigerated lorries and far less air transport, peaches or mangoes were unheard of, let alone competing apples and cherries from Italy, Turkey and the USA.

Despite the benefits of dwarfing stocks, which overcame the expense of picking from tall trees, the flown-in alternatives ensured that in the second half of the century two-thirds of our orchards were lost. The last of the Thames Valley orchards, where in 1830 Richard Cox raised his famous Orange Pippin, were felled by appropriate irony to make way for the expanding runways at Heathrow bringing in the imported apples. In Kent there were nearly 13,000 acres of commercial cherries in 1951. By 2000, there was a grand total of 186 acres in the whole of England and Wales. At home in Kent we used to sit around our fire of fragrant cherry

Grading apples at J. Day's mechanised farm at Staplehurst, Kent, 1930s.

logs munching imported apples and lamenting vaguely about the loss of the springtime spectacle.

Nonetheless, many Kentish apple orchards and even some cherries survive partly because farm payments from the EU prohibit further felling. The growers must choose between low or high-input, with rain shields and netting. With the latter costly investment they cannot afford to fail, and half-measures are the worst of both worlds. Risk management is everything. A few large cherry trees have been retained to enhance the ambience – and the earning power of pubs and rented cottages. A hillside of modern ten-foot cherries is still spectacular at blossom time and dwarf apple trees develop just as gnarled and crooked a character as their larger predecessors, their crusty bark silvered with lichen. Hares and partridges thrive in the orchards, which are sheltered with belts of alder or birch. Best of all, the apple pickers are still needed. You can't afford to bruise a Grade 1 Bramley for the supermarket and that means careful hand- picking either by locals or itinerant communities coming in from Europe.

There are alternatives to commercial farming for keeping some fruit trees in a landscape. The village of Lustleigh in Devon has its own community orchard, left by a parishioner in his will. It is four acres of public open space which would otherwise have gone for housing. The cider and mistletoe it produces cover the cost of the orchard, where children climb trees and, when the apple blossom is at its height, the Okehampton brass band celebrates May Day. In some countries fruit trees are harvested as common property in the way we pick blackberries from the hedgerows. Over the rolling hills of the Czech Republic, the tipsily weaving country lanes are lined with plum trees. Somebody presumably owns them but nobody seems to mind when, every harvest time, people arrive with sheets to catch the sweet and bursting fruit, which they shake down to make plum brandy. It was in this spirit of celebrating this natural abundance which is the hallmark of orchards that, in 1990, the environmental charity Common Ground launched National Apple

Day. This is now observed all over the country on 21 October with displays and sales of apples, consumption of apple dishes and the presence of an expert who will identify any fruit you might bring in from your orchard or garden. Apple Day has fuelled a movement which promoted community orchards, grant-aided apple growing and increased awareness of our locally grown varieties.

But the greatest apple success story has come from the unexpected quarter of big business and has resulted from the virtual reinvention of what was previously a very unpromising commodity: cider. For many years cider was a warm drink sold in a large plastic bottle and largely made from apple concentrate imported from China. It was cheap alcohol for drunks or used for boiling bacon. With such an image, if the traditional apple orchards were beleaguered in the 1990s, the cider orchards were rapidly becoming extinct. Into this situation, in 2007, stepped Magners, a brand of Bulmers Irish Cider, originally produced in County Tipperary by the Irish drinks company C and C Group. Capitalising on the landscape awareness of orchards fostered by Common Ground, Magners transformed the image of cider into something fashionable and metropolitan.

Suddenly cider was cool, marketed in elegantly labelled bottles and poured over ice. Much cider is now certified with a Protected Geographical Indicator (PGI), which guarantees that it doesn't use imported apple concentrate. What is more, small local growers, who flourish under the rules whereby excise duty is removed if the grower produces less than 7,000 litres, are branding their unique local cider like a rare and sought-after wine. Liqueur ciders can retail at £20 a bottle and specialist English ciders are now exported to the USA, while pears are also being grown for a resurging production of perry. In the apple-growing counties cider shops are opening and there are cider cycling routes. As a result of this new cider chic the felling and ploughing is reversed, and in Kent, the West Country and the Welsh Borders orchards are actually being planted again. Between 2009 and 2012, apple orchards expanded in England and Wales by 6.4 per cent, with cider orchards making up half the area at over 7,000 hectares. The Garden of England is starting to look like a garden again.

Hop gardens

Every September in my childhood the air of our village was saturated with the musty aroma of hops and the pub resounded with songs and raucous laughter. This was 'Hop Picking', perhaps the nearest England ever came to the great social event of the French grape harvest. The local workforce was supplemented by a great influx of East Enders, who came down from London for a traditional working holiday. A typical hop farm might have 500 hopper huts and that meant as many families. They worked all day, their arms and faces black with the hop resin, their children as young as six helping in the picking. This would now be frowned on, but there was seldom a crop which left so individual and positive a mark both on a community and a landscape. In the late-1960s, machines replaced the hop pickers and the hop gardens themselves began to vanish. A consumer switch to lager, imports from Germany and USA, improved storage and chemical alternatives radically reduced the hop gardens with their green colonnades of vines in high summer and their stark winter tracery of poles and wires. The circular brick oast houses no longer contained drying hops but London commuters.

Since 2010, however, English hop growing has been undergoing a steady renaissance due to the boom in microbreweries producing craft beer. For economy of scale and consistency of product, industrial-scale brewers use as few hops as possible. This is the complete opposite of craft beers, which require a wide range of hops that are produced locally. Especially popular are the aromatic varieties, which give a wide range of flavours. The resinous, peppery and fruity character of English hops is described in language previously associated with fine wines.

A Kentish Hop Garden.

Goulden & Wind, Ashford.

Souvenir postcard from a Kentish hop garden, 1905. Many Londoners had 'working holidays' picking hops in Kent.

The key to microbreweries' success is the tiny number of people needed to brew beer. Even in large breweries, the actual brewing process seldom employs more than ten people. Microbreweries might only need a couple of workers, while a small family business can restrict distribution to nearby pubs, shops and farmers' markets and do its own bottling in redundant farm buildings until it gets large enough to contract out. For these reasons, microbreweries which started with 20 pioneers in 1980 now number over 1,200 in the UK and are growing at around 10 per cent a year. This diverse small-scale economy has to be good for a diverse small-scale landscape and improve the market for hop poles out of the coppiced woodland. In 2015, an additional 20 hectares of hop gardens were planted in England, a relatively small increase but a record one to set against all the previous decades of decline. All is not entirely lost in Kent's farmland, despite the monocultures of wheat or Sitka spruce.

My own personal connection with Kent ended when in 1987 my sister finally died and my father soon after her. After my mother died, I sold the house. I have seldom been back. However, when I visited Sissinghurst again, the revival of its farmland and its bluebell woods gave me reasons for hope. Adam Nicolson, the grandson of Vita and Harold, had for a period returned to Sissinghurst Castle and became the driving force behind the restoration of the surrounding farm. As a tenant of the National Trust he lacked his grandparents' instant freedom to change things, but as a writer and journalist he could exploit the glamorous mantle of his Sackville ancestry to promote his ideas, which he documented in his book, *Sissinghurst: An Unfinished History*. As a result, the National Trust brought natural habitat back to the estate's Home Farm, a sympathetic blueprint that is now being used for the management of the Trust's estate farms throughout the country.

CHAPTER 3

Peat and wheat

The end of British farming?

The house of William Bunting, bleak and derelict, dominates the heart of the Yorkshire town of Thorne. Its name is Periplaneta, Latin for 'cockroach'. This was Bunting's little joke. In 1954 he was thrown out of his council house in Thorne because he was breeding cockroaches there for scientific research and use in school biology classes. When he bought his own home, he memorialised those misunderstood insects as part of his postal address. The house has stood empty for the twenty years or so since Bunting died in 1995, the windows boarded and the roof full of holes. Thorne itself is not exactly flourishing, having been stricken by the collapse of British coal-mining, but so extravagant is the dereliction of Periplaneta that, among the betting shops and bars of its town centre, it comes as a shock. Grass grows in the gutters. Burdock blocks up the door. A sleek young yew tree sprouts from the tottering chimney. A colony of pigeons is in proud possession of the house. They perch heraldically on the Gothic gables and, from to time, all rise to circle their home in a leisurely manner, scattering a pattern of wheeling shadows on the white peeling walls. Rats run in the cellars, which were the prison cells for what was once the police house and where Bunting used to keep his lethal home-brew known as 'witch's piss'.

The garden is impassable, choked with brambles and rosebay; and a large evergreen tree is in fact another substantial building, entirely concealed by ivy. Linnets perch on the coils of razor wire surveying the surrounding ruin and goldfinches flit over the thistle tops. The warm summer air is filled with floating thistledown and ripe with the peppery blackcurrant scent of buddleia. Arching over it all are the rank towers of hemlock that smell of death.

It must be thirty years since I came here to visit Mr Bunting with my friend Stephen Warburton, stalwart of the Yorkshire Wildlife Trust. We tapped tentatively on the front door. Immediately from the darkness within, there erupted the hollow baying of an unseen bloodhound, which hurled itself upon us the minute we entered. When eventually its owner troubled to restrain it, this horrifying beast retired to a corner, where with rolling eyes and slavering jaws it set about mauling a marrowbone. Only then was it possible to focus on Bunting himself. A chronic sufferer from tuberculosis and spondylitis, he was clearly very ill but mastered his infirmities with an iron will. He was smaller than I expected, given his terrifying reputation, and had pale almost blueish skin. But, like Coleridge's ancient mariner, he held you with his glittering eye and with an atmosphere of half-concealed violence. 'Poofs, pederasts, poseurs!' was his continual catchphrase, uttered with a broad Yorkshire accent. It was never very clear whether this was addressed to a particular enemy of the moment or the company in general. While he was a passionate conservationist, he vented his bitterness and rage on fellow naturalists and potential allies as much as on developers. I once met a farmer who encountered Bunting out walking. In response to a friendly greeting from the farmer, he unleashed a writhing mass of adders that he had collected on his wanderings. On another occasion Bunting drew the sword-stick, which he habitually carried with him, against an officer from the Nature Conservancy Council. And when he disagreed with the evidence given in a public inquiry by Professor David Bellamy he threw money in the famous ecologist's face with the accusation that

Bellamy's consultancy fees were the equivalent of thirty pieces of silver. Yet this dislikeable and frightening man was also one of the most inspirational and effective saviours of the English landscape in the late twentieth century.

To understand what he achieved it is necessary to visit the countryside around the town of Thorne. This is not the tourist Yorkshire of the Dales or the upland moors of the Brontë sisters. Altogether odder and quite as atmospheric, these are the levels east of Doncaster, which became known in the 1980s miners' strike as the People's Republic of South Yorkshire. At harvest time it is a landscape without a single leaf. The intensive arable farmland lies just below the level of the adjacent roads, so when you are driving along the road surface is flush with the top of the wheat, which gives the illusion of sailing on an infinite sea of cereals: the blond wheat, the bearded barley and the oilseed rape which, to walk through once cut, is like penetrating a field of knives. The gleaming wheat ears are packed in like an army of soldiers on parade, not a bristle or an awl out of place in their millions upon millions. It is perfection of a kind, if that is what you are after. Around these parts the farmers say they 'plough to the tarmac' and the cereals sweep up to the service station forecourts and the very doors of the gardenless farmhouses. The only other landscape elements here are the steel wind farms, wire pylons, concrete cooling towers and no fewer than three motorways. This is the landscape of the future and increasingly of the whole world. From Lincolnshire to Land's End and across Europe, America, China, and even Africa, where crop meets concrete and every last scrap of habitat is eliminated to squeeze out the last available commodity.

But there is one totally unexpected contrast to this unrelieved picture of exploitation, for right in the centre of this intensive agribusiness and industrialised control lie some of the largest and wildest wildernesses to be found anywhere in lowland Britain: the great wetlands of Thorne Moors and Hatfield Chase, collectively known as the Humberhead Levels.

Peat-mining: the Humberhead Levels

The Humberhead Levels comprise more than 3,300 hectares of birch, moss and water. They are ringed by fenced-off wind farms and impassable ditches, with public roads circling warily at a respectful distance, and so the moors both lure and taunt the traveller, forever unreachable beyond the next and then the next horizon. When you finally penetrate the wetland fastness, there are ticks in the bracken and adders in the heather. It is very easy to get lost even with an experienced guide and one false step in the wrong direction may land you up to your waist or worse, swallowed entirely, in the quaking bog. But the perils are worth it. This was William Bunting's playground and it is a mecca for all naturalists and lovers of England's wild places.

Perhaps the most astonishing thing about this natural phenomenon is its physical nature. Thorne Moors is a swamp which is also a hill and, what is more, a hill which continually grows. It is like an ever-expanding animal two miles wide, a kind of huge living sponge transplanted from the seabed, although it is actually a vast colony of plants fed by rain and peaceful neglect. Around three to four thousand years ago the great forests at the mouth of the Humber were inundated by rising seas and, at the lowest and deepest part of the swamp, the acid conditions favoured the growth of sphagnum moss. Their delicate but persistent fronds continually soak up rain and never rot in the Yorkshire cold. They are virtual machines for absorbing water and nutrients. So when the pyramids and Stonehenge were being built, while South Yorkshire was wild and untamed beyond imagination, the mosses began to grow. Patiently, inexorably, the little filaments swelled and expanded through the Romans to the Normans and into modern times.

Through 3,000 springs and 3,000 winters the bog continued to grow and it pickled and preserved everything that fell into it. You can pick up branches lying in the swamp which look as if

Important wetlands are destroyed by industrial-scale peat-mining, here in the Natural Regional Park of Volcans d'Auvergne, France.

they fell there yesterday. Peer closer and they are boughs of bog oak which leafed up in some long-forgotten springtime around the time Julius Caesar was invading Britain. Some of the living residents have also been around that long. Crawling through the mosses is a little beetle known as the 'bog hog'. Fossils of its ancestors have been found here dating back three millennia. The 'raised mires', as they are now called, were regarded as a wonder of nature by local diarists and antiquarians from as early as the seventeenth century. With every wet winter they visibly expanded. In the nineteenth century a local vicar, Adrian Woodruffe-Peacock, observed that the moors grew 6 to 8 feet every winter and another local botanist and miller stated that such was the growth of the bog that he could no longer see the tower of Crowle church from the village of Thorne.

Within this eccentric natural system all kinds of specialised wetland wildlife flourish. Among the glittering ranks of birch the mysterious nightjar churrs to its mate. In spring the inky pools reflect the butter- yellow flowers of the insectivorous bladderwort and a blizzard of snow-white cotton grass while the scarce large heath butterflies feast on the coconut–scented gorse.

But just over ten years ago Thorne Moors and Hatfield Chase presented a very different scene. Almost unbelievably the great wildernesses were as leafless and industrialised as the surrounding countryside. Thorne Moors resembled an airfield of black scoured mud extending to the horizon over which massive machinery systematically excavated the entire wetland system. This was because a by-product of the sphagnum which had created the raised mires also yielded a very lucrative commercial commodity: horticultural peat. Traditionally peat had been cut with spades for fuel on the moors, but because of the small scale of harvesting creating little pools and ditches, if anything this enhanced rather than damaged the ecosystem. But between the 1960s and the 1990s gardeners discovered the usefulness of this new wonder compost, leading to massive commercial investment. In 1963, the company Fisons plc took over the British Moss Litter Company which had received planning permission for peat extraction on Thorne Moors and Hatfield Chase in the 1950s. With huge profits at stake the technology of large-scale peat extraction was revolutionised. To remove large quantities of peat it needed to be partially dried, and huge drains were dug, which immediately dried up the pools and swamps along with with all their wetland wildlife. Then, in 1987, Fisons introduced a new technology: surface milling. This involved stripping off all the vegetation and deep-draining the bog. Machines could then skim off the peat from many hundreds of acres in a very short time.

This was the spectacle which confronted me when I first visited the Humberhead Levels. On Hatfield Chase, behind a discreet screen of wind-scorched Leyland cypresses, were the shabby huts, tramlines and stacked bales of the peat works. Beyond them extended 2,000 acres of totally stripped-out, black, gleaming peat: an area equivalent to that of a sizeable town. The surviving 1,000 acres of vegetation, where a few trees, birds and butterflies still held on, were also scheduled for destruction. The shifting light illuminated the great sweep of the milling fields, devoid of even a single bobtail of cotton grass, as the cranes and diggers, looming out on the moor like space age dinosaurs, picked over the wetland until there was nothing left. As we looked on horrified and helpless, it seemed that this extraordinary natural system which had taken 3,000 years to evolve would in ten years or less be gone, taken away bag by bag for brief summer crops of tomatoes.

The total miracle, that Thorne Moors have in fact survived this onslaught, is due in no small part to the tenacity of that bad-tempered old devil William Bunting. What Bunting brought to the situation was erudite legal cunning, a willingness to resort to direct physical action and a refusal to take no for an answer even when he was entirely isolated. His mantra was 'Say NO. Mean NO. Fight to retain the places we have.' A knowledgeable and observant naturalist, he was also a self-taught lawyer who could decipher ancient documents in medieval Latin and Norman French and who actually persuaded the High Court Chancery Division to move temporarily from London to Doncaster to hear one of his petitions concerning Thorne Moors. This was a first in legal history.

In 1972, Fisons excavated several deep drains in the heart of the bog to facilitate peat extraction. Bunting immediately convened a group of naturalists, local residents and students. Throughout the long hot summer they set out onto the moors with stones, clay and railway sleepers to dam the newly excavated drains. They were to become known as 'Bunting's Beavers'. In October that year, shortly after a BBC television crew filmed the 'Beavers' at work, Fisons dynamited eighteen of the dams. The Beavers repaired them but this time, under pressure from increasing bad publicity, Fisons let them stand, and in 1974 they agreed to stay off that core area of the bog, which was finally purchased by the Nature Conservancy Council. In 1985, it was declared a National Nature Reserve.

Meanwhile, Bunting played his other card: the legal argument that Thorne Moors was really common land and the peat extractors did not have proper legal ownership of it. In 1976, he lost his application to have the moors registered as common land, but in 1983 he took his appeal to the High Court, which upheld his application and granted William Bunting and the occupants of his house, Periplaneta, the right to cut peat on Thorne Moors under the noses of Fisons in perpetuity.

This was something of a pyrrhic victory, since Fisons was left in control of the surrounding system. Bunting told me that others in the community, who might all have claimed commoner's rights on the moors and so seriously challenged the development, were 'bought off with women and bottles of whisky'. Whether or not this was true, there was also an understandable lobby from those in Thorne employed in the peat industry to keep operations going. The core nature reserve land was physically threatened by the drying and milling of the surrounding peatlands and its legal status undermined by the fact that the planning permission granted in the 1950s could not be retrospectively overturned.

Bunting achieved nothing absolute to halt the advance of development on the moors but, in retrospect, it is clear that he bought time. By the late 1980s the spotlight of publicity was at last turning on this remote corner of South Yorkshire. In 1987, I led a small team from Channel 4 TV to film the peat-cutting. We drove over the single rusting bridge that gave access onto Hatfield Chase, past warning signs announcing that trespassers would be 'arrested and prosecuted'. We crawled under the barbed wire to get as close as we dared to film the machinery out on the moor.

This was part of a general wave of press coverage in which the National Peat Campaign, formed in 1990, encouraged gardeners to boycott the use of peat in nurseries and garden centres. It was the best possible weapon to use against Fisons but the race was now on. Everything depended on how much peat remained at the bottom of the mire. It needed to be deep enough and wet enough to allow the sphagnum to regrow once operations ceased. If too much was removed, the site would just become a lake, similar to the many flooded gravel pits up and down the country. The peat operators insisted that they were leaving sufficient depth of moss. The conservationists were certain that they were not. Learned papers and consultancy reports commissioned by the rival protagonists debated this arcane but crucial point while peat- milling on the moors moved into high gear. Would the gardening public realise and act in time before these extraordinary natural systems were irreversibly destroyed?

Quizzed about peat at the Chelsea Flower Show, Margaret Thatcher announced that she couldn't see how gardeners could manage without it. But finally in 1992 Fisons was brought to the negotiating table and agreed in principle to 'gift' Thorne Moors and Hatfield Chase to the nation and hand it over to English Nature, the heirs of the Nature Conservancy Council. The peat developers had their price and when eventually Fisons' successors, Scotts (UK) Ltd, presented the peatland to the nation, they were able to claim £17.3 million from the government in potential loss of earnings. But even after that agreement a leaseback negotiated behind closed doors allowed peat extraction to continue until 2004, when peat-mining finally ceased on Hatfield Chase, Thorne Moors and Wedholme Flow in Cumbria. The peat had been reduced to no more than a foot deep in places. It was the eleventh hour and fifty-ninth minute for Britain's finest raised mires but, after half a century of campaigning, they were saved.

The case of peat, a relatively small environmental issue, is surely a test case for the way we are torn between our love of nature and the inexorable law of unintended consequences. Before I had visited Thorne and Hatfield nobody was more insatiable for peat than I was. A passionate gardener, I absolutely poured it on my garden. I remember my local supplier in Birmingham saying: 'You can't have enough of this stuff!' Like millions of other gardeners I didn't make the connection, because I had only the vaguest idea how peat was obtained. Those of us who then witnessed the destruction of the raised mires were able to see the inherent contradiction of a nation of flower lovers destroying one of the country's finest and most extraordinary natural gardens. In the 1980s, I wrote that the ruining of the raised mires was 'the ecological equivalent of knocking down a cathedral and using the dust to line the garden path', a phrase which was printed on bags of peat-free compost.

But even now the progress on peat alternatives is far from successfully concluded. It is the old story of *What does it mean, and How do you know?* Your garden centre may proclaim a sustainable peat policy, but if you look carefully at the bags, many do contain peat, albeit with the disclaimer that this is not peat from Sites of Scientific Interest (SSSIs). This is hardly something to boast about, since peat from those protected nature reserves would be illegal.

On Friday 1 October 2004, following the deal between English Nature and the peat producers, the peat machines at Thorne Moors milled along a final strip for the press and television cameras, and in a small ceremonious procession departed the site for good. A week later a sharp-eyed local took a celebratory stroll on Hatfield Chase which, after being closed off for so long, was now open to the public. He immediately noticed a set of nine poles partially disinterred by the most recent peat working and all neatly laid out in parallel lines. Emerging from beneath what had previously been two metres of peat, clearly they were not the handiwork of any modern peat worker. Looking closer he saw that the ends of the poles had been chiselled sharp with a blunt axe. It was ultimately confirmed through carbon dating that this had been part of an ancient causeway laid down in the Neolithic period.

Now nature has returned. There are curlew, snipe and even breeding cranes while harriers and short-eared owls patrol the levels of dancing cotton grass. Best of all, only ten years since Thorne Moors was a scoured industrial wasteland the mosses are growing again, spilling out over the edges of the trackways and, like the corals of a reef, rebuilding the raised mires as they have

Cotton grass flourishes again in the restored Thorne Moors near Doncaster.

done for over three millennia. But there is something that has not changed. The old peat works at Hatfield Chase, behind the wind-scorched Leyland cypresses, is still there and appears to be as busy as ever. There are plenty of peat bales, although they are no longer scoured from the now protected wetlands of Hatfield and Thorne. This peat that is being packaged up and sent round the country has been shipped in across the North Sea via the nearby port of Goole from the magnificent and unprotected raised mires of Estonia on the Baltic.

In the UK, 52 per cent of our peat comes from Ireland, with the rest from Scotland, north-west England and the Baltic States. The argument concerning peat from British wetlands is that they are already so damaged that it doesn't matter if we finish them off.

While the surface habitat had been effectively destroyed on many British peatlands, the potential of recovery may remain, as was proved at Thorne, while all peatlands are an important carbon sink capable of helping to contain and even to reverse climate change. However, we seldom discuss the environmental issues concerning peat from the Baltic.

The scoured peatlands of Doncaster and their surrounding arable monocultures were both created by a desire for absolute maximum profit. But, while our avarice may be bottomless, there is always a limit to what we can squeeze out of the natural system. In the case of both peat and wheat, human greed has come up against the finite nature of the earth's resources. As we have seen in the first half of this chapter, once the raised mires have been entirely excavated, the peat will no longer regenerate. As we will see in the second half, the barley barons are now facing a whole range of ecological and economic challenges to their dreams of an infinite harvest. The sting in the tail of this chapter is also the way in which Britain attempts to solve these environmental problems by simply exporting them.

The perils of the plough

A hundred years ago the poet Edward Thomas sat in a fallen tree watching a ploughman and his team of horses with their shining brasses fixed to the harness. They talked of the Great War then raging in France, how everything was changed and one of the farmer's mates had been killed. Then

> *The horses started and for the last time*
> *I watched the clods crumble and topple over*
> *After the ploughshare and the stumbling team.*

So the poem ends. Within weeks of this incident Thomas had joined up, and the following year he too was killed in the maelstrom of war. With the convulsions of history the whole world would change but some things always remained the same. The rhythm of cereal farming could be relied upon as permanent and inevitable as the rhythm of the seasons.

Thomas Hardy, writing at the same time, saw this too in his poem 'In time of "The Breaking of Nations"'

> *Only a man harrowing clods*
> *In a slow silent walk*
> *With an old horse that stumbles and nods*
> *Half asleep as they stalk*
>
> *Only thin smoke without flame*
> *From the heaps of couch-grass*
> *Yet this will go onward the same*
> *Though Dynasties pass*

Arable farming is the great constant of European history and the plough and the harrow have been with us for millennia. If you take the boat from Felixstowe to Holland you will sail over an English Atlantis. It lies tantalisingly beneath the grey prosaic waters of the North Sea, whose bed is dense with archaeological remains. Scientists call it Doggerland after the Dogger Bank, which in this strange lost land was once the Dogger Hills. They are still there just below the waves and remain a peril to shipping. In deep time before 6500 BCE, mammoths and woolly rhinoceros roamed over this immense lowland basin which fused the present East Anglia with the present Netherlands. There were also people armed with axes with which, for the first time, they used to fell the primeval forest. The polished axes were crafted from stone obtained in exotically distant locations: greenstone from Cumbria and jadeite from the Italian Alps. They were exquisite and very efficient. In 2008, twenty-eight Paleolithic stone axes were rescued from the waters off Great Yarmouth, the first of an increasing number of archeological finds.

It was only a matter of time before the plough followed the axe and the unwilding of Britain began in earnest. But for six millennia this was more symbiosis than outright destruction. Around 4000 BCE wheat and barley arrived in Britain. These are Middle Eastern grasses far from ideally suited to this cold wet Atlantic island and yet with staggering conservatism we have stuck with them as a staple ever since. In the second millennium BCE Bronze Age farmers were industriously creating a familiar arable landscape of fields, boundaries and farmsteads. The plough that Shakespeare knew was not radically different from the one the Romans found when they arrived, and the good harvest, as reassuring as the seasons that he described in the sonnets, was to last through the centuries as the symbol of an eternal England.

> *When lofty trees I see barren of leaves,*
> *Which erst from heat did canopy the herd*
> *And summer's green all girded up in sheaves*
> *Born on the bier with white and bristly beard*

This was the landscape of mixed farming, with cereals on the best land, cattle in the lush valley bottoms, sheep on the hill and plenty of trees and woodlands. The golden corn which gleams out of the paintings of John Constable and Samuel Palmer was an essential part of farming's rightness and beauty, feeding the eye and also the body. The English farmland really was a symbol of what the British fought for in the two great wars. In the Second World War countless paintings, posters and films showed ploughmen and their teams. In the First World War soldiers took the poems of Housman's 'A Shropshire Lad' with them to the trenches as inspiration.

My father's family were all farmers and how they loved their shire horses! My father's cousin George told me that one of the saddest days of his life was when they came for the farm horses to take them to their certain destruction in the terrible trenches of the Great War. My uncle kept his horse brasses polished to perfection until the day he died. But they were sad silenced ornaments, relegated to the mantelpiece among the coronation mugs, no longer jingling on the harness of the team he used to drive in the days when practical farming and a glorious landscape were held in elegant balance. My grandfather, boasting that he was the last farmer in the Peak District to surrender to a new-fangled modern tractor, kept his Shires until the 1930s.

My father, born in 1912, fondly remembered the horses but he also remembered another side of farming less celebrated by poets and by townspeople who do not toil on the land – the narrow horizons and the sheer back-breaking hard work. Farming was and remains a brutal industry and a collapse in grain prices in the mid-nineteenth century fuelled agricultural decline and rural poverty. Between 1875 and 1900, over two million acres of arable land reverted to pasture and a further half million had gone by 1915.

In 1914, on the eve of the Great War, the writer Hilaire Belloc, driving through Sussex, came across abandoned plough land and the ruins of a corn mill at Halnaker in the South Downs. He wrote a poem which still resonates with the prevalent belief that farmers are the guardians of the landscape and that a landscape in decay is the mirror of a collapsing society.

> *Sally is gone that was so kindly*
> *Sally is gone from Ha'nacker Hill.*
> *And the briar grows ever since then so blindly*
> *And ever since then the clapper is still,*
> *And the sweeps have fallen from Ha'nacker Mill.*
>
> *Spirits that call and no one answers;*
> *Ha'nacker's down and England's done.*
> *Wind and Thistle for pipe and dancers*
> *And never a ploughman under the Sun.*
> *Never a ploughman. Never a one.*

The agricultural recession, which Belloc witnessed, continued through the 1920s and 1930s. At the end of the Second World War, when Britain had been besieged by German U-boats, the government, terrified of the possibility of food shortages, resolved that never again would farming be allowed to decline through lack of resources. British leaders were especially concerned about the staple commodity of cereals. In this they were part of a long tradition. The Roman Emperor Domitian (CE 81–96) ordered the destruction of vines in his British provinces on the grounds that they were taking land which should be used for producing bread. Back

Early spring ploughing with a team of horses on a West Lothian farm, near South Queensferry, 1930s.

in Rome, Emperor Augustus (27BCE–CE14) had done everything he could to ensure adequate supplies of imported wheat for his one million urban populace and guaranteed free grain to a minority of favoured consumers, the *plebs frumentaria*. Returning Roman veterans were given land and encouraged to produce corn in Italy but all they wanted to do was to sell up and enjoy the pleasures of Rome. While Augustus followed one failed agricultural reform after another, Virgil wrote timeless verse extolling the beauties of a working landscape, but it failed to alter lifestyles – like many a modern environmental polemic.

Back in post-war England, the 1947 Agriculture Act introduced comprehensive subsidies for cereals, milk and beef and in 1973 Britain joined the Common Market and so became eligible for the massive farming subsidies available from the Common Agricultural Policy (CAP). Agriculture, uniquely among British industries, became heavily subsidised by the state, providing farmers with an average additional 50 per cent income above what they would otherwise receive. Through the high-input/high-output farming technology, which this approach demanded, wetlands were drained, woods and hedges bulldozed and 97 per cent of our flower-rich meadows were lost. I remember in the early 1970s paying a visit to the family farm in Derbyshire. My father, who had pursued a successful career as a botanist and agriculturalist, originally inspired by the local flowers which he had found in those fields as a boy, bounded forward to show me the eyebright, harebells and yellow rattle where he had always remembered them. But they were no longer there. My uncle, in accordance with correct modern practice, had ploughed them up for a spanking new ley of well-fertilised ryegrass. In these small unregulated ways the balance between nature and exploitation was unravelling all over the countryside, and in that moment my father suddenly understood the real meaning of nature conservation.

The wild flowers were now exiled to nature reserves, which in turn have been reduced, in many parts of the country, to tiny islands in a sea of wheat. Farming has become an industrial operation in a rural locality. This is the real cost paid in partially hidden taxes and loss of landscape for supermarket food. But the worst consequence of agribusiness was arguably not the loss of wildlife but the destruction of that sector of the farming community which had most created and sustained the diverse mixed agricultural landscape: the small and medium-sized landowners, together with the tenant farmers. The resulting food surplus, together with the high-input trap which pushed up land prices and the cost of production, fuelled the remorseless march to ever larger farm units and ever fewer farmworkers.

There are now less than half the farms there were in the 1950s. In 1945, we had a million farmworkers, now reduced to a tenth of that number, many of whom are part-time. The trend continues. By restructuring tenancies and sharing contract labour, it is estimated that, apart from a significant number of small hobby farmers, many counties are parcelled up into only fifteen to twenty major arable units. Nowadays we prefer 'power harrowing' to ploughing as it leaves a finer tilth. It is still essentially a worker and a machine clearing the ground to grow corn, but the scale is altered beyond recognition. Contractors hire out a range of vast machines which resemble military tanks to harvest the crop and then harrow the field. The modern ploughman sits in a computer-driven cab on a heated seat listening to music or even watching a film. That is if he is even present at all. In 2016, trials were under way in the UK for driverless tractors which use mapping technology to follow a planned course, and tank-tracked robots are being hailed as a great agricultural saving of the future. Except for a tiny minority of winners, both farmers and the farmed landscape have been destroyed by the expectation of plenty. Our attempt to create a rich agricultural sector through massive investment and high-input technology offers a terrible lesson for the developing world. Hilaire Belloc's vision of an empty landscape has come true, but not for the reasons he imagined. *Never a ploughman. Never a one.*

Farms and floods

The price we pay for the arable intensification is not confined to the loss of landscape and farm employment. It is also the terror of the flood. The battle between farming and the floodwaters is as old as English history and is still unfolding. In Britain's latest flood crisis, which is exacerbated by climate change, the unmitigated mono-cultures of agribusiness are being directly blamed for catastrophic floods hitting the downstream towns.

This is a debate which goes back a very long way. The wetlands, which nowadays we increasingly conserve, were long seen as the enemy of agriculture, causing foot rot in sheep, diseases in cattle and above all as being hostile to those dry-loving Middle Eastern grasses, wheat and barley. When most of the country was engaged in farming, wetland had a bad name. Queen Elizabeth I, making her progress through Kent, was careful to avoid the malarial Romney Marsh, which her archivist, William Lambarde, described as 'evil in winter, grievous in summer and never good', while in 1629 the fens were vilified thus: 'The air, nebulous, gross and full of rotten gases; the water putrid and muddy, yea full of loathsome vermin; the earth spewing, unfast and boggy.' In King Lear, Shakespeare inveighs against the 'fen-sucked fogs'.

Our farmed landscape was drained and embanked from the earliest times. In 1252, the 'jurats' of Romney Marsh were recorded as having power to control the ditches 'from time out of mind' and in the Domesday Book the earliest recorded river engineer makes his appearance in the Somerset Levels. He was called Girard Fossarius, 'Gerard of the Drain'. Throughout the Middle Ages people were sent out in the misty mornings to inspect the Thames floodbanks and paid by a charge known as 'scottage'. Those who escaped these earliest water rates could be deemed to have got off 'scot-free'.

With each subsequent generation the systematic drying of England was under way. When I arrived in the British Water Industry in 1977, all this furious activity was being carried on with a will and on an unprecedented scale with revolutionary new budgets and technology. Massive machines stripped and straightened rivers, concreted their margins and encased them in raised banks so that high water levels could no longer escape into the adjacent valley bottoms and floodplains. There were some who congratulated themselves that the flood had been tamed at last. But not for long.

When I first became involved with river engineering I became convinced that traditional drainage, taken to its logical conclusion, contained within it the seeds of its own destruction. But I never suspected in those early days just how dangerous working against nature was to prove. Cage a river in cement and iron, and it will struggle to break out like a wild beast. In the bed of a gravel river the flowing water sorts the little stones into a stable fish-scale pattern, so by dredging it up the engineers destabilise the riverbed and accelerate the erosion they are trying to prevent. This is made even worse by the removal of the trees which had previously held the banks together. Meanwhile the intensive farming, which all this drainage was designed to promote, removed hedges, woods and wet corners which had helped hold back the run-off from the land at times of heavy rain. With nowhere else to go, the floodwater pours straight to the rivers, which are closely bounded by raised floodbanks. The banks then channel the water down to the nearest downstream towns. With 80 per cent of us in the UK now living in towns and cities and unprecedented rainfall resulting from climate change, we have tailor-made the perfect storm and the perfect flood.

And so it has happened. As climate change cuts in with unusually warm winters and intense summer thunderstorms, the prevailing south-westerly winds carry plumes of moist air out of the Caribbean and Atlantic to dump unprecedented rainfall on our shores. Major flooding affected the Midlands in 2007, the West Country and the Thames Valley in 2013–2014 and the North of England in 2015. As the floodwaters receded and the lessons began to be learned, there was a realisation that, although there is not much that we can do to stop the rain, a great deal can be achieved in terms of land use and land management to reduce its effects. Centuries of intensive drainage and farming would need to be reversed in order to hold back water in the upper catchments and then slowly store and disperse the rainwater at every stage on its long journey to the sea. This principle, known as natural flood management (NFM), is about working with nature and making space for water by blocking ditches, planting trees and removing raised floodbanks so that rivers can reconnect with the floodplains from which they have been separated for so long.

One of the best places I know to see these strategies working is an exceptionally beautiful farmed landscape away in the west.

The town of Tewkesbury, Gloucestershire, surrounded by floodwaters, following the torrential rain on July 22, 2007.

If you stand on the northern edge of Exmoor looking down on Porlock Bay in Somerset, below you extends the National Trust's Holnicote Estate. This comprises the catchment of two small rivers, Horner Water and the River Aller, which flow from the heathery moorland tops through dense woods, embanked pastures and down to the pebbled shore.

Nigel Hester, the National Trust's manager for its NFM project at Holnicote is a gentle giant of a man. He understands farming and engineering and has long gained the trust of his tenants on the estate, though, as with all farmers, this must have taken a bit of doing. His task was to persuade them to surrender parts of their land in order to store water at flood times along the entire length of the river system, and his leverage to achieve this was to reduce the rent. In this way he put small dams on the moorland headwaters, blocked some of the upper reaches in a steep gorge with tree trunks, and broke out some of the old floodbanks on the lower reaches so the water can deliberately spread out over low-lying fields at times of heavy rain. At the same time hydrologists installed devices along the streams to regularly measure the water flow. Then, on Christmas Eve 2013, the storm came. As the nearby Somerset Levels went underwater, the local floods lapped up to the doorsteps of the downstream village houses but never quite came in. Using the carefully gathered hydrological data it was possible to prove that the relatively small interventions costing £160,000 to install had saved £30 million of property assets from flooding. That was Nigel's best ever Christmas present.

Cereal questions

The next big question, in the absence of a benign landlord like the National Trust, is whether it is possible to run an efficient farm which can also make space for water and wildlife alongside the essential crop. To answer these questions I went to visit a couple of large cereal farms near Cambridge. The Allerton Project, run by the Game & Wildlife Conservation Trust (GWCT) consists of a 318- hectare farm astride the border between Rutland and Leicestershire. This is traditional sheep and corn country, a quilted landscape from whose blue distances church spires rise within a stipple of ash trees. Hedges and lanes loop over the steeply rolling hills and villages of golden stone nestle in the hollows. Hope Farm at Knapwell consisting of 180 hectares and run by the RSPB is in more open country of large arable fields in Cambridgeshire.

The protagonists in both operations clearly have an agenda to promote environmentally sympathetic farming, with the RSPB understandably focusing on birds. However, they both insist that they are ordinary commercial farms facing the same problems as all their neighbours and they are out to make a profit which compares favourably with the average for agriculture in their regions. If they did not do this they would have failed, since the whole point is to demonstrate that what they are doing can be achieved by any typical farmer. They are also content to use chemicals, provided they are used carefully. What they are both essentially doing, though in different ways, is taking ten per cent of their land out of active agricultural production. This relatively small sacrifice has made all the difference to the wildlife and landscape quality of their land, conserving topsoil, reducing flood run-off and – here comes the surprise – it pays for itself in the long run.

The killer point that they make is the familiar one that total intensive monocultures are ultimately unsustainable and self-destructive. When working with nature you cannot expect to go for broke. The great agricultural revolution of the late twentieth century was driven by the new technologies of mechanisation, crop breeding, agrochemicals and inorganic fertiliser imported from North Africa. The present generation of British farmers was trained to expect this technical fix would last forever. Now, forty years down the line, it is becoming clear that this is a dream that is coming to an end.

Black grass or mousetail grass is an innocent-looking little weed with tapering black spires which poke above the wheat and critically ripens and scatters its seeds before the cereals can be cut. Farmers have also long had another name for it: hungerweed. Relatively rare in the 1950s when it was confined to south-east England, this is a plant whose time has now arrived. Over the past decade the black grass has been evolving resistance to herbicides and is surviving on at least 80 per cent of the farms that try to spray it out. Given time, and without control, it will completely engulf a cereal crop.

More insidious but ultimately calamitous for arable agriculture is the massive damage and loss of precious topsoil, the long-term lifeblood of any farm. The ability of huge machines to 'power through' truly damaged soil has masked the problem of soil's bulk density which has increased by around 25 per cent since 1969 with insufficient organic matter and air constant in the soil matrix. Then there is the outright loss which you can simply observe from the gullies and crevasses on winter plough land, the deposited soil fanning out at the bottom of slopes and sometimes even blocking country lanes. It is estimated that 2.2 million tons of topsoil is lost from the land each year in the UK.

There are very few farms without a proportion of land that is too dry, too steep, too low-lying or simply too awkward to get at. For all these reasons, the strategy of keeping 10 per cent of fields out of agriculture adopted at Allerton and Hope Farm makes practical commercial sense. At Allerton the key principles are minimising soil disturbance during crop establishment, diversifying crop rotations and maintaining permanent soil cover with annual plants such as radish and phacelia in the period between harvesting the wheat and sowing of the next crop. Not only does this mean that the soil is no longer exposed to be washed away by autumn rains, but when they finally remove the annual cover crop, they can also remove the black grass which has germinated after harvest. Buffer strips known as 'beetle banks' slow extreme erosion and harbour

The RSPB's Hope Farm in Cambridgeshire combines productive cereals with plenty of hedges and lush field margins for farmland birds.

huge numbers of beetles and spiders, which stray 90 yards out into the cultivated fields to prey on pests such as slugs and aphids.

The wider margins also contribute an important addition to the farm income, as pheasants and partridges thrive in the set-aside land and so supply the regular shoots which earn between £25,000 and £40,000 a year. This is especially welcome in lean years when overproduction leads to a fall in the price of cereals. After the harvest of 2015, there was a national surplus of three million tonnes of wheat sitting in grain stores even before the following year's harvest had begun. Finally the wheat from Allerton achieves environmental certification from the Guild of Conservation Grade Producers and so commands a premium price.

The buffers, hedges and cover crops provide nesting areas and food for farmland birds such as barn owls, linnets, bullfinches and goldfinches. Between 2000 and 2016, the RSPB increased the yellow hammers on Hope Farm from two pairs to over 700 and skylarks from ten pairs to forty. In these ways even the notorious prairies of arable agribusiness can be gently modified to prove yet again that, if we are careful, we can have our environmental cake and eat it. If all arable farmers in Britain followed these practices there would be a landscape revolution. Currently the estimate of those following this approach is around two per cent of farmers. A major reason for this sad state of affairs is the subsidy offered to British farmers by the Common Agricultural Policy (CAP), of which 80 per cent simply encourages them to continue farming intensively. However, a new revolution now hangs over the British farmed landscape, which may change all that.

Driving round England in June 2016 you could see much of the countryside dominated by signs stating 'Vote Leave' and 'We Want our Country Back'. Many of them were posted on farmland. When referendum day arrived on 23 June, the country was lashed by appropriately apocalyptic storms of rain and hail. In London the equivalent of a month's rain fell in twenty-four hours. In Essex the River Rom burst its banks and many people had to be rescued from their homes by boat. In Newham voters hitched up their trousers and waded through the floodwater to reach their polling stations. Floods on the railway lines stranded huge crowds at Clapham Junction and Waterloo, causing some to miss the voting deadline. But it would probably not have changed the outcome. Britain voted to leave the European Union.

Future farming in a Britain without CAP

In December 2019 the Tory party won a landslide election on a mandate to take Britain out of Europe and as this edition goes to press the Brexit project is underway. What this means for British farming is loss of access to the Common Agricultural Policy which was originally designed to support the different circumstances of French agriculture and has driven Britain's agribusiness boom ever since it joined the EU in 1973. The CAP pays out £3 billion a year to British farmers, which is around 55 per cent of their income. The billion dollar question for them now is whether a Conservative government, which believes in free market forces, will match these extraordinary payouts; or a future Labour government, with virtually no rural seats. It seems unlikely. Agriculture has negligible pulling power in terms of votes and a relatively small contribution to the economy. There are only around 100,000 commercial farm businesses in the UK, with a steadily falling contribution to the gross domestic product (GDP) which ran between 0.8 per cent and 0.5 per cent in the years from 2000 to 2010.

Contrary to popular belief, importing food is far cheaper than growing our own, even if we remove the subsidy. Even unsubsidised New Zealand lamb costs less than ours, despite having come from the other end of the world, while the Ukraine or Canada can produce cheaper wheat than us due to their economies of scale. We are only 60 per cent self-sufficient in the food we can grow in our climate and most of that is dependent on fertiliser which we have to import from North Africa, so we will never have total food security in our small urbanised island. Nor will a major reduction in agriculture mean that the whole countryside disappears under bricks and mortar, since our existing urban areas are less than 15 per cent of land use. For all these reasons the Treasury, which has always been cynical about agriculture, cannot be relied upon to match the CAP payments. In addition the government has now pledged that in the event of Brexit, it will remove the Basic Payment, which pays all farmers to continue farming intensively.

In this situation agricultural land values fell by 7 per cent in 2016 and are almost certain to fall further. Our farmed countryside now faces the greatest political and economic revolution since the

Repeal of the Corn Laws in 1846. High-input farming, dependent on imported fertiliser and above all credit, is in serious trouble. With agricultural decline, the contracting businesses that hire out the massive combine harvesters could pull out of the industry, shipping their machines to mainland Europe and thereby removing the actual engines which drive intensive cereal farming.

Looking at the Farm Business Survey for July 2016, it is possible to estimate the typical profit made by different farming operations both currently and if the subsidy were removed. In these circumstances a very large high- performing cereal farm of 582 hectares has its profits halved to less than £300/hectare, while a moderately large cereal farm of 540 hectares has its profit dip from £376/hectare to £15/hectare. A small dairy farm of 57 hectares would make an absolute loss of £6/hectare.

At Hope Farm they confirm that their profit is equal to the subsidy. The problem is made worse by the fact that more than half of English farmland is tenanted and so the tenant farmers have to find the rent as well as making a profit. A final killer blow may be a possible trade deal with USA, which helps out British industry in exchange for a flood of cheap American food arriving in the UK.

It seems unlikely that the government will cease to subsidise agriculture altogether, but for the next few years there will be a tremendous battle to decide the new deal for British farming. There are no rules. There is no precedent and we cannot know what will happen across the landscape, which is bound to vary according to the personal circumstances of individual farmers, who may decide to either give up or plough on regardless.

Among a range of scenarios there are two fairly obvious ones. Large farms may buy up the smaller units and further intensify them or, elsewhere, farmland may be abandoned. In this second scenario we are looking at the previously unthinkable: the end of British farming. The eternal ploughing of the fields, celebrated by the poets, may prove not so eternal after all and the trees may move back to colonise the land from which they were first removed by those earliest settlers walking in from Doggerland with their stone axes. Already golf courses, amenity woodlands and some very large nature reserves have sprung up on farmland in recent years. There are also around 100,000 hobby farmers, which equal the number of commercial farm units. Supported by money from the urban economy, they keep horses, run a few sheep or cattle and happily watch their abandoned hedges luxuriate out into the fields. With a drop in land values, yet more will move in.

All this may prove a personal tragedy for many farmers, but it will also surely be an opportunity for the landscape. The Queen's Speech of December 2019 set out plans to replace the CAP with a system of subsidies rewarding farmers for promoting environmental enhancement, biodiversity, and flood control rather than yield. It will be critical to confirm these benefits, which have been only available from 20 percent of the subsidy.

For the last forty years the British, those superlative gardeners, have cultivated and embellished every corner of their green and pleasant land. The slag-heaps and ruins of the Industrial Revolution have been reafforested. The historic landscaped gardens of Capability Brown and Repton, which in the 1960s were threatened and decayed, have been exquisitely restored. Landscape techniques have been evolved to transform what was hideous urban infrastructure into positive ecological engineering. Green walls clothe the facades of tower blocks. Green bridges span motorways which are also adorned with lavish planting and newly created flowery meadows.

And nowadays we are not just growing flowers and trees but cultivating animals and birds. Through legal reform and proactive intervention, the otter has returned to our rivers and the peregrine stoops once more from cathedral spires and city towers. Over 450 pairs of marsh harriers patrol our re-created reed beds where in 1971 there was only one breeding pair in Britain. The red kite which for generations was confined to central Wales is now a commonplace sight over much of the country. We have seen how our heavily mined peatlands have been turned back into nature reserves, and it may be that we will now watch the woods and wetlands reclaim at least part of our beleaguered farmland.

The next challenge is to control the impact we have on the harvests of more distant lands as we import the commodities which we no longer produce. This leads us to the embattled rainforests of tropical America and to another chapter in my childhood.

CHAPTER 4

The chocolate forest

Harvesting the habitat: forests of cocoa and wetlands of rice

When my father left Singapore in 1957 he bought our house in Kent and took up a job in Trinidad, to which I returned with my family on a work assignment almost forty years later. Soon after arriving I went to seek out my old childhood home. I knew what it must feel like to be a ghost when I revisited the silent garden. If you had passed your hand right through me I would not have been surprised. A familiar chip in the step, a crack in the drain, leaping back into focus after so long an absence, were more real than all the preoccupations of the present. The flamboyant tree, long since felled, reared up in my memory where it used to stand, shedding its bent black husks of seedpods and magically concealing a lime-green iguana among its light-dappled branches. The great Saman tree, festooned in orchids and epiphytes, casting its half-acre umbrella of shade, endured unaltered, a symbol of stability. When I lifted my daughter onto the branch I used to climb, a new generation of ants came out to defend the colony that had once bitten me.

The cavernous colonial bungalow, so often remembered in dreams, still offered a shadowy haven beneath its zinc roof, which used to rattle like a tin drum under the sudden rains or creaked through the warm hours of darkness in symphony with the distant howl of dogs and the babble of frogs and cicadas emanating from the tropical night. Here, in the cool cockerelling dawns, my father, sustained by successive cups of tea, would set to work on his volumes of botanical scholarship, and here, when the huge velvet butterflies, known for their punctuality as 'Six o'clock Blues', blundered out of the dusk into the lamplight, he would pour himself the first of an ever more impressive and seemingly endless succession of rum and sodas, stained with a splash of Angostura bitters. Here, in the solitary still afternoons, while my mother pined for England and the sun on the verandah blistered the old numbers of the *Illustrated London News*, I would trace the Indian files of the leafcutter ants which staggered under their silken parasols of leaf and petal, or else crawl beneath the stilted bungalow, where the cavities were too low even for a small boy to crouch comfortably, and return the gaze of the impassive mysterious toads which inhabited that cellared darkness.

When I returned to work on the environmental impact of road improvements throughout the island of Trinidad in 1994, my homecoming gave me a teasing perspective on time. In the briefest space of years, the governor generals in their plumes and epaulettes and the garden-partying memsahibs in their elbow-length kid gloves had departed and now seemed as distant historical figures as Raleigh and his troops adventuring in pursuit of El Dorado. My father's post in Trinidad had been Professor of Tropical Agriculture in the University of the West Indies (UWI), but when we first arrived this was still called the Imperial College of Tropical Agriculture (ICTA) and it was one of the main training grounds for all the agriculturalists in the British Empire. Colonies such as Trinidad were expected to supply food and other primary materials such as minerals for the mother country, which in turn grew rich on manufactured goods and financial services.

In Trinidad, agriculture principally meant sugar. The most notorious of all commodities, sugar was the driver of the slave trade until its abolition in 1833 and, even after that, plantation owners imported indentured labour from India, which was almost as unjust. Now the empire has gone, but throughout the tropics the sterile monocultures of sugarcane remain. In the 1990s Trinidad airport was periodically closed because the island lay under a pall of smoke when the cane fields were burned at harvest time. In Brazil, much of the Caribbean and increasingly in Africa immense intensive sugar plantations are run by large corporations and imposed by outsiders. In many ways these resemble the palm oil plantations of the Far East and the arable agribusiness of the UK. We have seen how these can be moderated with the addition of careful management, but what I discovered when I returned to Trinidad was an older, subtler and more radical approach to farming whereby crops such as cocoa are actually grown beneath the forest canopy so there is an intrinsic connection between cultivation and habitat. This different model for using and saving the wild places of the world forms the main subject matter of this chapter. But first we will explore the qualities of the island and the pressures they are under.

The New World tropics are anything but new, despite the shallow roots of their modern culture. The Old World may pride itself on scenes recognisable from the Middle Ages, the classics or the Bible, but in tropical America you gaze beyond the historical past into prehistory. To stand in the rainforest is to experience a world not radically different from the Pleistocene, when giant sloths and armadillos moved among the majestic palm trees. Much of the coast of Trinidad looks exactly as it must have done long before Columbus saw it. To the east, backed by humid swamps, are beaches of a wildness to challenge the conquistadors and make the modern tourist tremble. This is no bland paradise from the travel brochures. Propelled by the full fetch of the Atlantic, extending unbroken from Africa, the boiling ocean slams into the beach. Carcasses of ripped-up trees and the occasional fly-blown shark lie bedded in the sand, which is strewn with the still pulsing

A leatherback turtle lays her eggs on a Trinidad beach and then hides them under the sand.

bodies of jellyfish like bubbles of violet gum. Pelicans, angular as pterodactyls, cruise the riptide.

Out of this wild sea, there emerge once a year, under the cover of darkness, creatures that were at home in the ancient oceans 25 million years before the high noon of the dinosaurs. To see them, you should go in May and be prepared for disappointment. The hours pass and there is nothing but the pounding midnight surf. Moonlight marbles the rippled sand. A star twinkles. Then you think you see an upturned dinghy moving slowly and silently up the beach. It is a giant leather-backed turtle returning to her birthplace to lay her eggs. Once the turtle has scooped her nest in the sand and started to lay what resembles clusters of ping-pong balls, she can be approached without disturbance. To trace a finger on her sea-smoothed shell or her huge scaly flipper is to contact a remoteness beyond imagination. Then, inch by inch, she slips back into the cold dark sea, where she will move among squids and whales as far as northern Canada and beyond.

The forest

Leatherback turtles can live for thirty to fifty years. Within this turtle's lifetime, the rainforest of tropical America including Trinidad, which has seen all the empires come and go, has suffered some notorious changes. Brazil accounts for 60 per cent of the Amazon rainforest and of that almost 20 per cent has been lost since 1970. By the late 1980s, an area the size of the UK was being removed annually. Between 2000 and 2006, Brazil lost nearly 150,000 square kilometres of forest. All this has afflicted a system which has more species of plants and animals than any other terrestrial ecosystem on the planet. Rainforest clearance contributes to the current unprecedented extinction taking place in the world. It is estimated that we are losing up to five thousand species a year. In 2018, Brazil recorded the worst annual deforestation in a decade, and with the arrival of President Bolsonaro in January 2019 this is likely to get much worse.

The forces of destruction on Trinidad have also been and remain serious. Large tracts of lowland forest have been cleared for mineral workings and illegal loggers have been removing trees from the remote fastness of the Northern Range with their own portable sawmills. Most depressing of all is the collective carelessness of 'slash and burn'.

Its consequences can be seen in the Melajo Forest, which is dominated by white-flowered *Mora* trees and is a home to possums, armadillos and some very large boa constrictors. Along the sandy paths you may pick out the trails of agouti, outsized guinea pigs,

A Trinidad cocoa farmer shows off the cocoa pods growing on his trees. The trunk and branches are crusted with a rich growth of moss and lichen.

followed closely by the feline prints of ocelot, stalking it on velvet paws. The experience of being in these high woods could never be captured by photographs or film. Nothing could replicate the pleasurable shock of instant coolness, as if chilled air is breathed from some natural airconditioning whose workings sigh and churr with shrill crescendos of cicadas or the precarious paths which cunningly follow a knife-edge route along the narrow ridge tops, nor the dim green twilight, through which the occasional dazzle of a sunbeam spotlights a morpho butterfly, midnight blue and big as a bird, waltzing down the buttressed aisles.

The great enemy of these places is fire. All the fires are set by humans but no one ever knows precisely who started them. In 1987, 600 acres of the Melajo burned. Soon poor settlers arrived, desperate for homes. In a few years they had cleared a town-sized wasteland, in which the dunes of eroded sand, too acid and poor to support any crops without a continual reapplication of fertiliser, grade into low sterile scrub. Today, in the dusty glare, there is an unnatural stillness. The barking of a tethered dog echoes against the silence and the air has the bitter smell of burning. Thin smoke without flame rises from the edge of the clearing. Here a six-month melon crop grows on the leaf mould accumulated over a thousand years as the protagonists of slash and burn move further into the forest and the land dies behind them.

The chocolate

Wisely used, the rainforests of Trinidad can produce resources to benefit local inhabitants and central governments indefinitely. Honey, charcoal and wild fruits such as balata are sold by the roadside. Traditional crops such as cocoa and coffee, grown beneath the existing trees, have long helped the forest earn its keep without devastating the environment. While coffee must be the most fragrant of tropical crops, its white flowers outrivalling orange blossom in their sweetness, cocoa is surely the most beautiful. It is a low tree from whose trunk and inner branches hang glossy pods like chestnut and yellow gourds, glowing like lanterns from the shady heart of the tree. To increase the shade the cocoa prefers, farmers often plant trees such as the *madre de cacao* or immortelle, whose flowers create a flame-coloured haze through the forest canopy and a feast for nectar-eating birds. The cocoa trees themselves are crusted and filmed with epiphytic growth, their stems spangled with the threads of cocoa mint, while beneath them flower scented spider lilies, white and fragile within the darkness of the forest floor. The managed balance of light and shade which makes an English hazel coppice so rich for wildlife is echoed in these subtly manipulated tropical woodlands, where the cocoa bushes occupy the same level in the woodland storey taken by the hazel. There are few better places for birdwatching in Trinidad than a cocoa plantation. From among the moist veils of vines and bromeliads, a top-heavy toucan peers down with curiosity. A lime-and-lemon-coloured trogon perches motionless in the leaf-framed darkness and vanishes.

Best of all, the export value of the cocoa beans, however marginal, keeps the otherwise unpoliceable activities of slash and burn at bay. The cocoa farmers will always come out and defend their forests from passing arsonists, whereas national parks and nature reserves never have the armies of staff required to protect them; indeed, in some countries forests are even being sold off for development by their own environment ministries.

The way the cocoa farmers grow their crop within the forest may broadly be described as 'agroforestry'. This is defined as a land use system in which crops or animals are raised beneath or around trees. Alongside the offsetting of intensive monocultures such as palm oil with corridors and buffers of protected forest, agroforestry is another classic model for sustainable agriculture. (A British example would be a traditional apple orchard in which sheep graze beneath the apple trees. On a hot day the sheep will benefit from the shade and the sheep droppings will help enrich the ground for the apple trees.) In Trinidad, even in this very basic mixed system, there will also be many more birds and insects than in a field containing a single crop. Forest-certificated cocoa can also be marketed as contributing to the salvation of the rainforest, in contrast to that produced in monocultural plantations in West Africa and Brazil.

I first witnessed the certification of chocolate in the late 1990s in Belize, a slice of Central America where the Caribbean culture of Bob Marley meets the ancient world of the Maya with the melancholy undertow of Latin America thrown in. In the forests of southern Belize there survive not only varieties of cocoa propagated from plants found growing on remote Mayan ruins, but also the original Mayan people, descended from the civilisation which first brought us chocolate. They scrape a living with some small support from over-stretched schools and clinics. In 1993, the British company Green & Black arrived in Belize under their idealistic founder Craig Sams and provided a guaranteed market for organic cocoa, which commanded three times the value of conventionally produced beans. In this way the twin pillars of ecological and social good practice supports truly sustainable production. In 1994 Green and Black's 'Maya Gold' bar was awarded the Fairtrade mark – the first British product to carry it.

Since then Green and Black was sold to Cadbury Schweppes in 2005 and then to Kraft Foods, which in 2012 became Mondelez International. Green and Black still market their bars as sustainable, although some environmentalists say that the huge parent company's poor environmental reputation has put a question mark over their current claims. I believe that if the largest corporations take on high standards that is the best news of all, but it is the familiar dilemma of certification: *What does it mean, and How do you know?* However, the principle that forests can defend themselves by marketing their own products is not going away. A number of new small producers of organic chocolate are springing up in Belize and elsewhere. In 2016 a cocoa farming co-operative in the central hills of Trinidad became the first farm operation in the English-speaking Caribbean to obtain the certification of the green frog seal from the NGO Rainforest Alliance.

The savannah

The Belizean landscape contains another element, which I love as much as any forest, and which has almost entirely disappeared from Trinidad: the savannah. These flat tropical prairies, baked in the dry season and flooded under rain, support a specialised ecology of insect-eating plants such as sundews; birds including vermilion and scissor-tailed flycatchers; together with tapirs, armadillos and anteaters. The landscape quality of these places is as remarkable as their ecology. In the evening as you travel along the Southern Highway in Belize, you can see a hundred night hawks wheeling and veering over the savannah. The sun sets on a wilderness of grass and pine, which extends virtually unbroken between the sea and the Maya Mountains. Savannahs are perhaps best seen from horseback, as appreciated by the Victorian author Charles Kingsley. In Trinidad in 1869 he cantered into the freedom of their immense 'sheets of grey-green grass, as far as the eye could see, weltered in mirage'. But even from the road the shimmering levels of these pristine grasslands, seemingly infinite beneath the towering cumulus clouds, can be admired as the greatest open spaces of a still largely unspoiled country. They are the perfect foil to the steamy dark interior world of the rainforest, but they are far less well defended.

The Trinidad savannahs admired by Charles Kingsley have been reduced to one tiny nature reserve at Aripo, which is now zealously guarded as an isolated jewel equal to, if not exceeding, the island's most precious rainforests in terms of nature conservation importance. Even more than the forest, savannahs, which are notoriously acid and subject to a climatic regime of alternative bake and soak, make very poor agricultural land. All over the Caribbean you can see their remains reduced to goat-grazed scrub. Their lack of fertility hasn't saved them from destruction. Lowland habitats, so much more accessible than mountains, are often the first to go. In England some of the first nature reserves to gain statutory protection were the coastal precipices, where puffins and guillemots breed. This was because their conservation was correctly judged as not standing in the way of development. You can't plough or build on a seabird cliff.

The savannah suffers from another problem in terms of perception. Compared to rainforest it is flat, empty and contains fewer species, although many are unique to the savannah. In Belize, where much of the best forest is protected, there are no legally protected savannahs because they are generally regarded as 'waste land'. They are so little surveyed that, when they are gone, we will not even know what we have lost. They vanish under housing and monocultures of mechanised rice growing, which in Trinidad, together with subsequent melon cultivation, has drastically reduced the Nariva Swamp, the island's last stronghold of the legendary blue and yellow macaws. Elsewhere in the world mechanised rice cultivation threatens precious wetlands, as in the Camargue in Southern France and the Everglades in Florida. But of course all over the world monocultures of high-yielding rice varieties also feed hungry populations and provide exports. In Belize, however, the savannahs are also lost to one of the most apparently innocuous of harvests, prawns.

The real price of a prawn cocktail

It is unfortunate that prawns are so delicious, for their environmental cost – both in terms of destruction of ecosystems and ruination of the poor – is one of the highest of any commodities consumed in the developed world. As consumers we use the terms 'shrimp' and 'prawn' in an interchangeable way. Scientists more precisely describe shrimps as coming from the sea and prawns as living in freshwater. Remembering my childhood holidays with a shrimping net, I vaguely assumed that harvesting seafood was an agreeable business. Alas, this is not the case. As modern industrial fishing has reduced the world's fish stocks, cheaply produced seafood, either trawled or farmed, has moved into the vacuum.

Trawling in particular seems almost worse than the most extreme agribusiness. In his classic book *The End of the Line*, Charles Clover asks us to imagine what we would say if we saw huge machines dragging a mile-long net across the plains of Africa or indeed the savannahs of South America and scraping up everything in their wake: rocks, trees and every single living creature including juveniles and pregnant females, many of which would then be thrown out and left to die since they didn't taste good or were too damaged to use. This horrifying scenario would be the equivalent on land of modern trawling, which happens all over the world but conveniently out of sight at the bottom of the sea. This all-consuming and indiscriminate version of hunter gathering is the marine equivalent of clear felling and burning the rainforest.

Shrimp trawling is especially destructive because the small mesh used to retain the little shrimps also traps all the other larger species. A particular casualty are turtles, which need to reach the surface to breathe. Alas, many drown once they are caught in the shrimp trawl nets. In 2007, shrimp trawlers in Belize were estimated by the Food and Agriculture Organization (FAO) to have landed only 19 metric tonnes of fish, while between 76 and 190 metric tonnes of other marine life were thrown away.

Therefore, as an alternative to trawling, shrimp *farming* and other forms of fish farming have to be a good idea – provided they are done carefully. A good example can be seen on the savannahs of southern Belize, which have begun to be excavated for large rectangular prawn ponds and associated infrastructure. Seawater is pumped into the ponds. The juvenile shrimp are then stocked and chemicals are added, both to fatten up the prawns and to kill off diseases.

But shrimp farming can also create serious problems if there is no regard to the scale and location of the particular operation.

Throughout the tropics, coastal areas not only of savannah, but even more commonly of mangrove, the stilt-rooted estuarine forests of the tropics, are being drained and replaced by the familiar grid-works of shrimp ponds. With their tank-like ponds, pump houses and concrete drains, this new industrial landscape resembles an immense sewage works. The mangroves are often vital flood defences, as well as hosting an astonishing array of herons, ibis and manatees, and acting as nurseries of many offshore fish stocks, which provide the livelihood for the local fishing communities. However, throughout the tropics, fishing communities are losing their living or given paltry compensation in order to make way for the big companies, which can afford the freezing plants and other infrastructure to help get the shrimp to your table. In Ecuador, protesting fishermen have been killed.

But the problem doesn't even end with the loss of mangroves. Concentrated populations of farmed shrimps deposit huge quantities of acid faeces at the bottom of their ponds. Every few years this has to be cleaned out and neutralised with quantities of lime, obtained by opening quarries in the forest or digging up the white sands of the beaches. An even greater problem worldwide is the source of the fishmeal fed to the shrimp. Like farmed salmon and trout, shrimp are carnivorous and so need other fish to live on. This often comes from small wild fish trawled up from the world's oceans and then ground into innocuous-looking pellets which are thrown into the shrimp tanks. Even leaving aside the damage from trawling, there is a limit to the availability of small wild fish in the sea, which are also the basis of the entire marine food chain.

Despite the problems, shrimp farming is yet another monoculture that can be carefully moderated. Shrimps can be produced by properly controlled fishing and farming, according to responsible guidelines, which minimise social disruption and ecological damage. There are plenty of places to locate fish farms outside mangrove swamps. There can be proper controls and monitoring of the source of fish food, and, as with the palm oil mills in South

East Asia, the pollution can be carefully managed too. In Belize, appropriate treatment by the operator, subject to monitoring by the Ministry of the Environment, reduces the pollution, which would otherwise pour out of the waste ditches and back into the sea. As with timber, palm oil and chocolate, certification of the product can then take place, in this context by the Marine Stewardship Council (MSC) and the Aquaculture Stewardship Council (ASC).

The rice and bamboo landscapes

To see a more joined-up and elegant model for harvesting fish and rice I had to cross the world from the Caribbean and visit Bangladesh, the steamy Bay of Bengal where the Indian subcontinent merges almost imperceptibly into Indo-China. I was sent there to report on the links between habitat conservation and poverty alleviation, two aspirations all too often regarded as mutually exclusive. All over the world it is assumed that prosperity can only be achieved through intensive high-input farming which at best is moderated by offsetting and at worst has marginalised the natural world and replaced diverse landscapes with the industrialised deserts of monoculture. In Bangladesh I found a different approach to agriculture which, even more than cocoa farming, has turned this assumption on its head. Here is the rice and bamboo landscape, where the use of every available natural element sustains the local people and where the familiar divorce between humanity and nature is replaced by a true marriage.

All over the tropics you may hear the seductive rustle of the bamboo around the settlements and glimpse the silken counterpanes of the rice paddies, so saturated with colour that they seem to radiate their own grasshopper-green glow beneath grey tropical rain clouds. This is the greenest landscape in the world. Much traditional farmland can be understood in terms of its complementary elements. 'Chalk and Cheese' has long been used to describe the downland of southern England. There the 'chalk' is exactly what it sounds like, the whale-backed chalk hills which swoop down to the lush dairy-farmed 'cheese' landscapes of the valley bottoms. For centuries people adapted the local geology and ecology for their livelihoods and so concentrated the character of these places. The sheep and corn were farmed on the dry Downs. Cattle grazed in the well-watered meadows where willows were grown for basketmaking and flints brought down from the hill for building material. Now modern development has eroded these practical harmonies. But in the Far East, where people live closer to the land, the landscape is still shaped in infinitely subtle ways by its life-supporting raw materials, pre-eminent of which are two closely related plants of the grass family, the rice and the bamboo.

Rice has been grown in South East Asia for more than 7,000 years and is estimated to sustain around half the human race. It is also used in cosmetics, alcohol, exquisite textiles and porcelain. But the people who depend on it also love and celebrate it as a symbol of life itself. Rice is far more than just a commodity. It is a culture, a way of life and the precious grain believed by Hindus to have been created by Vishnu. The Western custom of scattering rice at weddings is a pale echo of the many rituals, legends and Gods which bear tribute to it in the East. Rice farming has been the impctus for magnificent buildings such as the high-prowed rice granaries of Indonesia. Rice flour was a key ingredient in the mortar for the Great Wall of China, which has outlasted many of the bricks around which it was bonded. Most rice requires growing in water, and in Indonesia and the Philippines terraces to create the flooded paddy fields along the contours of mountainsides are one of the landscape and engineering wonders of the world.

Although not a staple crop like rice, bamboo also has a rich folklore and is almost more versatile. The shoots are eaten and just a few of its other uses include scaffolding, fences, paper, fuel, buckets, sun hats, chopsticks and musical instruments. Bamboo is used to craft the cradle and construct the grave.

Sustainable agriculture in Bangladesh. Pumpkins are trained across a bamboo trellis projecting over a rice paddy.

When I first arrived in Bangladesh, I braced myself for a grim experience, based on the country's image and economic facts. Apart from city states such as Singapore and Hong Kong, Bangladesh is the most densely populated country on earth, with a population of around 164 million by 2016. Of these, 46 million were living below the poverty line in 2010 and the landless poor were estimated at 65 per cent. Lying at the mouth of the mighty Ganges and Brahmaputra rivers, it is also famously flood-prone and threatened by sea-level rise.

What I actually found in the countryside gave me a very different picture. Despite its huge long-term problems Bangladesh is currently one of the best examples in the world of sustainable land use in the tropics. Imagine one of the great wetlands of the world, the greatest delta in the Indian subcontinent, which is now refined and adapted into a nationwide kitchen garden. A mixed system of rice, bamboo, vegetables, fruit trees, cattle and fish is dovetailed within a complex network of wild waterways and deltas. Ironically, in view of its image and genuine poverty, Bangladesh is a kind of tropical model for the 'good life' of the sustainable vernacular countryside now largely vanished from Europe and North America. What amazed me was the knowledge and cheerfulness of the farmers, who used what little they had to build a world in which the potential of each plant and creature was ingeniously combined to maximise their benefits. 'Why are they always laughing?' I asked my guide. 'Because they cannot afford not to' came the reply.

My first surprise was to find that the fish were cultivated *in* the rice. The flooded paddy fields double as fish ponds and from this logical economy there expands a whole series of remarkable synergies. Just as rice is far more than food, the rice paddy is far more than a crop. It is a complex self-regulating habitat. If you pause beside a rice field you can hardly miss the croaking frogs, which throb like Harley-Davidsons, and the dragonflies and swifts, which hawk over the glittering water. Algae in the flooded fields stimulate nitrogen and oxygenate the water. This process is accelerated by the fish, which also enrich the rice with their droppings. They fatten up on duckweed, which might otherwise compete with the rice, and on mosquito larvae, which might otherwise bring malaria. Plump tilapia are cultivated for the market and, since they live on aquatic plants, they do not present the problems associated with farming carnivorous shrimps or salmon. The highly nutritious little wild fish are caught by the women to be eaten – head, bones and all – as the family meal.

Rice is subject to many insect pests, but pesticides can have undesirable side effects as well as creating a costly reliance on chemicals among the poorer farmers. Around the rice paddies there are plenty of alternative agents of control at hand. The villagers know the value of bats, which roost in the bamboo and can consume a third of their body weight of insects in a single night. They are especially partial to moths, whose caterpillars are notorious predators of rice. In the miniature world among the rice shoots, wolf spiders hunt the destructive leafhoppers. Stepping delicately through the shallow water, pond herons glean their harvest of mole crickets, which can damage the base of the rice plants. But perhaps the most remarkable biological control of all is the strategy known as 'bird on a stick'.

All over Bangladesh you will see bamboo poles projecting at rakish angles from the level rice paddies. Invariably perched on top, or dexterously sallying out after its prey, is a black crow-like bird with a striking forked tail. This is the drongo, an aggressive consumer of insects which, to be effective, needs a perch seldom found in the open rice paddy. How this neat reverse of the scarecrow, a kind of real live 'guardcrow' was first adopted is unknown and it is suspected that drongos consume both beneficial and destructive insects. But these charming sentinels have certainly benefited and expanded their population as a result of their home-made perches. They cost nothing and are obviously valued as they gulp down plenty of damaging caterpillars and stemborers.

The bamboo pole in the rice paddy is just one example of the seemingly endless combinations of these two plants, which create a kind of signature tune for the local sense of place. The connection has been enshrined in folklore and religion. In Sarawak, the Iban people traditionally lay a bamboo pole from the harvested rice paddies to the new fields to provide a bridge for the rice spirit to ensure the success of the next crop. In Bangladesh, the tall bamboo thickets and the dramatic parabolas of the great bamboo fish weirs create a firm vertical framework for the fluid energy of the level rice fields. Everywhere houses are constructed with bamboo and roofed with rice straw. Bamboo is woven into bins for rice storage and made into traditional rice steamers. Glutinous rice is often cooked in a bamboo joint over the fire. Where land is limited, bamboo trellises project out over the rice paddy to support marrows, pumpkins and climbing Indian spinach. Who would have thought that pumpkins could reduce road accidents? Scientists have observed that the vitamin A which they provide can reduce night blindness, a common cause of car crashes in Bangladesh.

In my study hangs a little bamboo fish trap given to me by a tumultuously enthusiastic crowd of Bangladeshi villagers. It is the neatest thing. Two deftly woven funnels guide the hapless fish down a one-way tunnel and there is a little hinged door to allow you to extract your catch once you have secured it. When I returned home through Dhaka airport, I was harassed by the customs officials. That was until they spotted the fish trap. Then, in that pressured urban environment of bag checks and security, it was all delighted smiles, rural reminiscence and national pride. A love of harvesting our local resources must be one of the oldest impulses in humanity.

The solutions I describe here can be found all over the tropics. What is impressive in Bangladesh is the way that non-government organisations (NGOs) work at the grass roots level of the rural communities to rediscover these traditions of good husbandry and develop new ones so that people can be as self-sufficient as possible with minimal investment of chemicals and cash. I visited the international NGO Cooperative for Assistance and Relief Everywhere (CARE), which was employing local people and equipping them with motor scooters to travel around the delta spreading the word. In time these missionaries will no longer be needed as their converts carry the message of what they call 'creative farming' deeper into the community. They were even running hugely popular travelling theatre groups, which graphically demonstrate the practical lessons of sustainability to the local community. In Bangladesh the NGOs working 'bottom-up' have become so influential as to be almost an alternative form of government to the remote bureaucratic hierarchies operated by the state.

Of course it would be naive to sentimentalise poor rural life. The rice farmers have no illusions about the sheer toil of planting and hoeing their crop. As with the subsistence cocoa farmers, the rice and bamboo landscape depends on abundant cheap labour, and so on relative poverty. But Bangladesh's paddy fields will always remain my dream of the ideal working landscape and a gold standard of sustainable agriculture. It may also foreshadow the ultimate in high-tech farming. The algae, which feeds the fish in the rice paddies, can be grown for animal feed, vitamin pills and juices and may prove a neat way of mass-producing food with less land consumption than conventional agriculture.

I also found it impossible to witness the Bangladeshis' cheerful resourcefulness in the face of their problems and not feel optimistic about how future generations might enjoy making an elegantly sustainable living from the land. This is a model that we should try to support whenever it arises – not the severance between farming and landscape, which we see with the intensive monocultures, but one in which the actual working of the land concentrates its beauty and totally involves the community that creates it. The way that a landscape can trade on the richness of its scenery and wildlife, so often regarded as something to be swept away in pursuit of profit, also takes us to one of our most potentially creative modern industries – that of tourism.

A Valkyrie among the vampires

In Belize forests, mangroves and even savannahs have been able to pay for themselves – and so survive – as a tourist attraction. Of course, tourism is a double-edged sword, and when uncontrolled it has had a disastrous impact on landscapes, habitats and communities in the Caribbean. Since the days when I first swam over it as a child, Tobago's Buccoo Reef has been severely damaged by generations of tourists walking on the coral and anchoring their boats to it, as well as by the sewage outfalls from the nearby hotels.

In addition, some bays in Tobago were reduced to mud through the activities of sand mining, whereby beaches were bulldozed to provide aggregate for the concrete needed to extend beachside hotels. As well as ruining the further tourist potential of the adjacent coast, this also destroyed the sands in which the great marine turtles lay their eggs. Beach mining has now long ceased in Tobago but continues on some Caribbean islands such as Montserrat. Worst of all are the Caribbean cruise ships, for whose passage gaps have been bulldozed in the reefs.

Yet, in both Trinidad and Tobago, tourism offers one of the best allies for nature conservation. In the past shark fishers commonly poached the nesting turtles, to use their severed flippers as bait. With the arrival of visitors, the money generated by turtles provided a practical disincentive to such butchery. Now attitudes are greatly changed and Trinidad is proud of its conservation. The island has long marketed its wildlife and the consequence is a steady and lucrative stream of birdwatching holidaymakers, especially from the USA. At one of the most spectacular palm-fringed beaches, the only international tourists you are likely to see are little groups in safari suits peering into the nearest thicket for a glimpse of a howler monkey. Not that this attention always saves the monkeys. One old man told me how he shot a red howler. It held a leaf against its wound, he explained, before it died. He felt sufficiently uncomfortable about this to resolve never to shoot one again.

Belize is also full of small tourist operators, who are given special government facility to run rainforest lodges or small beach hotels employing local people. I have spent some years battling to save a rainforest in Belize from extended quarrying and the ravages of slash and burn. The best solution was to register it with the government for a small tourist development. If this then attracts an investor, the resulting lodge may employ the local people, who would otherwise burn the bush, and it should attract visitors, who come in the hope of seeing a jaguar or a macaw as well as snorkelling off the nearby beach. There are dozens of such operations in Belize and this is a product where we as consumers don't need to wait for a certification system to come into being. We just have to choose the right kind of holiday.

One of the best places in the tropics to see eco-tourism in action is the Arima Valley. Arima is a typical ramshackle Trinidad town, with some fine specimens of local graffiti. One wall exhorts:

Say NO to drugs. SAY YES TO JESUS!
STAND UP FOR THE LORD!
No urinating here.

Behind the town a road climbs the mountainside to an old estate house, embowered in hibiscus and yellow *Allemanda*, commanding views over the forested valley. The cool elegance of the house, with its mahogany doors and frosted gilt mirrors counterpoints the steaming forests pressing in on every side. It is now a hotel and nature centre, named after Asa Wright, its previous owner.

I remember Asa Wright. So does everyone else who was around in Trinidad before the mid-1960s. She was a personality in scale with her exotic surroundings. An Icelander, straight from the pages of the Sagas, she was a huge flat-footed, big-jawed woman. Strong men would marvel at the ease with which she swung cement bags into the back of the Jeep in which she sped up the mountain pass, like some tropical Valkyrie. She was generally surrounded by a retinue of American zoologists, who could be found in various corners of the house, writing learned papers or playing with the tree porcupine which was a regular inmate of the place.

I can still picture Asa pouring tea on the verandah, as the waxy pink candelabras of the Amherstia tree shed their silky petals through the windows onto the polished mahogany floors. When the teatime porcelain gave way to the chilled dewy glasses of rum and soda, the house on its hill was a cool refuge from the sweltering anarchy of the surrounding tropical dusk. But the furniture creaked ominously, consumed from within by armies of termites. 'When the

Birdwatchers look out over the rainforest from the verandah of the Asa Wright Nature Centre in Trinidad.

termites stop holding hands,' it is said in Trinidad, 'the works of man will collapse.' I recall the momentous crash when my mother's china cabinet imploded in this way. 'The poor little things,' said Asa, in her Icelandic accent, brushing aside the problem and the termite dust from the tablecloth with an airy wave of her enormous hand, 'They must have somewhere to live.'

Now the great colonial verandah acts as what must be the most stylish birdhide in the world. Fruit and sugarwater are put out as bait. Downy and delicate, the birds flutter within inches of the watchers' heads: glittering malachite hummingbirds and tanagers, soft and purple as ripe plums. Squirrels and rugby-striped lizards catch the crumbs from the bird tables. Behind the rail are ranked the batteries of tripods and long lenses. As irresistibly as the melon rinds lure the wildlife, the visitors pour past the cash desk in pursuit of the spectacle. Eco-tourism, which uses wildlife as bait for the tourists, is our most modern and sophisticated example of the ancient art of angling. The Asa Wright Nature Centre is a model of its kind and the guided walks through the old cocoa plantations instantly reveal a world of birds and insects, which would take the casual visitors many days to glimpse if they trudged, uninstructed, through the rainforest.

Yet something of the spontaneity and eccentricity which I remembered from the past was lacking. As it turned out, I didn't have to go far to find it. Simla is Trinidad's best-kept secret. The other great house in the Arima Valley, it is the research and scientific wing of the Asa Wright Nature Centre. A long low building, superbly situated along the end of a ridge, with forested cliffs plunging away on three sides, it was built in colonial times as the governor generals' summer residence and named after the more famous hill retreat of the Indian Raj. It was also the final home of William Beebe, zoologist of Darwinian range, prolific author and one of the great explorers of the century. It was Dr Beebe who descended the deep sea off Bermuda in a bathysphere and was the first man to gaze at the luminous hatchet-jawed monsters of those sunless depths. Beebe designed his own craft and set off with minimal back-up. It was also he who established the still-persisting connection between the Arima Valley and the New York Zoological Society of which he was an early director.

When I visited, the old house had withdrawn into itself, besieged from without by the forest which crowds to its shuttered windows, and mined ever deeper from within by the invincible termites. But the atmosphere I remembered from Beebe's time had not changed. The main item pinned to the noticeboard was the skin of a pit viper. Tethered in what was once the governor's herbaceous border was a large goat, kept, we were told, to feed April's vampires. That explained the large bowl of blood in the fridge, where we stored our provisions. April, the only resident, an appropriately pale but deceptively demure biologist, was studying bats.

At feeding time, we processed along a moonlit forest path bearing their supper. They flickered around the ceiling of an outhouse: the big fruit bats swooping on piles of ripe mangoes; the little carnivores sipping delicately. Next came an alarming discovery. The door of the outhouse had been bolted from the outside. We were locked in with vampire bats. Retreat was only possible by crawling through a hole in the wall out into the tropical night. Old man Beebe used to joke about the vampires which regularly quartered his bedroom, and the need to keep his big toe well inside the mosquito net. With the passing years the bats had clearly flourished and more alarmingly there was now no sign of mosquito nets.

Trinidad oilbirds nest in caves from which they emerge at night to feed on oily forest fruit.

The chocolate forest

What sums up for me, more than anything, the special quality of Trinidad are the oilbird caves which lie in the heart of its rainforest. Oilbirds are relatives of the nightjar, which roost by day in limestone caverns. Their screams, likened to the cries of tortured prisoners, are underscored by a clicking sound by which they navigate the darkness with the aid of echolocation. At night they emerge to feed on oily forest fruit, advance scouts leading the way, followed by wave after wave, feeding like giant hawks hovering up and down the shaft of fruit-laden palms. At dawn they stream homeward to vanish into the bowels of the earth. Small wonder they are regarded traditionally as evil spirits.

Walking to the oilbird caves you crest the hill to gaze over valleys beyond valleys untouched by any road or house. Mud sucks at your ankles and the local farmers have to get their cocoa out by muleback. Nothing has changed here. The call of the bellbird, like the twang of a Jew's harp, resonates across five miles of blue remembered cloud forest. Descending into the steam bath of the valley bottom, you hear the cave before you see it: a distant collective scream like the thin hiss of tearing metal. Then you smell the hen-house whiff of guano. Half concealed by lianes and elephants' ear is a crack in the rock like a pitch-black lightning bolt. An ice-cold river pours from the vent. Inside, the packed flocks of birds thrash against the stalactited roof, their eyes glowing like red coals. The senses are overwhelmed by the noise, the stink and the swirling knee-deep water. Whip scorpions hunt along the slippery cavern walls, so it is best to grope your way down the centre of the stream, whose source remains uncharted. An attempted exploration by the Trinidad potholers' club ended in disaster: the skull of one diver was eventually washed up in the mouth of the cave.

The survival of the chocolate forests of Trinidad and Belize is a cause for celebration. Whether they will still be there for the next thirty years is another question. Ironically, one factor that has saved some forests is fossil fuel. Trinidad's oil wealth has, through the electricity network, long been providing a fuel alternative to the wholesale felling of trees, while some of the best blocks of forest in the south of the island owe their protection from slash and burn to ownership by the oil companies. A road along the north coast has been debated and fought off as long as I can remember and the forested slopes of the Northern Range still plunge to the reef with nothing to diminish the pristine meeting of jungle green and aquamarine.

Other circumstances make Trinidad and Belize something of a special case. Their bubbling Caribbean culture includes among its unlikely legacies from Britain and the US a love of hiking, so for many of their citizens the wilderness is not a threat but a resource. Both countries have led the way in the field of eco-tourism, with their English-speaking traditions and their comparative accessibility. They both have an increasing potential for exporting sustainably certified forest products.

Finally, there is their position: Belize at the threshold of Central America and Trinidad facing the South American continent. On a clear day, the crumpled blue coastline of the Spanish Main is alluringly visible from Port of Spain, whence the Elizabethans set off up the Orinoco in search of wealth beyond the dreams of avarice. Scientists, especially from the USA, have also used both Trinidad and Belize with their universities and easy access as first base for Amazonia and Central America. Forest loss in Trinidad is steadily decreasing and the terrible fires of the 1980s have proved to be the exception rather than the rule. If this succeeds, then something more valuable to humanity than all the gold of El Dorado can be achieved in these places: they will help to set a standard for the sustainable use of all the South American rainforest, the most fabulous natural system on earth.

Not only the Trinidad cocoa groves, but the whole world, is a chocolate forest, with its finite resources which we may nibble carefully without consuming the lot. But the luxurious nature of chocolate, with its high price and low nutritional value, also points to a deeper question that will always hang over any discussion of sustainable commodities: the distinction between need and desire. For the Maya and Aztec civilisations of Central America, foaming cups of drinking chocolate were the prerogative of a warrior elite, who engaged in chocolate wars for the best cocoa-growing territories. Among their burial goods, bowls of cocoa take pride of place beside the jade, jaguar skins, gold and quetzal feathers. In Central America from around 1000 BCE until the nineteenth century, cocoa beans were counted out as currency.

In 1987, Mrs Brundtland, the prime minister of Norway, made a brave and early attempt to define sustainability as follows:

> *Development which meets the needs of the present without compromising the ability of future generations to meet their own needs.*

The problem with this much-quoted definition is that word 'need'. Who is going to adjudicate exactly what each of us need? 'Reason not the need', as Shakespeare put it in *King Lear*. The billion-dollar question is exactly how far each individual should modify their lifestyle. I have sat through countless lectures on sustainability but I have never heard a speaker exhort their audience to embrace poverty in order to reduce their environmental footprint. Such a speaker would soon be out of a job. We can be sure that our descendants and the currently excluded poor of the developing world will demand more than the bare minimum and will fight, if need be, as the Aztecs did, for every last luxurious commodity. This now takes us to the real cost of creating the fashion items of cotton in the beguiling, terrifying deserts of the Middle East.

CHAPTER 5

Watering the desert

The use and misuse of water in Asia

'My name is Ozymandias, king of kings;
Look on my works, ye Mighty, and despair!'
Nothing beside remains. Round the decay
Of that colossal wreck, boundless and bare
The lone and level sands stretch far away.

Percy Bysshe Shelley

Fast asleep on a pile of buffalo heads, a boy in the back of a pickup jolts his way across a bridge over the River Indus in Pakistan. The river, pearly grey under a white-hot sky, seems to dissolve in the blazing light. Beyond it and aloof from the malarial slime and stench of the streets, the offices of the Water Board stand among dusty gardens. Hedges enclose powdery rectangles of grass, creating formal spaces like tanks of hot air, scented of drains and jasmine and never stirred except by the hoopoes, which float away like startled butterflies.

Within, pyjamaed attendants lounge in ante rooms, creating the atmosphere of a mughal court rather than a modern bureaucracy. From time to time, they rise to glide back and forth with contract documents, specifications and tea. The photocopier is the centre of an elaborate ritual involving a dozen attendants. Forms are duplicated and quintuplicated, while in inner sanctums meetings are held, promises made, the minutes filed away. With the passing years, the layers of dust and the files themselves slowly thicken until, so swollen as to become unopenable, they are bundled together in sheets and stacked to the ceiling in airless rooms whose only value is as a habitat for bats and geckos. Secure from the stinking furnace outside, the cool closed world of the Water Board remains unchanged, preoccupied with the business of looking busy.

Offices like this control one of the great irrigation systems of the world, a labyrinth of canals and channels, dispersing the river waters along 30,000 level green miles of wheat, rice and cotton, shaded by spreading mango trees and patched with the crimson rectangles of roses cultivated for their perfume. But the real flowers of this landscape are the people. Parakeet- and kingfisher-coloured, they move through the fields, their clothes flashing in the sunlight with a brilliance matched only by the wild birds. Over ten million of them depend on this watered wealth created out of dusty camel-thorn scrub during the past 150 years.

This landscape at first appears a perfect example of moderate sustainable land use, but if you look harder you begin to see a very different picture. This chapter is about the law of unintended consequences which arises from a belief that technology can somehow unlock a world of infinite resources. In Pakistan the magic technology, which is seen as the key to limitless riches, is modern water engineering, but as we will discover there is a dangerous fallacy in the assumption that sophisticated agriculture offers the opportunity of unlimited consumption.

A surfeit of salt

The Indus Valley is an irrigation engineer's dream come true. But it is a dream that always hovers on the edge of nightmare. Poised elegantly around every puddle are black and white birds with

The Indus Valley in Pakistan where the river supplies the water for massive irrigation schemes to grow cotton.

immensely long shrimp-pink legs. They step cautiously out into the shallows or line up reflected in the milky pools, motionless as decoys. They are the engineers' birds, known to ornithologists as black-winged stilts, the commonest wader in the Indus Valley and a kind of symbol of its problems. Where the stilts gather, large areas of cracked mud extend around the briny white-rimmed pools. This is salinity, a consequence of irrigation when it is applied with insufficient accompanying drainage.

If you dig a hole, the level the water reaches in the bottom of your hole is the water table. The water below that is the groundwater. This consists of a vast underground body of water, which can fall if it is pumped up for drinking through abstraction wells. In the case of irrigation, which involves constantly pouring water onto the desert to grow crops, the water table rises. This situation is made much worse in the Indus Valley, where salts were laid down millions of years ago when the land lay beneath the sea. As the groundwater is drawn up to the surface, so the dissolved salts rise with it. The fierce heat further warms the water and the salt is distilled out over the land as if in an immense pressure cooker. The result is a bald white snow-scape beneath a blazing sky, as hostile to crops as it is to most other forms of life. As the land sickens, often exacerbated by the leaking irrigation canals, it comes to resemble a vast airfield powdered with crystals, which, according to Asian legend, are the dried tears of the despairing inhabitants. Worldwide, around 1.5 million hectares of previously irrigated land are lost every year to salinity. When irrigation fails in this way, despite the millions of pounds spent on it, the only real winners are the black-winged stilts.

As the saline water table rises, first the mango trees die and then the salts appear. Over the past half-century, the water table has risen from 40 feet below the surface to five feet or less. If you walk into the hotels in the town of Sukkur, near the great Indus barrage, even the carpets are sodden. In Egypt the Colossi of Memnon, which have gazed impassively across the Nile for over 3,000 years are now threatened by rising irrigation water which eats away at their foundations. When farmers pour yet more water on the land to wash away the salt, neighbouring fields without the resources of drainage become waterlogged and sour.

It is easier to supply water than to manage it. Everybody likes building new canals or reservoirs, which create high interest for the lending banks, easy money for the consultants and a small empire for the Water Board. Removing the surplus water, on the other hand, involves an unglamorous interminable process of negotiating with farmers and installing pumps whose maintenance presents almost insuperable problems. Perhaps most importantly these are dependent on electricity, which is only available for part of the day, even in major towns, and is notoriously diverted by the local power pirates in the countryside. The pumps themselves are linked with wells to draw away the saline groundwater, but they are also an irresistible magnet for small boys, whose delight is to fill them with stones. Many are the sophisticated projects hatched in the corridors of Washington and Brussels which have come to grief as target practice for the local ten-year-olds. And of course there is bureaucracy and poor managment. Of the 2,000 pumps scheduled for operation by 1995 on one scheme I worked on, ten were known to be working, while 500 were still in boxes awaiting their delivery.

The obstacles to large-scale irrigation range from such practical problems to the rise and fall of empires. The British constructed the Indus barrages in the 1930s with a realistic understanding of the problems of salinity. Their impeccable master plan envisaged accompanying drainage works, whose construction was designed to peak in the 1960s. What they did not foresee was the hasty departure of the Raj in 1947. Yet the previous generations of worthy irrigation engineers had contributed to that historic turning point, since the immense new population of the Indus Valley, providing the power base for an independent Pakistan, had largely been created by their efforts. Without the irrigation of the previously empty desert, Muhammad Ali Jinnah would never have had a nation from which to create an independent nation state. Within a decade, India was planning the diversion of the Indus headwaters in order to destroy her hated downstream neighbour.

Symptomatic of the way in which this immense invention appears to be expanding beyond the control of its creators is the apparent impossibility of even properly comprehending it. The keys to the overall complexity of relatively modest components may have been understood by their originators, now retired or deceased, or else they are irretrievably buried in the mouldering archives. Predictions for the future of this classically unsustainable juggernaut, which is nonetheless still sustaining the rural population of Pakistan and a large part of India, are equally uncertain despite the relative ease of satellite monitoring. What is certain is that no-one can afford to allow it to fail and environmentalists who dismiss its follies must still answer the harder question of how else the ever-expanding population that now depends upon it is to be fed.

Their answer to these life and death questions will be an unhesitating 'Inshallah' or 'God willing', an essential survival mechanism if the system is not to drive you mad, and a brand of fatalism that ensures the survival of that system. It is both the weakness and the fundamental strength of the people of the Indus.

Another hallmark of this subtle complicated culture is a love of concealing ornament, which verges on the obsessive. You never saw so great a dedication to decoration. The people are Elizabethan in their finery. Everything is painted. The men, robed and turbaned, dye their beards with henna and etch their eyes with kohl. The desert women, when you glimpse them, are so armoured with jewellery that they move as with the clashing of cutlery. The camels are clipped and branded with stars, moons and arabesques, while brass bells are hung from the horns of the dewlapped cattle. The white farmyard doves are stained with rose madder and catch the eye like tumbling cockatoos. Even the hooded crows are dyed scarlet. The bicycles and horse-drawn carriages are decked out like Christmas trees, while the patterned paintwork of the lorries elevates them to a level of folk art.

There never was a culture that is closer to the absolutes of nature and yet more given to fantastical embroidery. The people of the Indus sit in the desert on tinsel cushions, drinking from patterned teacups beneath the immense night skies. Nothing is what it seems, especially not the truth, which is always concealed beneath a brocade of allusion, evasion and disguise.

Marooned in the desert

My own first challenge here was to unearth hard facts about my project, a new reservoir for irrigation water, designed to flood 100 square miles and so inundate a complex chain of existing lakes, extending into the remote heart of the Thar Desert in southern Sindh. The innermost pool affected is called the Makhi Dhand, which means 'Lake of Honey'. It is guarded by two hunting lodges: one, a whitewashed fort, is inhabited by leaf-green parakeets which swoop screaming from the battlements; while the other totters on a sandy island half-shrouded in trees, a mere ruin. But what a ruin! Arcaded and balustraded, it rises from the water's edge like a playful eighteenth- century Trianon. The walls of this shell are decorated with swagging stone garlands, rose-coloured tiles and plaster putti, while the topmost pediment provides a regular perch, not for some heraldic stone beast but for a real live Pallas's fish eagle, as he watches over his precarious rooftop nest. From time to time he soars from his rococo eyrie to plunge on an unsuspecting fish, cause havoc in the local heronry, or snatch a gallinule from where it crouches among the lotus leaves like an iridescent blue

The author at work, surveying in the Thar Desert, Pakistan, watched over by local children.

moorhen. In the reeds, a dust storm of little birds parts to reveal a patrolling harrier, gliding forward on silent wings, while out on the water the fishermen balance effortlessly on their tiny craft, a trained cormorant at the wrist with its throat loosely tied to prevent it swallowing the catch. If you visit the nearby fishing villages, you are regaled with traditional desert hospitality. In the middle of nowhere, rugs and tasselled pillows are produced and sequined quilts laid out on the sand. Plump carp are speared on stakes and grilled over a fire. Tea is provided and water from the well.

But this natural paradise is not quite what it seems. The local people acknowledge the sovereignty of a traditional leader, a middle-aged businessman and living god called the Pir of Pagaro. When he comes hunting, they erect triumphal arches of reed and tissue paper and cast their bangles and bracelets before him. Acceptable tribute is said to be a man's own weight in gold. With suitable majesty he acknowledges the adoration of his people and his retainers collect the loot. Relations between central government and such feudal chiefs have always been uneasy. In 1942, the British Raj was on the defensive, with a world war at its front and the Mahatma at its back. The Pir saw his chance and encouraged his fiefs to rise in rebellion. They fell upon the outlying irrigation bungalows and cut the occupants to pieces.

The British dealt swiftly with the Pir of Pagaro by a well-tried stratagem. They executed the father and sent his son to Eton. To destroy the remaining centres of resistance, all that was required was redirection of the irrigation water, whose management they had now perfected. They diverted the largest canal and flooded the rebels out. Fifty years later I found myself defending this sizeable lake district, which they had created by this act of sabotage, now a valuable fishing and grazing resource, from the latest army of British engineers bent on its further inundation. This new water body, annually emptied and refilled like a gigantic bathtub, would create a twenty foot drawdown of sterile silt, whose regime of alternate flooding and drying would prevent the re-establishment of the existing sinuous margins of grass and reed.

The loss of this 'edge effect', the point where land and water meet, is a disaster for the ecosystem since the grassy margins and weedy shallows are the main food source for the insects. These in turn feed the fish, without which the wetland predators of otters, herons and eagles would all perish. Since cattle cannot eat mud, the local communities who depend on the lakeshores would also have to wander off into the desert. This is one of the greatest problems of most dams and, on well-designed schemes, subsidiary lakes with a stable water level should be created to offset the problem.

I was faced here with a reservoir which would submerge the hunting lodge, the lake margins, seasonal pools and scrub forest. The real challenge of such a project in Pakistan, where you cannot save everything, is to explain why it matters. 'It's just an old house' was the engineer's view of the hunting lodge and in one sense he was right. How important is it to save such landscapes, when for all you know they extend for hundreds of miles? In the developing world, the environmentalist is firefighting with insufficient contextual information to establish a site's overall importance against the insistent pressures of development. Environmental law in developing countries seldom offers much support, either. Very few areas have National Park status and only certain animals are listed as protected. All the latter means is that it is illegal to kill and eat them, which poses far less of a threat than habitat destruction against which there is little legal redress.

In these circumstances, the imperative action before irreversible engineering decisions are taken is to get out and have a look. In rough country a major factor dictating the location of large developments is accessibility. Sites are seldom chosen because they are the best option, but more often because the person doing the initial assessment wants to get home in time for tea. After that the chosen location begins to take on a life of its own, reinforced by successive surveyors, who take samples within easy reach of the access track, rather than trudging across burning sands or swamps infested with crocodiles. The latter, reaching up to fourteen feet, were a genuine hazard on this site, despite the reassurances of my guide. 'They are only really ferocious in the nesting season', he casually remarked as he pointed out a nest. For the remoter parts of my study area, a topographic survey had been produced by the local team, eager to please but equally anxious to remain in their air-conditioned office. The result was an elaborate piece of fiction, its swirling contours bearing no relation to what existed on the ground. But when I tried to explore the place for myself, I came to understand their attitude.

At first, the desert seemed entirely delightful. Its pristine immensity of rolling dune glows dusky pink with tamarisk and silver with the olive-like *Salvadora* trees. In the hollows of the dunes lie yellow gourds and every plume of wild sugarcane is etched with a brilliant halo of evening light. But it is at night that the desert really comes into its own. I slept in the open on a charpoy or string bed, perched on the dunes. In the gathering dusk you glimpse the fluttering forms of nightjars and the great dusky horned owl. Soon our lamps and firelight were attracting other residents. Three species of scorpion encircled the edge of the campsite. Above us blazed the starry heavens, the milky way streaming across the firmament. A chill pink dawn revealed fresh snakes' tracks in the sand beneath my charpoy, a fat grasshopper on my spangled pillow and cold goat's brains in the skull for breakfast.

The problems of getting around our site explained why so little was known about it. The trackless terrain across the grain of the steep dunes neatly overturned the Jeep, from which we gingerly emerged before righting it. Our driver had no experience of desert driving and was terrified of the dacoits or bandits, who were certainly in the area. A busload of people had been kidnapped that week in the nearest town to the north. In the end my experienced colleague from the Game Department took the wheel. This did, however, mean breaking the golden rule of driving in convoy. Instead we took only one vehicle without a radio.

On the last day, fifty miles from base, the battery died. The hours passed and midday approached as my companions failed to stir the vehicle into any kind of life. Our salvation, I thought, would be the famous desert hospitality. The turbaned leader of a camel train duly appeared. Never had I been so glad to see a camel. Then came a shock as he grinned sheepishly and led away his train. My companions explained that he had refused to help. This meant that the nearest little settlements, which he represented, would also fail us. They were clearly afraid of something, but as usual the truth was hard to establish. Most likely, by helping our official-looking party, they would suffer from the dacoits. We faced the prospect of walking out by night or, if we were lucky, two days on camelback. I looked at our supplies: half a barrel of water, four apples and a jar of Cooper's Oxford marmalade. The heat seemed undefeatable. Crouching in the shrinking shade of a *Salvadora* tree and looking at the bleached noonday dustlands, I focused on a landscape rather different from the picturesque place, which had previously seemed the reality, and wept. 'Inshallah', said my friends, 'Do not worry'.

After a very long day, their faith was justified, though it was the trick of hammering a nail into the positive terminal of the battery that saved us. We pushed the Jeep down the dune, holding our breath. The engine stuttered back to life and again the world seemed a different place. But never again have I felt quite the same about water.

Drinking the world dry

When I worked in the British water industry I once attended a public meeting in which there was uproar over increased water charges. An old lady stood up. 'Why should we pay for water which God gives us with His rain from Heaven?' 'Indeed He does, madam', responded my chairman. 'But you should just see where He puts it.'

Most rain falls on the sea or on regions and communities already blessed with abundant water. If the total volume of water on earth were represented by one gallon, available freshwater would only comprise one seventh of a teaspoon.

Water is one of the most pressurised and depleted of world commodities and not only in the obvious dry spots. In 1995, the rainy but populous county of Yorkshire had to resort to bringing in water by lorry. One tanker appeared at the water authority offices daubed with the slogan 'To the Poor People of Yorkshire: A Present from Ethiopia'. The most critical measure of water availability is that of water use per person per day. The Indian subcontinent combines a lack of natural resources with a booming population and is therefore using far more water than it has sustainably available. However, the average citizen of the developed world, who uses between 200 and 500 litres of water a day, sets a terrible example to the world's poor whose typical daily consumption is just five litres a head. For the poor to catch up with the rich using current technologies by 2050 will require eight more planets' worth of water resources to sustain us all. This situation is made far worse by the likelihood of unprecedented droughts due to climate change, which could create a major world water crisis in the not too distant future.

There can be few things more inflammatory than watching others drink when you are thirsty. In villages around the developing world the rural poor queue at the pump beside pipes and reservoirs, which bypass them to supply water straight to the bathrooms of city dwellers and to irrigate crops, providing a profit for local businessmen and luxuries for distant supermarket shelves. Inequity in water resources is often worsened by the engineering infrastructure. In India giant water pipes, which are seldom buried, march across the landscape severing farmland and causing the removal of houses and shrines which lie in their path. Reservoirs are even more unpopular. The glittering untouchable lakes of officialdom, they evaporate in the heat, silt up and starve the flows of rivers downstream of them. This is even more maddening if the upstream river is controlled by another country which is holding the water back from you.

So innocuous, so apparently abundant, water is the ultimate commodity we cannot do without, but like everything else we must use it moderately. The perils of hydro-politics have always flowed through history. Water, especially as used for agricultural irrigation, has been the nurse and destroyer of civilisations, the tool and ultimate prize of war. And, what is more, from the dawn of organised society to the present day the problems of sustainable water management, creating world-changing consequences, have generally emanated from the same particular places.

If you stand on the bare mountaintops in eastern Turkey with the wild barley blowing around your feet and look over the unfolding purple hills, you can see far below you a silver ribbon snaking its way to the south. Pointed out by the locals as 'the Frat', this is the Euphrates, which, with its easterly sister, the Tigris, flows down through ancient Mesopotamia, now modern Iraq. Here around 5500 BCE irrigation was initiated as a way of intensifying the production of cereals which earlier people had brought down from those Turkish uplands. By 3100 BCE writing had emerged as a means of recording and administering the harvests of an increasingly ambitious system of reservoirs and feeder canals. The earliest known script appears as marks on small clay tablets attached as labels to sacks of grain. Among the world's first laws is Hammurabi's Code, which includes a stipulation that farmers who fail to maintain the dams and sluices should be sold into slavery.

Soon after, similar developments took place in ancient Egypt and the Indus Valley. In Egypt the peasant farmers paid rent to the pharaoh according to the area of irrigated land they farmed. To survey these productive acres, trigonometry was invented. Out of the harvests of irrigation mathematics was born. The key to these breakthroughs and to the whole existence of the societies that produced them was agricultural surplus, which in turn depended on water. Without a food surplus it would be impossible to feed priests, an army, industrial workers, administrators and intellectuals. In short, a surplus of commodities, perhaps even an appetite for them, is the first basis of civilisation. And that, of course, is also where all our modern environmental problems begin.

Water wars

Flowing from Turkey to Syria and Iraq, the Euphrates, like many a vexed waterway, rises in one country and benefits another. In the ancient world, when it flowed through the heart of Babylon there were even more countries upstream, many of them hostile. In this way the life-giving river could be used as an instrument of death. In 689 BCE Sennacherib of Nineveh fell upon Babylon, when, it is said, he dammed the Euphrates, built up a head of water and then broke the dam, sending down a tidal wave to engulf the city. A century and a half later, the Persian King Cyrus tried a different tactic. According to Herodotus,: 'he dug a channel to divert the river into a marshy lake...and when the Euphrates had subsided until the water reached more or less the middle of a man's thigh, they waded into Babylon along the river.'

Sometimes nature did the job for the invaders. The beginning of the end for the Roman Empire was the last day of 406 CE when the Vandals walked over the frozen Rhine into Gaul. Water played a less incidental role in the fall of the British Empire. In 1956, Colonel Nasser, concerned that Ethiopia and the Sudan might capture the upstream waters of the Nile upon which Egypt depended, conceived the High Aswan Dam, which could store almost two years' worth of flow. When Britain refused to pay for the dam, Nasser nationalised the Suez Canal. Anthony Eden's retaliatory invasion was the debacle of Suez.

Civil and military engineers have always shared common ground, manipulating water to drown or starve their enemies. In 1503, the Florentines besieging Pisa assembled one of the

Boats grounded on the Euphrates River near Fallujah, Iraq, as a result of low water levels caused by insurgents, 2014.

most formidable design teams in history. Cesare Borgia was the client. Machiavelli provided the strategy and business plan. The engineer was Leonardo da Vinci. Their project was nothing less than the diversion of the Arno to deprive the Pisans of water and cut off their route to the sea. But, as with many a lesser proposal it foundered on cost cutting and political expediency. But if water makes a terrifying weapon, it could prove even more dangerous as an embattled resource in the water wars and water terrorism of the future.

The current turmoil in the Middle East has more than a little to do with water. Israel's desire to control the River Jordan, which sustains its orange and avocado orchards, is a dominant factor in its determination to hold the land on the West Bank, with all the wider consequences for instability in the region. Moving a little further east, the Tigris and the Euphrates are now entering yet another violent chapter in their long and embattled history. Both rivers rise in Turkey, which is theoretically capable of preventing the entire Euphrates flow from entering Syria, which lies immediately downstream. Both Syria and Iraq are entirely dependent on their downstream flows for water supply, irrigated agriculture and hydro-electricity. Since the 1970s, those flows have been reduced by 40 per cent due in major part to water storage by some 141 dams in the Turkish headwaters. Between 2007 and 2009, intense drought in Syria, caused in part by the withholding of the headwaters, led to massive crop failures and soaring food prices in the cities, which were in turn invaded by large numbers of angry unemployed farmers coming in from the abandoned countryside. This is now seen to have been a major catalyst for the Syrian Civil War.

In the ensuing struggle the fundamentalist group calling itself ISIS had taken control of many dams on the Euphrates in both Syria and Iraq by 2014. In 2013, ISIS captured the Tabqah Dam which supplies water to Aleppo, and announced that it had placed explosives in the body of the dam and that it would detonate them if it were to come under attack. The fact that ISIS was more than willing to carry out its threats was demonstrated by its use of the Fallujah Dam near Baghdad to withhold water to downstream Shiite cities and also deliberately flood around 500 square kilometres of farmland upstream. Most frightening of all so far was ISIS's control in the summer of 2014 of the Mosul Dam on the Tigris, the largest reservoir in Iraq. If the dam were breached, it is estimated that a flood wave 20 metres high would destroy Mosul and other downstream cities, killing up to 1.5 million people before it finally hit Baghdad, still about four metres high. In August 2014, the Mosul Dam was recaptured from ISIS with the help of American air strikes and, in a letter to Congress, Barack Obama cited the risk to the dam as a justification for his intervention. But the problem of the Mosul Dam is not over yet. Built on the cheap by Saddam Hussein on a foundation of highly soluble gypsum, if it is not to fall down of its own accord, the dam constantly requires highly specialised engineering maintenance, something which is easier said than done in the midst of war.

The Dammed

The 'water cycle' is the process of how water is evaporated from the sea and then falls on the land, where it replenishes rivers, crops, groundwater and even reservoirs. Groundwater in particular is an immense renewable resource if it is not polluted or over-abstracted. Careful management can easily prevent this. Over the years I have been involved in closing down boreholes in the UK when they were exploiting too much water. Even dams are not neccessarily bad. Like all other forms of engineering they can be done well or badly. All over Asia and Africa small reservoirs act as wetland nature reserves, which are a habitat for birds and a resource for the local people. In the dry season the margins are often used to grow vegetables, which thrive in the damp silt and are an important local earner. Cherry tomatoes, which reach our shops from West Africa in winter, are often produced in this way. All reservoirs should be properly designed and very carefully located and nowadays this is generally done through an environmental impact assessment. This should address and resolve two of the main problems they create: reduced downstream flows and inappropriate size and location.

The point of dams is to capture water so when they are built across rivers, not surprisingly, there is less water to flow down to the sea. In the late 1980s in France, the pressure group Loire Vivante collected water from the source of the River Loire. They carried it all the way downstream, where they poured it into the estuary, announcing in a successful publicity exercise that this was the first time in decades that, the pure waters of the Loire had reached their proper destination. In the case of the Rhône, which is one long succession of reservoirs, hardly any water at all flows out. The same is true of the Indus, where, as with many impounded tropical rivers, there are serious negative consequences for the coastal mangroves which need a regular supply of fresh water to create the brackish rather than pure salt water in which they thrive. The fishermen who depend on the dwindling mangroves are among the many downstream residents who pay the real cost of upstream reservoirs.

A modern dam is now normally designed to release adequate downstream slows and in some cases inappropriate dams are actually removed. One other consolation in relation to our terrible heritage of badly designed dams is that all reservoirs are perfect silt traps, so that in 50 to 150 years they will fill with sediment. Indeed, no engineer expects them to last forever.

The worst thing about reservoirs is the land take. As the waters rose behind the grand new dams of the 1950s, world-famous rescue attempts saved the animals at Lake Kariba in Southern Africa and the monuments at Abu Simbel, south of Aswan. The people whose homes and land were all submerged were simply forgotten. In India the Narmada Dam and its sister reservoir, the Sardar Sarovar, have inundated 700 kilometres of river valley and, according to the three state governments involved, displaced at least 200,000 people. In 1990, a 5,000-strong protest march faced police blockades, resulting in arrests and a death. The following year the World Bank withdrew support from what had become the world's most notorious dam. Nowadays most schemes are subject to very elaborate compensation and resettlement schemes carried out by experienced socio-economists. And, with international aid agencies now largely terrified of involvement in such projects, the age of mega-dams appears largely over. Apart from anything else there are hardly any appropriate sites left.

In the coming water crisis we cannot afford to neglect any sustainable supplies. In Chile, villagers living on misty ridges lay out polypropylene mesh and collect sufficient high-quality water for all their needs. In Oman, the sea fog has been studied as a resource for forestry and is critical in sustaining the coastal vegetation of wild frankincense trees, which continue to yield one of the most ecumenical of commodities. Their resinous gum was offered up before both the infant Jesus and the crocodile-headed gods of Egypt, and its incense still spices the air in Hindu temples But frankincense is not the only ancient Islamic resin still reaching a global market. In the Sudan, white-flowered *Acacia* trees are tapped for gum arabic, which has been exported to Europe for over 2,000 years. It is used in shoe polish, sweets, soft drinks and especially printing, since it helps newspaper ink stick to printing presses. Around 1993, Osama bin Laden acquired major shareholdings in Gum Arabic Company Ltd, a Khartoum-based firm which had a virtual monopoly over Sudan's gum arabic export, in turn comprising around 80 per cent of world supplies. It is likely that as people all round the world read in horror about the events of September 11, the very newspapers reporting it were materially contributing to its protagonist.

It is a good idea to understand where our commodities come from, and this is no more so than with one of the planet's mightiest monocultures: the irrigated cotton fields of Asia.

The cost of a cotton shirt

When economists grapple with the question of how much water is needed for energy and food, they always return to that fundamental consumer issue: the distinction between need and desire. If uncertainty about our real needs apply to food, how much more so in the world of clothes and fashion? In 1663, Samuel Pepys took his wife shopping and was subject to familiar agonising decisions over purchase but 'after many tryalls bought my wife a chinke [chintz]; that is a paynted Indian callico'. Indian cotton imported by the East India Company, founded in 1600 by Elizabeth I, was a colourful flexible material for tailors, and above all it was cheap. A constant

theme in the history of dress is the desire to look posh. The Elizabethans were so aware of this that they enacted sumptuary laws
forbidding ordinary citizens to dress in the style of the court. The
main cost of garments was not the tailoring but the materials. Pepys
could only afford to *hire* the silk morning gown in which he had
his portrait painted. The accessibility of ready-made cotton clothes,
one of the earliest mass consumer commodities, was to change
all that. The craze for calico, originally from the city of Calicut in
southern India, dominated British fashion in the late seventeenth
and eighteenth centuries. But not without a struggle. For cotton was
not only democratic but also dangerous. The cotton boom made
the merchants of the East India Company rich but it threatened the
home textile industry, especially the wool weavers. In 1719, riots
swept through London when the weavers attacked cotton-printing
shops and destroyed imported cloth. Political agitation from the
silk and wool lobbies led to a series of statutes banning imported
cotton, culminating in the Calico Act of 1721.

But legislation seldom overcomes the force of human desire.
The earliest cotton legislation of 1701 only prohibited the import
of ready-dyed cotton. Entrepreneurs saw their chance, and by 1712
small businesses in north-west England were dyeing the plain
cotton. The Lancashire cotton trade was under way and with it the
Industrial Revolution. But the delight and liberation enjoyed by
all sectors of society in simple cotton clothes was to have a terrible
price in human misery on both sides of the Atlantic. The first half
of the nineteenth century saw an eightfold increase in African
slaves growing the cotton in America and a similar increase in
the number of women and children toiling in the brutal mills
of northern England in order to process it. Modern Britain was
forged by industry in which cotton was a key commodity just as
the United States was defined by the American Civil War which
grew out of the debate over slavery in the cotton plantations. A
major factor in the formulation of Marxism was Engels' horror at
the social conditions of the Manchester cotton industry.

These days, cotton is principally grown only in the southern states of America and the Islamic world. But to see the real environmental cost of cotton and one of the worst water-related disasters the world has ever known, you must travel to the heart of Asia: to Uzbekistan and the old silk road.

Here, the ancient oasis city of Bokhara makes a fine first impression. It is built of pale brick to which egg yolk and camel's milk were traditionally added, enriching the local clay. Above the bulging mud-coloured walls, the blue porcelain domes of the great mosque seem to float like bubbles of sky. In the cat-haunted alleys there are muffled greetings and the clink of vodka glasses. The warm air smells of baking bread and kebabs on braziers. Traders beat the dust from carpets as richly crimson as the embers of a dying fire. Over the oven-like city a cool wind blows in from the desert and at dusk a crescent moon hangs above the minarets and

Farmers unloading cotton in Uzbekistan.

the mulberry trees. Brown and blue, the colours of earth and air are the dominant tones of Bokhara's breathtaking architecture. But, as in all the great cities of Central Asia, a third element completes the severe yet sensuous harmonies of Islam: water. This is a place of echoing cisterns, inkily reflecting wells and gardens sustained and intersected by water channels. Here the green light of a well-watered pomegranate orchard, filled with the twittering of bee-eaters and the piping of doves, is the best refreshment after days of desert travel.

Today in Bokhara you may drink tea and recline on rug-draped divans around the Lyab-i-Hauz or old town reservoir, a formal rectangle of copper-green water where Chinese geese glide and ripples betray the presence of a surfacing carp. But something is not quite right. The pool looks oily. The Shah Rud or Royal Canal which fed it carries only an evil-smelling trickle along its slimy concrete bed: all that is left of the local River Zerefshan. The quality and quantity of Bokhara's salty drinking water is also notorious. This is now pumped from the River Amu, known upstream as the Pyanj. It is famous in legend and history as the Oxus, but infamous in modern times as one of the most over-abstracted rivers in the world.

If you walk out from Bokhara, between lines of salad-green poplars, where goats trot briskly by in a cloud of dust, on either side lie cotton fields with their yellow hibiscus flowers and bursting 'bols' like fleecy buds of cottonwool. For one of the world's staple crops, cotton is a remarkably fussy plant. Temperate climes are too cold for it and the tropics are too wet for it. What it likes is semi-desert. At the same time it is extremely thirsty and also prone to a whole catalogue of pests and diseases. Farmers have even found it necessary to strip the leaves to facilitate harvesting by spraying them with weedkiller. If you set out to look for a plant that demands maximum chemicals and irrigation, you could hardly invent a more unsustainable one than cotton.

The Central Asian countries such as Uzbekistan, which used to comprise the southern USSR, are now fundamentally dependent on irrigated rice and cotton as a cornerstone of their economy. The cotton lands of Central Asia depend on two rivers: the Amu, and its sister river, the Syr Darya or River Syr, known in classical times as the Jaxartes. They both flow north from the high Pamir mountains before emptying into the landlocked Aral Sea. The Amu flows into the southern Aral Sea within Uzbekistan, but before emptying into the north end of the sea, the Syr takes a 1,600-kilometre detour through the vast open grasslands of Kazakhstan. Here it flows through clay desert and steppe of the utmost emptiness and tranquillity. In late summer the steppe is grey-gold and the desert is straw-gold. In spring they are aflame with Oriental poppies. The only punctuation marks in this boundless space are the horsemen with their flocks, which are harried by wolves, and the Islamic graveyards, which, with their domes and battlements, seem like small forgotten citadels cresting the horizon. If you travel for days through these great silences, you eventually come upon a milky blue haze where the steppe melts into the sky. This is the fast-vanishing Aral Sea.

Large-scale cotton growing first reached Central Asia from tsarist Russia in the 1860s. Farmers in the Ferghana valley were ordered to surrender mixed farmland for a less rewarding cotton economy, in which they were paid in kind. Revolt was ruthlessly suppressed. In 1898, eighteen troublemakers were hanged and 300 exiled to Siberia. In 1918, Lenin signalled the further expansion of cotton with funds for irrigation around the Amu, and in the 1930s cotton production was a major part of Stalin's five-year plans. This was the territory of the gulags and many irrigation canals were dug with slave labour. In Uzbekistan orchards, vineyards and even villages were bulldozed to make way for the 'white gold'. But the familiar pattern of seepage and salinity ensured that accelerated expansion was met with proportionally diminished returns. In 1933, famine claimed more than seven million lives. Meanwhile, the teeming fish of the Aral Sea, salted and exported along the railway line, massively alleviated starvation throughout the Stalin era.

The protagonists of irrigation had always known that the real cost of cotton could be the sacrifice of the Aral Sea. Under the Tsar, geographers recommended tapping the rivers, which flowed 'uselessly' into the landlocked sea, a sentiment echoed by Yusupov in 1939, under personal orders of life and death from Stalin to increase the cotton yield. As real evidence of environmental degradation emerged in the 1960s, irrigation pressed on regardless. Between 1962 and 1992, the area of the sea halved from 67,388 square kilometres to 33,300 square kilometres. The fishing and grazing industries collapsed and there was mass emigration from its shores. Without the moderating impact of the water body, the climate changed. The hotter summers force up the evaporation rate as the cycle of decline feeds on itself. There are terrible dust storms made worse by the high level of pesticides washed down from the cotton fields and accumulated in the dry seabed, all creating acute health problems. When the first concerted attempts were made to address the problem in 1995, it was too late. By this time millions of people had of course become dependent on the irrigated cotton fields for their economic survival.

But in the last decade attitudes have begun to change. The international green cotton movement promotes organically grown cotton, cultivated with the use of biological control using predatory insects rather than chemicals to destroy the pests. Hemp, more familiar to us as cannabis, is increasingly grown under licence even in England and provides an alternative fibre without the need for irrigation. In Arizona, scientists are developing the weeds of salt deserts (known as halophytes) as a food crop, and in Uzbekistan they are being developed as fodder, so perhaps one day we will be able to harvest the desert in a sustainable way without the need for irrigation engineers.

In Central Asia, since the collapse of communism, the farmers fending for themselves can no longer afford the high-inputs of chemicals and maximum irrigation and even in Uzbekistan the cotton quota has dropped. Throughout the old USSR farmers are seldom paid for their cotton until after it has been processed in the government- owned ginneries. They rarely cover their costs, let alone make a profit. 'At least I can eat the wheat I grow', remarked one embittered cotton farmer to me in Tajikistan in 2007.

In 1987, the dwindling Aral Sea split into two, leaving a small sea to the north and a larger water body to the south. The smaller Northern Sea fed by the River Syr appears increasingly viable although only a twentieth the size of the original sea. A properly engineered bund is now being constructed to hold it in and it was to this project that I was assigned as the environmentalist in 2002. The local people described to me how they had spent their lives watching the waves froth and bubble and their shores retreat but they were now positive about the recovery of the Northern Sea. They insisted that climate and even health had begun to improve, at least in their region. And when I asked about the notorious decline of fish stocks I was in for a surprise. While flounders and Baltic herring have long been introduced, native fish had been pronounced extinct in the Aral Sea except for a solitary species of stickleback. However, after repeated toasts of vodka, the village chief presented me with a large pungent parcel wrapped in newspaper. With a flourish he unwrapped two bronze-gold haddock-like specimens and slapped them down beside the samovar. 'Would Mr Jeremy like to take this rare delicacy back to his family in England?' They were subsequently identified as the endangered pike-asp, unique to the Aral catchment.

When we had begun work in Kazakhstan on the Northern Aral Sea project, the local chief of police was making difficulties. Tensions between the USA and Iraq were brewing and the road to the sea was blocked by road checks near the space centre at Baykonur, where excessive rocket fuel is listed as a pollution hazard. We were therefore obliged to slip through the restricted zone by taking the train. Loaded with the obligatory vodka, teapots for brews en route and a Geiger counter to check out the sinister radiation symbols on our site map, we boarded the grimy grandeur of the Moscow

Fishing boats left high and dry in the Aral Sea in Kazakhstan as the sea has been drained away to grow irrigated cotton.

to Mongolia line. At dead of night we reached our destination and climbed down from the train, a trundling leviathan of grease and iron with tasselled velvet curtains in the cab. Platforms are a rare luxury in the old USSR and we stumbled across the tracks under a high searchlight. The unlit station house, with its classical urns and columns was like an orangery from the Tsar's summer palace, stranded in the steppe. Beyond came the howling of dogs and the sound of dancing.

We woke next morning in Aralsk, the former main port on the Aral Sea. As with many Kazakh towns the only available paint seems to be turquoise blue, which on doors and shutters in the deserted high street has blistered and bleached to shades of faded denim. At the end of the road the harbour gates and rails stand against the sky. They had been designed in a jaunty motif of seagulls and sailing boats, but as you crest the ridge they swing open to reveal one of the most surreal sights in the world: a harbour that has lost its sea. The hollow space extends below you, like an amphitheatre, ringed with silent cranes and littered with tilted ships, stranded 30 kilometres from the nearest shore. The perfect summer morning is quite still except for the distant clank of trains going from nowhere to nowhere and someone hammering out galvanised tin. From pools of liquid salt, oozing like molten icing sugar, protrude the cabs of trucks and a child's iron cot, its filigree design crusted with a hoar frost of salt. But, as ever with human disasters, nature has found a toehold. The ships lie beached on juicy lawns of glasswort and samphire, lead-grey, rust and crimson, spilling out like a woven carpet. Wheatears guard their territories, perched on the eminence of long silent funnels. Beyond the port, the empty seabed extends purple with tamarisk and sea lavender, and dromedaries browse among the rusting fleets.

The restoration of the Northern Sea will never reach quite as far as the port, and the main Southern Sea is becoming ever shallower and saltier since the waters of the Amu are locked up in irrigated fields to grow cotton, sold to us on the world market. If they ask in Aralsk where their sea has gone, our main answer has to be: 'We are wearing it.' However, by 2006, four years after my visit, our bund was brimful and fishing fleets were setting out again on the little northern sea. It is a nice irony that rescue has come from that much-reviled object, a dam, and good to know that the golden fish of the shrinking sea are returning at last.

The reservoir revisited

The dream of all architects and engineers is to be immortalised by some mighty project. For environmentalists and conservationists the opposite often holds true. Their great achievements are to stop such projects in their tracks: their far more discreet monuments, a simple absence soon overlooked after projects are dropped and forgotten. Although I am proud of some of my schemes, many of the best things I have done have been simply to stop things happening. In 1989, I helped fight a battle to stop a dam on the upper Loire. Now you can visit the valley at Serre de la Fare in the Auvergne and still enjoy the river cliffs, the meadows, the rock shelters with their extraordinary Neolithic art and the forests where the eagle owl, known locally as 'le grand duc', still reigns supreme. You would never guess that, but for some long-forgotten controversy, the whole place would have vanished under the waters of a reservoir built to support the nuclear power stations downstream.

Such triumphs are more commonly achieved by the ineffectiveness of the developers than by the determination of the opposition. In the Lar Valley in the Elburz mountains of Iran a mighty dam was proposed by the Shah in the 1970s and would probably been completed by the Ayatollah but for an accident of geology overlooked by the engineers at the time. So porous was the local limestone that no dam would ever hold the water in. Now tulips and Oriental poppies grow over the foundations of the abandoned engineering, standing Ozymandias-like below the glittering snow peak of Mount Demavand.

Far more schemes are planned than ever built around the world. The money runs out and the engineers go home. When I was working on a water supply project in India, I once walked into an empty office to see the unattended computer printing out a lengthy report which had been written with much toil for an indifferent client. As the pages were fed out of the printer, they drifted gently onto the floor, and, activated by the whirling ceiling fans, floated down the stairs or out of the window. One was caught in the branches of a tree. Such inertia can have its compensations for the landscapes of the planet.

In 2011, I returned to Pakistan after an absence of fifteen years. At first glance Lahore was the same old city with the nostalgic familiar hallmarks of the subcontinent: the long dusty avenues; the muezzins rising in ever wilder crescendos; the smell of charcoal and unrefined petrol; the tiny garage workshops with each carefully polished wheel hub stacked ready for use; the street hawkers dwarfed by their giant bunches of balloons half floating above them as if they were Chinese dragons in a festival; and the lethal traffic with its boy racers, suicidal cyclists and tinselled trucks. The familiar evasion and disguise is more impenetrable than ever. Pakistan now harbours the highest concentration of terrorist organisations on the planet. But of course nobody ever mentions this and it is routinely denied if they do. It doesn't take long to realise that since 9/11 this is a new and sadder Lahore. Everyone declares too much that wherever you happen to be is 'really safe place'. This jewel of a city, beloved of Kipling, which I remember as a carefree place where I could wander at will beside the marble fountains of the Shalimar Gardens or climb the rooftops of private houses at their owners' insistent invitation to watch the sun set behind a sky of a thousand kites flown by every small boy in Lahore and dancing like a symphony over the city – is now besieged within and without. No foreigner would dream now of walking out alone, since Pakistan is one of the worst countries in the world for kidnapping. Even kite flying is subject to a prison sentence, since their razor-sharp strings used for cutting rival kites have led to fatal injuries. Throughout Lahore there are roadblocks and soldiers crouch with their guns in fortified pillboxes. Along with the winter mist which steals in from the canals of the surrounding Punjab, there is a pervasive climate of fear.

As for the new reservoir, after ten years of standing empty it was finally filled by the major rains in 2010. Its hard-won water is subject to illegal offtakes and there is, as ever, no clear plan for its use for effective irrigation or for the control of salinity. It may be that with little comprehensive drawdown the reservoir may develop as a reed-fringed lake similar to the one it drowned out – yet another failed scheme, a colossal waste of money but not a major disaster to the environment after all. Nearby, in the interminable plain, there is a square mile of bricks. Some say these are remains of the earliest Indus civilisation, famously destroyed by unsustainable irrigation. But the site may be more recent. It is not in the guidebooks. No one knows its name. The point of this place is its anonymity. There is no obvious clue to link it with any age or culture. Rather, it seems like some lost city of the future. The ancient bricks have been manufactured, straight, rectangular, impersonal and in their millions. They could have been made yesterday. A goatherd picks his way over the rubble and beyond, some new green fields appear to be winning their struggle for life in the desert. Inshallah.

CHAPTER 6

The red roads of Africa

Poaching Africa's riches

In 2010, I travelled 600 miles across Mozambique with two local biologists to help plan the route of a proposed power line. We drove in a pickup on roads that were seldom more than footpaths, pitching camp wherever we had reached by nightfall and cooking on an open fire. We encountered lions, landmines, cobras and rebels but they were generally at a comfortable distance.

I was born in Africa but was too small to remember it as a child and, though working there frequently over the previous twenty years, it had taken me to the age of sixty to have such a prolonged adventure in the African bush. It was one of the great journeys of my life. Here was my diary entry for 15 March:

In a small hamlet of round houses. A peaceful morning with merciful grey skies keeping the heat at bay. There is a smell of wood smoke and the regular 'bong' as an old man in a ragged t-shirt chops wood. His axe handle is a bent tree branch and with this he is building a house. It is circular, 2 metres in diameter with 12 post holes. The first thing to go up is the door frame: a door into emptiness. In another ten minutes he has erected five more posts. 'How long will you take to do it?' I ask. 'Two hours,' he says.

There are a few children. A dog sleeps and chickens scratch under the mango trees: an enclosed quiet domestic world within a seeming infinity of bush and many miles from electricity. Water has to be brought in jerry cans from a distant well. By western standards the poverty is shocking but there is an atmosphere of genial cheerfulness and home. It is March and gathering swallows twitter in the skies, some of them perhaps bound for England. The head man is glad to be back from 20 years working in the South African gold mines.

Of this book's two chapters on Africa, the second one looks at the debate about agricultural land use and compares indigenous agroforestry with an imported monoculture. This first African chapter considers the commodity of minerals. Mining in Africa ranges from large well-run quarries with security fences, heavy machinery and teams of professional engineers and environmentalists to unsupervised artisanal mining carried out by little groups of Africans with picks and pails.

I have never witnessed the gold mines of South Africa, but working in Ghana I did stumble on small-scale illegal gold mining. Carried out in broad daylight beside the road it certainly didn't feel like an illegal activity and in Ghana such operations are often blessed by the local chiefs. Bikes were propped against a tree and there were perhaps thirty people, including women in brightly coloured clothes and many small boys in Wellington boots. Buckets were being hauled up out of a pit with the use of a home-made pulley. A woman wearing bright pink flashed a huge smile and revealed the contents of her bucket. There in the dark earth were tiny glinting worms and curlicues of brightest gold. Despite myself I could feel my pulse quicken in primal anticipation. There is nothing wrong with mining, provided (like everything else) it is carried out carefully and with moderation. The problem arises when unscrupulous outsiders dominate the industry, and to understand how this happens in Africa we need to examine the continent's communications and travel down the red roads of Africa.

The red and rolling road

When I think of Africa the first things I recall are thunderstorms and getting stuck in the mud. The one is generally the consequence of the other when the rains turn the roads to axle-deep rivers of liquid clay. But such are the roads that, even without the rain, there hovers over any day's expedition the possibility of a night marooned in the bush. One evening in Burkina Faso, the corner of French West Africa previously known as Upper Volta, I crashed my vehicle up a bank to avoid a pothole. And there I was in the grey thorn scrub that rolls beyond the next and the next horizon to the furthest limits of Africa. The moon was rising. Mackerel-coloured guinea fowl were scratching in the dust. In the cool stillness of the night, children and women materialised from the bush to smile, then vanish. There was a pale echo of voices calling in a distant village and, like a second sunset, a faraway glow of bush fires. Eventually, rescue arrived: a man on a motorbike with a gun over his shoulder and a live chicken upended in a plastic bag slung from the handlebars. I hopped on the back clutching my briefcase and we set off under the stars.

The earth roads of Africa uncoil across the continent, varying only with the regional geology and climate. In Uganda, the red roads loop across the wet green landscape of Central African Equatoria. As the towering cumulus gives way to the smoking indigo backdrop of an approaching storm, the light intensifies and the roads turn to sunset-coloured ribbons, flame and salmon on the polished mud, chocolate in the shadows or coolest violet where they are strewn with the fallen petals of the jacaranda tree. At night, red coals reflecting the headlights are the eyes of dust-bathing nightjars and a long low ripple of black and cream stripes is a giant genet, out hunting.

Where the roads cut through the forest, the black and white colobus monkeys sit on the overhanging branches and watch the world go by. All life travels along the roads of Uganda, much of it at a leisurely pace. Along these roads you will see files of schoolchildren, immaculate in their candy-pink and canary-yellow uniforms (100 highly motivated children to every un-resourced class); a pregnant woman, bent double beneath a load of sticks while her husband strolls beside her, twirling his jacket from his index finger; or, if you are lucky, the local witch doctor, not got up in beads and hornbill feathers but in shades and a sharp suit, as he is the richest man in the community. There will be the consultants like me with their notebooks, laptops and little bottles of hand cleaner, the ones in open pickups looking enviously at those in air-conditioned Land Cruisers. More recently there are the Chinese, big businessmen in suits, small traders in jeans and an army of workers in dungarees. They are the biggest force for change in Africa since the arrival of Dr Livingstone and the villains in his wake.

Then there are the bicycles. The cycles themselves are a marvel with their burnished chrome and long-worn-out plastic pedals replaced by wooden blocks which are polished and rounded by use. Even more marvellous are the loads they carry, which include mothers and babies riding pillion, crates, beds and fridges. The possibilities of what can be balanced on the flat rack above the rear wheel appear inexhaustible: a live goat, its legs tied beneath it; a giant Nile perch, its gaping mouth and scaly tail trailing in the dust on either side of the wheel. In 1945, many black African troops, in lieu of an army pension, were given a bicycle, some of which are still doing service. When Uganda was on its knees, in the aftermath of Idi Amin, the old bicycle tyres were stuffed with straw.

The roads, with their roadside markets piled high with glossy tomatoes, limes, dusty yams and purple passion fruit, are the lifeblood of the rural communities. In Britain, many avoid living by the main road and mount a protest when road widening comes too close to them. In Africa, the worst thing you can do to a village is to give it a bypass. If you do, the houses may simply be dismantled and rebuilt hard on the highway. In the West, dislocated from its own economic roots, it is often the road itself (and above all its impact on the view) which is opposed, an attitude found entirely baffling by people from less developed countries. In Africa, communication and easy access to markets is everything. In 2013, I was consulting a local chief in Ghana about developments near his community. 'The main thing is the road,' he insisted. 'If we have the road it's abundance here, full stop'.

But in the longer term the goods travelling along the road are often not so much the lifeblood of Africa as a haemorrhage of its resources. The roads have always carried the continent's riches down to the nearest port, which swallows its raw materials and sends them overseas, enriching the world and leaving Africa still poor. And the plunder is far from exhausted, especially the minerals. Gold and diamonds still pour from the African earth and

The red roads of Africa uncoil across the continent and everybody travels along the road. Here, a cyclist takes home a load of firewood.

there is copper from Zambia, aluminium from Ghana, coltan for smart phones from the Democratic Republic of Congo and oil from Nigeria. In return, back along the road come the world's castoffs. Lorryload after lorryload of second-hand bikes travel north through Ghana to Burkina Faso and Mali, lost or stolen in Europe and shipped from Dutch ports. There are third-hand computers and Singer sewing machines, all repaired and pressed into service. This is a pattern that has stayed the same over the past forty years as China, India and the Far East have learned to process their raw materials before exporting them, and so have overtaken Africa, which is left behind as the least developed continent on the planet. When did you last see the label 'Made in Africa'?

The influence of roads is, however, far greater than these specific commodities. Roads are the great agents of change, neutral arteries which can bring to desperately poor and isolated communities their only hope of improvement, or else final disaster. They bring medicine and trade, together with tourists whose money funds wardens to police poaching in remote beleaguered game parks. The roads also bring occasional rebel incursions. At Christmas in Uganda, when cashflows are tight, they bring armed robbers who wait patiently while the bus passengers empty their pockets. Travelling in Africa is time travelling. There are still highwaymen on the high road and pirates on the high seas. The only difference is that the uniform of cocked hat and pistols has been replaced by T-shirts and a Kalashnikov.

But a steadily improving road system brings one advantage which perhaps outweighs all the problems: an end to isolation. Rural Africa often seems like the remotest place on earth. Here is another Mozambique diary entry, from 25 March 2010:

After a long day of interminable wilderness we decided to stop at a little village deep in the bush and asked permission of the head man to camp there. The usual dusty clearing with a scatter of huts and rubbish grading into scrub. Large numbers of fiery-necked nightjar

swoop and trill in the dusk. The headmaster from the adjacent
school came and talked to us, presenting us with a water melon.
He has 150 children in the school many making very long walks
to the school each day. He insists that the villagers are happy in
their remote world despite the malaria and the distance of clinics.
But for him it is a hard posting. His wife is in Maputo and he sees
her for a week every few months. It is a 15km walk to get a signal
to phone her. His loneliness is palpable. The Mozambicans all feel
sorry for him. But he has to earn the money, he says.

The problem of isolation was something I should have known
about from my father. Along the roads of Uganda in the 1940s
and 1950s also came a cavalcade of colonial administrators. In
one of these processions I was borne along as a small baby. There
were no adequate vehicles, so everyone went on foot. My father
walked in front, leading the way. An army of porters then carried
all that an English agricultural officer might require on a six-week
safari to inspect his district: the canteen of cutlery, the collapsible
bath, the copies of *Country Life*, the dachshund and the Singer
sewing machine. My mother liked nothing better than to stitch up
curtains on safari. But there was another darker side to the story
of my father's African career, one that took me half a lifetime to
discover. One day, not long after he died, I found a photograph of
him on his wedding day, but the bride beside him was definitely
not my mother. I had never heard the remotest rumour about
this from him or anyone else. I taxed my mother about it. 'Oh, he
was married before I met him,' she explained airily. 'During the
war. But she ran off with a planter.' No further explanation was
forthcoming.

My mother herself arrived along those red earth roads soon
after the end of the Second World War, a small but feisty Falkland
Islander looking for a new life after years of teaching through the
London Blitz. I wonder now how such matches were arranged.
In the war years, it took letters about six weeks to reach Britain

from the depths of Uganda. In the remoter parts of Africa postal communications remain as bad today. But that no longer matters, as the whole continent has jumped a generation of technology. When I first worked in Africa in the 1990s, it used to be a major challenge to ring home from a landline and access to internet was rare. Now plastic scratch cards to pay as you go on the mobile are available in almost any town or village.

Between 1999 and 2004, mobile subscribers in Africa jumped from 7.5 million to 76.8 million, and today the number of mobile users in sub-Saharan Africa is estimated at more than 420 million, almost half the adult population. Banking by mobile phone is universal. Even before the mass advent of mobiles in Africa, war torn Somalia in the 1990s kick-started its own economy through a worldwide telephone banking system using a few satellite dishes in Somalia and working through the large and loyal Somali communities overseas. This was done without any help from the west, after the 1994 debacle in which US troops were killed in Mogadishu and President Clinton pulled out US forces, followed by the withdrawal of all international aid.

In the twenty-first century, communications and energy generation comprise the greatest material challenge to Africa's progress, while the continent's immense mineral wealth offers one of the best ways of paying for these badly needed improvements. One problem is that the profit from minerals so often benefits outsiders rather than Africans. In Zambia foreign mining companies helping the country out when it was bankrupt secured profitable indefinitely long-term deals from the copper mines. In 2011, the Swiss-based company Glencore was reported as paying little or no corporation tax in Zambia and weak Zambian laws allowed overseas investors to transfer all their profits abroad without any ceiling or restriction. In Nigeria, such was the incompetence and lack of investment by the greedy elite who controlled the country's oil in 1998 that so many refineries were allowed to close that Nigeria (awash with oil) had to import its own fuel.

Ghana, known as the Gold Coast in colonial times, is very rich in minerals, including one of the world's largest supplies of bauxite. The raw material for aluminium, this must first be processed and then smelted, requiring a high-input of energy. In 1957 Kwame Nkrumah of Ghana was the first African president to lead his country to independence. That was also the year of the Suez crisis and large dams were what every new leader wanted in order to modernise the country. He proposed a huge reservoir at Akosombo to drive an aluminium smelter, drowning out an area of fertile land the size of Lebanon. A key player in the financing of all this was Edgar Kaiser of the Kaiser Corporation, the US aluminium combine. The reservoir was built and the smelter supplied but without a processor, as Kaiser already had an existing one in Jamaica. The dam has other benefits as a fishery and as a crucial power source for Accra, keeping the lights of the capital going. But to this day half a century after it was constructed, there are still claims coming in for resettlement at Akosombo and Ghana still sends its bauxite to Jamaica for processing, so failing to realise the full value of its most precious raw material.

An even greater problem with minerals such as gold, diamonds and oil is that they are among the most double-edged commodities a country can be blessed or cursed with, familiar through history for their legacy of corruption, exploitation and war. But, to trace the sustainable origins of any commodity, we must answer the teasing questions about certification: *What does it mean, and How do you know?* To understand how difficult that can be to answer in Africa, I will first take you to the misty mountains of Equatoria.

Guerillas in the mist

Rwanda and Burundi, once a joint kingdom and now two very different republics, share many things in common: a landscape wreathed in low cloud; cool dripping hills patchworked with plots of pale green banana, dark glossy oil palms and red earth

Children work with their bare hands to mine coltan ore used in mobile phones. These boys are in South Kivu, Democratic Republic of Congo.

fields of cassava where the distant farmers work their hanging gardens like beetles inching up a wall. Tumbling streams chase down the ravines from mountains whose constant mist conceals both gorillas and guerrillas. The great apes migrate across borders to avoid the ebb and flow of civil war. This is a camouflage landscape of unexpected surprises, aptly echoing the pervasive atmosphere of political uncertainty. Chameleons twine their tails among the vine tendrils. Sunbirds and glossy starlings, jet black against the light, suddenly pulse electric blue as the sun catches their iridescence. At the city lakeside in Burundi, crocodiles lie in wait for late-night revellers; our driver told us of a friend who paused to wash his face one Saturday night – and was knocked in by a great reptilian tail.

Rwanda and Burundi face the dark heart of eastern Congo, its mountains looming ever visible across the Great Lakes with their lure of riches and capacity for terror. Above all they share the long-running revenge tragedy of the Hutu/Tutsi conflict. In 1993, a civil war began in Burundi which still rumbles on. The Rwanda genocide of 1994 was one of the great mass crimes of the twentieth century and also notoriously a tragedy of failed communication, as the world ignored what was happening until it was too late. In reconciled post-genocide Rwanda it is totally taboo to even mention the words 'Hutu' and 'Tutsi' but nonetheless a deep seated fear and mutual hostility has not gone away. In the 1994 genocide a million Tutsi were killed by Hutu aggressors, who were also the government in power. This was then overthrown by the Tutsi-dominated Rwandan Patriotic Front led by Paul Kagame who rules Rwanda from the base of a narrow 13 per cent Tutsi minority.

But there are major differences. Slick-suited Rwanda feels like a fledgling dictatorship haunted by its terrible ghosts. It is relatively stable and crime-free as Kagame is bent on rebuilding his country to erase its troubled history. He dreams of a tidy tropical Manhattan based on the internet, trade and banking, and has made plastic bags, bare feet and begging illegal. Sanitation is properly revered. Environmental workshops exhort the need for Open Defecation Free Communities (ODFCs) or failing that Emergency Defecation Areas (EDAs). Thatched African houses (could harbour rats) and slum communities (could harbour almost anything) are ruthlessly cleared for the glossy glass towers of real estate. This is a place where the creases on uniforms are razor-sharp, the ubiquitous portraits of the steel-spectacled president might just conceal a microphone and every dusk the streets bristle with armed soldiers for the 'evening patrol'. In one small town I was woken in the middle of the night by the tramp of yomping soldiers, singing and yodelling the high-pitched ululations usually heard at African funerals. It was the regular 'police exercise' letting us know who was in charge. In a country where most of the surviving population over the age of thirty had either acquiesced in the genocide or been perpetrators, the resolve to create a very clean slate is profoundly understandable and the reconciliation has been admirable. But it's not all benign. The boss of a colleague of ours was found by the roadside minus his head.

Hutu-ruled Burundi is anarchic compared with Rwanda, politically volatile and with a high level of crime, and its capital Bujumbura is a tense city. In 2010 the then current incumbent, President Nkurunziza, won an election in which the opposition refused to take part due to alleged vote rigging. Many Tutsis moved out to the hills around the city. Following a failed coup against Nkurunziza in 2015, more than 400 people have been killed and 260,000 have fled the country. When I worked on water projects in Burundi in 2011, the opposition leader Rwasa was said to be in Congo mustering forces. North of the city there were major raids on police posts and to the south an island in Lake Tanganyika was held by the Congolese as a possible stepping stone to Rumonge, whence they could advance close enough to mortar the capital.

In those circumstances, simply gauging how safe it was to make a site visit was beset by mixed messages and counter-rumours. The government said the only problem in the countryside was petty crime. The Hutu said the Tutsis were terrorising the hills. The Tutsi said violence was by Hutu government forces raiding the countryside. Britain's Foreign and Commonwealth Office, famous for its caution, insisted that there was 'extreme risk'. We were referred to EU's 'man in Burundi', a former legionnaire named Colonel Dreyfus with shaved head, broad shoulders and a hand grenade as a paperweight on his desk. He waved aside the rumours and pronounced it 'safe as Surrey'. Despite this, the local governor offered to accompany us with an armed escort. The next morning he was nowhere to be seen. Finally there was a phone call: 'J'arrive!', an airy Gallicism which broadly translates as 'I may be somewhere on the way. I might or might not turn up eventually.' After some hours, we set off alone.

To me all this uncertainty is made palpable by the cool tropical fog which shrouds every hill. From somewhere in the mists comes a bird's voice, a querulous four-note wail; the deep 'Bou! Bou!' of a mourning dove beats like a muffled gong in the thicket. Is it a lament or is it a warning? Every leaf and stem is beaded with water drops as if the whole cloud forest has broken out into a cold sweat. Then suddenly lurching up the track comes a vehicle of heavily armed troops. 'Bonjour! Ça va?' I ask nervously, waiting for them to shoot at me. They dismount and run past me up a mountain path swiftly vaporising into the mist. Their heads vanish first, followed finally by their boots like a nightmare war film version of the Cheshire cat. Who are they? What are they doing? Are they keeping the peace or attacking the locals? Only our guide's gesture of a finger drawn across his throat is unambivalent. On almost every night families in the hill villages are beaten up, raped and sometimes killed. When we reach our site, journalists are ahead of us taking notes. It transpires that last night an attempt was made on the life of the governor's brother, who lives locally. I felt relieved that the governor had not accompanied us, after all. We didn't hang around and were soon back in our hotel for a lunch of *salade de tomates* seated among the hibiscus. Of course no one there believed our story at all.

In the red earth of the mountainsides, thrown up over geological time by the Virunga volcanoes which loom like a vast light stopping shadow over Equatoria, is a mineral that drives all this anarchic and bloody activity. This convenient commodity sits snugly beneath your fingers each time you use a laptop or nestles beside your ear whenever you use a mobile phone. For an older generation, some of whom may be less reliant on such technology, it is also integral to hearing aids. 'Coltan' is short for 'columbite-tantalite', known industrially as tantalite. It is a dark metallic ore, which when refined becomes a heat-resistant powder holding a high electric charge. This facilitates the manufacture of compact electronic devices and has therefore become a necessity for modern communications. Coltan mining has become an indispensable and lucrative industry. Prices are around $100 per kilogramme. Between 60 per cent and 70 per cent of the world's coltan is produced in the ungoverned vacuum which is the Democratic Republic of Congo, the most dangerous country on earth. Rwanda and Burundi also produce coltan but in far smaller quantities, partly because they are tiny compared to the DRC. The DRC is two-thirds the size of Europe, while Rwanda, which lies beside it, is the size of Wales, and Burundi is even smaller. The two little landlocked states have few natural resources to exploit and their agriculture is at capacity, so they are heavily dependent on their neighbours. The DRC has no coastal outlet near its coltan-rich eastern territories, so does not export its coltan directly. Instead it is smuggled out through Rwanda and Burundi.

The relationship between Rwanda and the DRC is fraught with complications. After the 1994 genocide around 1.5 million Hutu refugees fled Rwanda into what is now the DRC, thus creating a permanent threat to Kagame's Tutsi government. The refugees included independent Hutu extremist groups known as Interhamwe, who were intent on returning to power in Rwanda. To destabilise things even further, already present in the Congo since pre-colonial times is a large Tutsi community called the Banyamulenge who regularly call upon Rwanda for support. In 1996, Rwanda invaded its huge anarchic neighbour, helping replace the decades-long dictatorship of Mobutu with the rebel leader Laurent-Désiré Kabila. In 1998, it invaded again, initiating what is known as the Second Congo War, which in its aftermath, by 2008, had killed an estimated 5.4 million people, mostly from disease and starvation. The cause of these conflicts was partly fuelled by the trade in coltan.

The rival militia groups who range unchecked through this tropical maelstrom are largely the people who extract the coltan in the DRC and whose continued existence is partly supported by the money they make from it. In the case of coltan the scale of operation will typically be small-scale mining and panning of rivers, carried out by little groups of local people. It is said that children are sometimes supervised at the point of a gun. Most Congolese coltan ends up in China, where it is processed for export to the rest of the world, thereby making it very difficult for us in the West to identify whether we are using 'conflict' material. It is, however, a fact that uncertified consumption of coltan does contribute to the terrifying instability in the heart of Africa. In our globalised world few things epitomise the unintended link between self-indulgence and slaughter more than the way in which the craze for Game Boys and the growth of mobile phones in the late 1990s led to an unprecedented boom in the price of coltan at the height of the Congo Wars.

Diamonds are for ever

In the town centre of Koidu in Sierra Leone, there is a large silk cotton tree known as the chopping tree. It acquired its name because the buttress roots made a convenient block for chopping off hands, a routine atrocity in Sierra Leone's civil war during the 1990s. Without hands you cannot vote, the victims were told. Sierra Leone is blessed with lush rainforests, a climate where everything grows, and rivers which are seamed with diamonds. So small, so valuable and so easy to smuggle, they are the symbol of love but, like coltan in the Congo, they are also the catalyst of war. Being reasonably abundant, diamonds should not be especially expensive. From the 1890s until the start of the twenty-first century the price of diamonds was kept artificially high by De Beers, the British-based South African company. From their elegant offices in Holborn they controlled all the outlets and stockpiled diamonds whenever overproduction threatened a drop in the market.

Suffering from gross inequality, corrupt government and invasion from neighbouring warlords such as Charles Taylor of

Liberia, Sierra Leone was racked by a brutal war in 1992–1998 with diamonds funding the weapons for the rival armies. This was the background to Leonardo di Caprio's film 'Blood Diamond', which aimed to waken the conscience of anyone entering a jeweler's shop. In 2000 De Beers responded by setting up a certification system known as the Kimberly Process so that the purchaser could be reassured that the diamonds on offer had been legitimately mined. This has improved matters but not entirely solved the problem, since conflict diamonds can be slipped in with a legitimate batch under cover of the Kimberly Process. However, diamond-rich countries with good governance such as Namibia and Botswana, not to mention Canada, have tightly controlled mining operations, well-used revenues and resulting economic benefits.

Bloody ivory

'Throw my legs in the boot', said Richard Leakey when I gave him a lift to the railway station. He is a large man with a red face and an absolutely hand-withering handshake. The legs in question were spare artificial ones supplied by a British hospital, where he had been sent in a critical condition to have his real ones amputated after a plane crash. Even before this dramatic turn of events, Leakey was an African legend in his own lifetime. The son of Louis and Mary Leakey, the anthropologists who discovered some of the earliest known human remains in the Olduvai Gorge and at Lake Turkana, he was actively involved in continuing the ground-breaking research of his parents.

In 1989, he became the head of the Kenya Wildlife Service (KWS) for President Daniel arap Moi and that year famously persuaded Moi to light a bonfire of ivory tusks in front of the TV cameras. The film went round the world successfully increasing awareness at least in the West that the purchase of ivory goods led directly to the poaching of elephants. However, in the early 1990s Leakey became increasingly critical of the corruption in the Moi administration and a focus for opposition to the President. His courageous stand against the government is said to have inspired John le Carre's novel *The Constant Gardener*.

In contrast to most commodities, there is, of course, no moderate way of harvesting ivory. No one needs ivory, but people have always desired it. A luxury traditionally used for billiard balls, piano keys and cutlery handles, more recently 40 per cent of Kenya's ivory has gone to the West as trinkets and curios, while 40 per cent went to Japan for *hankos*, the traditional Japanese name seals. Before 1977, when Kenya banned its internal trade in wildlife products, the tourist shops were full of ivory mementos. The elephants provided a safari experience and then you took a bit of them home. But the internal contradictions were even more profound. The first thing that Leakey found when he took over the Kenya Wildlife Service was that it relied heavily on the sale of confiscated tusks for revenue and that some park rangers supplemented their poor pay with a bit of poaching. With no vehicles, no fuel and no money, the morale in the KWS was rock-bottom. Armed with AK47s from the war zone of adjacent Somalia, the poachers were seen as invincible by a park service merely equipped with First World War Enfield rifles.

Inside a year Richard Leakey turned this dismal situation round. With his international charisma he raised funds for proper equipment and, with his inspirational style, staff morale soared. Ivory gained absolute prohibition under Appendix I of the Convention on International Trade in Endangered Species (CITES) and huge press coverage following the ivory burning underpinned the ban. President Bush banned the import of ivory into USA and Mrs Thatcher followed suit in the UK. The value of a pound of unworked ivory fell from $100 to $20. In 1990, Kenya only lost fifty-eight elephants to poaching, compared to several thousand taken annually in previous years. Leakey's reputation soared as an environmental saviour especially in the West.

Richard Leakey is the great pioneer of the ivory debate and his head-on approach made him the only person capable of taking

The conservationist Richard Leakey presides over the burning of ivory which has been confiscated from poachers in a Kenyan game reserve.

on that impossible role. But by his own admission he doesn't do unobtrusive or subtly tactful. In some ways he is like the elephants he so rightly loves. In my small experience, inside an hour he had us both thrown out of the Institute of Civil Engineers in London where we convened for a meeting – he lurching down the steps on his artificial legs, me wondering how on earth we would manage in a much more cramped café in Victoria Street without being hurled onto the street again.

Leakey had challenged a deep vein of corruption and vested interest and now his enemies were circling like vultures on the African plain. It began to look as if Richard Leakey's story was to be a classic tale of rise and fall. To rid the KWS of deadwood and corruption he sacked 1,640 employees who had seen themselves as safe for life on a civil service salary. The right-wing white Rhodesians and South Africans who still dominated the game services in Southern Africa saw him as a dangerous liberal trying to impose his policies on them. Liberal Western opinion was outraged at his strategy of shooting poachers on sight and in Kenya the Masai claimed they were losing their tribal homelands to a pampered wildlife industry. Even the elephants made matters worse by straying onto farmland and so unleashing a general chorus that they were a pest in need of culling. Most dangerous of all, when President Moi appeared at his hospital bedside offering to pray for him after his plane crash, Leakey brushed the President aside, proclaiming his own atheism – never a good idea in Africa at the best of times.

The Leakey family had close links with the Kikuyu and, as Leakey built up a fighting force of rangers, it was said that he was massing a private Kikuyu army to overturn President Moi who was from the Kalenjin tribe. Early in his career he found a note pinned to an *Acacia* tree which read 'Leakey we are going to kill you.' In 1993, when his light aircraft suddenly lost power and came down in the Kenyan bush, it was widely rumoured to have been an attempt on his life. When I asked him about this he didn't reply. If he had died that day he would surely have been canonised like an environmental version of Princess Diana. As it was, he resigned from the Wildlife Service in 1994, and in 1995 he was horsewhipped by government thugs when on the political campaign trail. His own brother, a Kenyan politician, denounced him as a traitor. After a comeback, he was sacked from his post as the head of the Civil Service in 2001. The very name Leakey, which has heroic status among Western journalists, was re-coined in the Kenyan press as a verb 'leakey-ise', meaning 'to vilify'. He became a half-forgotten icon, but neither he nor the awareness he created over ivory had gone away.

For a decade after Leakey's 1989 initiatives the elephant population in Kenya stabilised. However, with an affluent Chinese market the value of ivory has subsequently soared. The appetite for ivory is not confined to China. You can buy ivory saints without any trouble in St Peter's Square in Rome, where the Vatican has not signed up to CITES, and there is great demand for ivory crucifixes in the Catholic Philippines, where the word for ivory, *garing*, has a second meaning of: 'religious statue'. The most important strategy will be to persuade the Chinese to close down their licensed carving factories and then make ivory illegal and unacceptable across the world. Otherwise, the legal ivory provides a cover for the illegal material and it is yet another case of *What does it mean, and How do you know?* As it is, between 2000 and 2016, at least 30,000 African elephants have been killed each year for their tusks. Continued slaughter at this rate will cause their extinction within a decade.

In this crisis Richard Leakey, at the age of seventy, was called back to chair the Kenya Wildlife Service in 2015 and, with protracted negotiations for Brad Pitt to play him in Hollywood, we can be sure that the battle for the elephants is not over yet.

Death in the Delta

Being so embattled on the home front, you would imagine Leakey would lack the energy to become embroiled in further controversy in other dangerous parts of Africa. But in the spring of 1995 I had a call from Richard asking me to accompany him to Ogoni-land in Nigeria to work on environmental issues which had been highlighted by a local activist called Ken Saro-Wiwa. I knew little about Ogoniland and was only vaguely aware of Saro-Wiwa as a name that came up from time to time in the press. He was currently in jail.

Nigeria is Africa's largest (and the world's sixth largest) oil producer. The Niger Delta, where the oil is chiefly found, is a watery maze of creeks, islands and mangrove swamps and home to ten million impoverished villagers and shanty town folk. Amongst them are the Ogoni, who inhabit a small parcel of land of only 400 square miles which, ever since extraction began in the 1950s, has been increasingly polluted by oil. You can smell a badly managed oil operation before you see the rusted toppling derricks, the viscous pools of crude and the saturated earth. This results from poor maintenance, poorly controlled drilling and also from 'bunkering', whereby local people in remote areas puncture holes in the supply lines to siphon off the oil for themselves. All this typically makes farmland unusable for twenty-five to thirty years. A further problem is 'flaring' which is the process of burning off the gas that comes out of the ground with the crude and, unless removed, builds up, risking explosions in the oil well. Many flares run twenty-fiour hours a day and have been active for twenty-five years. The carbon dioxide and methane emissions have had enormous impacts on noise, habitats and communities. As a result Human Rights Watch claims that 40 per cent of the delta will be uninhabitable within thirty years.

This was the state of affairs confronted by Ken Saro-Wiwa, a native of Ogoniland, in the 1980s and 1990s. Small of stature and weak of heart, this fastidious middle aged novelist was not an obvious prototype for an eco-warrior. He made his name as author and producer of a witty TV soap opera, *Basi and Co*, about a bunch of feckless Lagos wide-boys, which took Africa by storm and was watched by an audience of 30 million. When he was appointed local minister for the Ogoni in 1968, he witnessed their conflict with the oil industry, which awakened passions that were to drive him to the bitter end of his life. In 1990, he made a speech in Lagos in which he outlined his central manifesto:

The insensitivity of the Nigerian elite has turned the delta and its environs into an ecological disaster and dehumanised its inhabitants. The notion that the oil-bearing areas can provide the revenue of the country and yet be denied a proper share of that revenue because it is perceived that the inhabitants are few in number is unjust, immoral, unnatural and ungodly. Why are they entitled to but five per cent of their resources? Why has the money not been paid as and when due? The peoples of Rivers State sit very heavy on the conscience of Nigeria. The silence of Nigeria's social reformers, writers and legal men over this issue is deafening. Therefore the affected peoples must immediately gird their loins and demand without equivocation their rightful patrimony.

Not surprisingly, after some years of campaigning in this style, in 1993 Ken Saro-Wiwa was arrested. His prison diary, which was later published as *A Month and a Day*, makes harrowing but also grimly humorous reading as he mocks his own squeamishness ('Mosquitoes make mincemeat of my beautiful body'). Wherever he was taken, driven in police vans or dumped in vile barracks, he observes the weedy gardens, the broken cars on broken roads, the filthy offices and the smell of excrement as a physical manifestation of the moral squalor of a country run by savage bullies whose orders are carried out by terrified henchmen:

I had been detained for a month and a day during which I had witnessed the efficiency of evil. In a country where virtually nothing worked, the security services, armed with all the gadgets of modern invention, made sure that all orders were carried out with military precision. And the men were marvellously faithful to their instructions.

Eventually Saro-Wiwa was released as a result of intense international pressure. Like Richard Leakey at around the same time, he was the darling of the NGOs and revered throughout Europe and America, while feared and hated by many of his own establishment at home. He was loud in his condemnation of General Babangida, known as the Prince of the Niger, who had incarcerated but then released him. Worse was to come. Four months after Saro-Wiwa's release Babangida was replaced by the terrifying General Sani Abacha, who stands out amongst the worst African leaders of the twentieth century as a monster of cruelty, corruption and greed. In 1994, Saro-Wiwa was imprisoned again, this time for much longer. In 1995, pressure mounted for his release and it was then that Richard Leakey approached me with his plan to go to Port Harcourt.

I have sometimes wondered whether Leakey's interest in Ken Saro-Wiwa was fed by a fascination with martyrdom. The European Union, rattled by the furore, asked us to help them make an environmental case for withdrawing their money from the Delta. The air tickets were bought and the arrangements made but at the last minute I could not obtain visas from the Nigerian High Commission. To this day I have never known which good angel blocked those visas and what would have happened to us if we had made the trip. On 10 November, in the same week that we were to be in the same town campaigning on his behalf, Ken Saro-Wiwa along with eight co-defendants, was taken to Port Harcourt jail in leg irons and hanged. The world reacted with stunned disbelief.

Ken Saro-Wiwa stood not only for the people of his homeland but also for all Africans fighting against injustice and for all communities whose environment is ruined in order to benefit central government and more privileged outsiders. Three years after his execution, General Abacha died of a heart attack while having sex with three women. In 2013, Shell returned to Ogoniland having previously pulled out in 1993 and, in 2015, they announced a payout of £55 million compensation to the Ogoni people. But it is estimated that it will take at least thirty years to clear up oil spills in the Delta. The pollution continues and much inequality remains.

A major agent of climate change, oil is the commodity for which few of us in the West can assume the high moral ground, since it underpins our entire lifestyle. Environmental certification scarcely applies to fuel, apart from the 'unleaded' label, which gives us a hypocritical green glow at the petrol pumps. However, having worked on oil extraction in the Middle East, I can attest that the pollution experienced in Nigeria is far from an inevitable part of the process. A properly run oil operation is reasonably clean and largely invisible, a nodding donkey behind a neat fence, with far less impact on the ground than dams or motorways let alone intensive farming. Nor is the fabled 'curse of oil' an automatic consequence of its extraction. Gross inequality and war have not arisen in relatively well-governed African countries such as Ghana and Uganda (where it is also found), not to mention Norway (where it underpins one of the world's strongest economies). Only where there is poor governance does oil add fuel to the flames. Finally a revolution in the technology, production and storage of solar energy has made it increasingly competitive with fossil fuels. Solar is now cheaper than coal and by 2030 oil and gas will be fighting for survival.

But if the story of oil and ivory is a sobering one yet worse is to come. An attack is now beginning on something even more precious than all Africa's fabulous mineral wealth: an assault on the land itself and the whole way of life it supports. Asked about nature in Africa, the average person would name the endlessly filmed and photographed National Parks such as the Serengeti. Yet Africa's ordinary extraordinary settled landscapes probably have more intrinsic biodiversity than all the continent's protected areas put together and it is they that are now coming under pressure from intensive agriculture. To understand what is at stake, I will first take you to the great grasslands of West Africa.

CHAPTER 7

Gardens of Africa

Shea nut, shambas and land grabs

When the summer rains come to the savannahs of northern Ghana they are received with so much happiness. Women gather along the road to sow their patches of maize and peanut under the trees, laughing as they work. The children shriek with excitement as they belly-flop into the river. The grey humpbacked cattle swish their tails amid the grasses which will soon be as tall as they are. Flocks of little birds swoop and chatter in the sunshine. The earth steams and all around the skeletal bush breaks into tenderest green.

At first glance, this landscape could be English parkland, the trees dotted across the rolling grassland, their lower branches trimmed to a level browse-line by the ever-nibbling cattle. But these trees are far more productive than those of any English park. They are shea nut trees with long crinkly leaves, their bark ridged and crusted like the back of a crocodile and with smooth brown nuts about the shape and size of an olive. When broken open, the nuts reveal white creamy oil which is the basis of shea butter, long used in Africa to moisten the hair and skin and now exported world-wide as a lucrative cash crop for cosmetics.

The shea nut trees are not planted but grow wild as a native part of the savannah. They are hard to transplant and slow to mature, so not easily tamed into plantations and, with so much wild abundance, there seems little point. Working in the shea nut country in northern Ghana I had to consult with a local chief. He received us seated outside among the round thatched houses of his village. We bowed as is customary and a small boy darted off from the cluster of children and puppies round his feet to fetch his ceremonial staff of office. Tall, grizzled and majestic, he was clad in a long Ghanaian smock, stripy turban and, like almost everyone else in Africa, blue flip-flops made in China. 'We do not have to sow the shea nuts. Simply harvest', he explained. 'We need no weedkiller or fertiliser. The only expenses are gloves to protect the pickers from snakes. Everyone picks. There are so many nuts that by September we are fed up with it but it is a huge export for us. The shea nuts earn us the equivalent of $25 US a sack.'

Shea butter from Africa is the exact opposite of palm oil from South East Asia, though both produce similar products, including margarine, lipstick, soap and face cream. Whereas the intensively cultivated palm plantations generally spell disaster for habitats and local communities, the shea nut groves are an example of benign agroforestry – like the Trinidad cocoa forests, an African Garden of Eden from which everyone and everything benefits, especially the landscape and the ecosystem. Alongside the shea nuts there is room for plenty of other trees, the stately domed *Parkia*, the great Savannah mahoganies, the tall silk cottons and the mighty baobab. The white-flowered *Acacia* trees seem to draw the light, standing like pale torches in the African bush. Fragrant as honeysuckle, they lure the sunbirds which swarm over the blossom like sleek iridescent mice to feast on the nectar.

All this diverse vegetation supports an abundance of wildlife. From cowpats and puddles rise dancing clouds of butterflies, yellow, velvet black and palest apple green. There are monkeys, duiker and a host of brilliantly coloured birds: bright green barbets, violet turacos and carmine bee-eaters all under the watchful gaze of a whole hierarchy of hawks and buzzards. Vermilion bishop birds

A shea nut tree in Gulu District, Uganda. The wild trees provide high- value nuts used in cosmetics .

flit fluorescently through the grasses, while hornbills like Jurassic magpies sail overhead on creaking wings.

Among the shea nut trees grow many other wild plants, which also provide benefits for people. The roots of the *Cochlospermum*, handsome shrubs with flowers like giant buttercups, stain the shea butter yellow and create those wonderful green Ghanaian robes when mixed with that most legendary of dye plants found both wild and cultivated throughout West Africa: the *Indigofera* shrub which gives us indigo. The *Parkia* trees known in Ghana as *dawa-dawa* produce a nutritious fruit beloved of children. Because the shea nut in particular is such a valuable resource, the whole ecosystem is defended by the community. The commonest threat to woodland and savannah in Africa is charcoal burning, which steadily reduces the tree cover. But the Ghanaian villagers well understand those consequences, as the chief explained: 'We quarrel with the charcoal burners so they don't dare cut around here.'

Among the shea nut trees cultivated areas produce maize, sweet potato and vegetables. In the dry season there are sea-green patches of irrigated onions gleaming among the golden grasses and a lifeline in that time of scarcity. But perhaps the greatest resource is the grass itself, silky as the finest barley you ever saw rolling away under the trees. This supports the local cattle, provides thatch for houses and as the dry season advances sustains huge herds for the nomadic pastoralists migrating south from Mali and Burkina Faso.

Shea nut trees are not confined to Ghana. They are an especially important export for Burkina Faso and grow wild throughout the savannah belt of West and Central Africa, from Senegal in the west to the Ethiopian foothills in the east. But more extraordinary is that the shea nut savannahs are only one of a whole range of African landscapes in which the interface between the wild and the domestic is wonderfully intertwined. If you look at a simplified vegetation map of Africa you will see a succession of broad stripes travelling from west to east across the continent. Immediately below the Sahara Desert is a band of dry grassland and savannah gradually getting moister as it extends south towards the equator. Further south across central Equatoria extends a band of rainforest, although it does not stretch quite as far east as the Indian Ocean due to the drier climates of Kenya and Tanzania. Even further south is more dry grassland and scattered woodland.

These natural systems relate to the way the climate becomes drier further away from the equator. They have long been settled and managed by people, but, in contrast to their equivalent in Europe and North America, they have been modified rather than obliterated. In the landscapes of the developed world the wilder areas tend to be island nature reserves in a sea of monocultural farming, either cereals or intensive grassland for sheep or cattle. Africa does have its protected forests and its famous game reserves, but around them extends what seems like a whole continent's worth of orchards, gardens and semi-cultivated bush.

Shamba landscapes

In East Africa the word 'shamba' is universally used to describe a small subsistence farm with crops and fruit trees. My father's old Swahili–English dictionary simply translates it as 'kitchen garden'. Typically there will be pawpaw, avocados and mango trees with patches of vegetables and cleared areas for millet or maize. There may also be some cash crops such as coffee, fuelwood trees, fodder plants, medicinal plants and hedges to keep out grazing animals. Everywhere the broad pattern is the same, though varying with the local regions. In the dry savannahs of Tanzania sisal is grown for ropes for cattle. All along the Indian Ocean cashew nut trees flourish. In Uganda, there are wild bananas and as many as sixty cultivated varieties. They are cooked, made into beer or simply peeled and munched, while their waste products are fed to live-stock. The canopy structure of a traditional banana grove reflects the natural multi-storey system of a tropical forest, where birds and insects flourish along with the vegetables, which are intercropped among the trees.

These productive farm gardens, found all over the continent, together with the managed bushlands into which they merge, everywhere enhance the sense of place of Africa's varied landscapes. They range from the rustling silver-green miombo woodlands of Mozambique to the highland valleys of Uganda, where the morning mist unrolls like a solid white fleece below the sunlit uplands, doubly aflame with the sunrise and the scarlet-tongued *Erythrina* trees. It is only when they are replaced by intensive agriculture that you realise their practical value and beauty. Standing in the huge irrigated wheat fields of northern Zimbabwe, I felt that I might have been in Lincolnshire.

In his book *Island Africa*, Jonathan Kingdon explains how much of Africa's wildlife has evolved to create a huge diversity of different species, but also how many are vulnerable, since they are only found in relatively localised corners of the continent. There are some eighty-five species of sunbird alone, some confined to tiny isolated areas. Alongside the smallholder farmers and pastoralists who also live off the shambas and scrublands are scores of different and individually unique species of jewel weeds, tree frogs, kingfishers, butterflies, chameleons, water shrews and a host of other creatures. I have found the scarlet flowers of *Gloriosa*, which in the West is prized as an exotic hothouse plant, happily flourishing on shambas in Tanzania as if it were bindweed on an English allotment. Africa's big-game animals are also sometimes found in these legally unprotected settled lands. Elephants regularly migrate from Burkina Faso down into Ghana along the course of the River Volta. Buffalo have always migrated across Mozambique from South Africa to the mouth of the Zambezi at Marrameo where 10,000 animals were recorded in 2008. Since the end of the war there twenty years ago, numbers of buffalo crossing the settled land between reserves have steadily increased and are largely tolerated, despite their ferocity.

The spirits of place

For me the great glory of these uncelebrated 'standard' landscapes of rural Africa is not their wilderness quality, though they often feel pretty wild, but the touching way that there always seems to be a marriage between humanity and nature. This contrasts to the absolute divorce which has so often taken place in the developed world between rural communities and the way their surrounding land is farmed. What is more, that relationship is deeply embedded in culture and spirituality. Alongside Christianity, traditional African religion which reveres local spirits inhabiting special rocks, trees, rivers, springs and animals is an absolute and universal part of rural life. One reason that we go to the Lake District is because of the cultural value of the landscape endorsed by the poetry of William Wordsworth, but the spiritual value of landscape for Africans makes Wordsworth's pantheism look mild indeed. A common practice in Uganda at the time I was born was to bury the afterbirth under the *Erythrina* tree. It was often said that the African midwives secretly continued this practice when British colonial babies were born so they would return one day. If that happened in my case it certainly worked for me and I have always had deep respect for African magic.

Here's my diary entry from that surveying trip to Mozambique, dated 17 March 2010:

Working out the best corridor for pylons we were assessing within well wooded ridges, we set off on very hot walk among granite kopjes and majestic Borassus palms. Wade a lovely cool river (hopefully too small for crocs) shaded by figs and tamarinds, their roots locked into the river rocks. More uphill walking. Midday creeps up like a migraine. Feel faint and very wobbly in the knees. Reach a family in a very remote place sitting under the shade of their circular straw roofed shelter. They give us some corn on the cob for our supper. When Valerio, our animals expert gets out his snake book to record what species they know locally, they all (including the Catholic pastor who was with them) solemnly explain that in the nearby sacred hill there is a snake which sometimes has three heads, sometimes six heads and sometimes nine heads: clearly new to science and not in the Collins Guide to African Reptiles. Carlos our leader points out that this universal animism together with the landmines is one of the greatest benefits to nature conservation in Mozambique.

Another time, in 2013, I was working on a project to assess the impact of a proposed dam on the River Volta in Ghana. Trying to preserve the pristine glossiness of his new silver Land Cruiser on treacherous tracks of sticky black mud, our driver refused to continue. The only option was to walk to the river through the steamy mosquito forest. After a long march, the cool grey Volta came in sight. Dripping with sweat we rushed towards the water but were suddenly stopped by the presence of a tremendous tree. It was shaped like the oldest craggiest oak, but mightier than any oak I had ever seen. Its lower branches propped on their elbows on the ground with some limbs like severed arms reaching towards the river. Somewhere in the immense bat-reeking canopy, which created its own permanent twilight in the blazing African afternoon, a bird gurgled. Giant cobwebs were slung from the branches, spangled by the occasional shaft of light. A rope had been carefully tied round the tree's enormous waist and there were other offerings: a tin bowl of dried blood, presumably goat, and the breast feathers of guinea fowl smeared on the great buttress roots. On a protruding knuckle of the mighty trunk lay a carefully deposited animal's tail, reduced by the omnivorous ants to a plume of ginger fur and the tiny tailbone like a flawless ivory spindle. I felt myself doubly cursed by the tree itself and by the job I do, for this forest giant was standing in the centre of the proposed reservoir. Suddenly, emanating from the heart of the sacred tree I became aware of a weird unearthly hum. I stepped back with due reverence, peering politely under the cavernous armpits of the giant's limbs. Sizzling with a steady boil

I found this sacred tree growing beside the River Volta in northern Ghana. A rope had been tied round the trunk and there were offerings of goat blood and feathers at its foot.

of indignation was a huge swarm of vociferous wild bees. I beat a hasty and unceremonious retreat.

If the reservoir we were planning is ever built, the sacred tree will vanish beneath its waters. Before this happens the local people will sacrifice cattle at each of its four corners, as the Gods must be consulted and propitiated. It is not just this particular tree, however. As you look around and get your eye in, you realise that the whole landscape is littered with standing stones, sacred groves and many other trees like this one. The archaeologists also know to look beneath them for beads and pottery dating back five centuries or more. Africa is a continent-sized Stonehenge but, what is more, the Druids are still there.

The Great African Land Grab

Africa's traditional agriculture represents one of the finest examples of integrated land use on the planet. Beautiful and productive, it is a classic landscape which supports communities, wildlife and a rich cultural heritage. But it is profoundly under threat. This threat often comes from the well intentioned, keen to make poverty history, as well as from the new investors who see Africa simply as a business opportunity. They argue that there are 20 million people in Africa who cannot afford to feed themselves. Half the planet's underexploited farmland lies in Africa. To them this unintensive agriculture represents insufficiently productive farming and backbreaking work for poor farmers, especially women. They point out that every plot and shamba subdivided by successive generations will finally dwindle to a single pawpaw tree each owned by just one individual, which will ensure an inevitable drift of people to the towns. Their solution is intensive monocultures and factory farming that could feed Africa's poor and provide a surplus to sell to the rest of our shrinking world. As these arguments are followed through, the Great African Land Grab of the twenty-first century is getting under way. I saw this for myself in Mozambique in 2010:

> As we approach the coast and draw nearer to the capital the silvery rustling miombo woodlands dwindle. Systematic logging and also mining by the Chinese has been evident even in the remotest places. The Mozambicans say the presence of land mines will never prevent the Chinese from logging. They explain that Chinese contractors arrive in Mozambique with gangs of prisoners who walk in to clear the mines, sometimes with loss of life. The bleak straight corridor of the Limpopo railway line is the worst combination of rural remoteness and urban squalor. Gone are the neat self-sufficient bush villages. Our first view of civilisation is Combumune, a railway town whose name translates as 'Oh what bad luck!' It is

the definitive dump with dust, flies, women queuing for water and rubbish everywhere. Beyond extend vast fields of maize, rice and sometimes sugarcane. In another place it is just pineapples as far as the eye can see. In a similar rail and road corridor through Manica Province to the north annual land leases for new plantations have risen from a mere 562 hectares in 2007 to a staggering 58,880 in 2009 while overall Mozambique has signed deals with foreign growers for over 20 per cent of its land.

To me the acquisition of Africa for monoculture crops would be the worst environmental disaster I could imagine. To see what this would involve in Africa, I only have to look around Cambridge where I live and travel to the edge of the city. Everywhere is a huge field of wheat. There is the occasional chemically sprayed and severed hedge. There are no flowers, no birds, and above all no people. It is totally silent except for a distant tractor driven by a contractor for the pension fund that owns the land. This arrangement is typical of the way a tiny minority of absentee businesses run much of British farmland. The process that created this alienated farmland developed over 300 years in England and may be about to be repeated over perhaps three decades in Africa.

In Britain in the seventeenth century, many wetlands were drained and commons taken over by outsiders. A largely unwritten land tenure system was ignored and 'the tragedy of the commons' whereby poor farmers were seen as doomed to ever greater poverty by their inefficient practices was invoked. In the eighteenth and early nineteenth centuries, enclosure by the rich landowners evicted commoners and carved up the farmland. In the second half of the twentieth century, a combination of economic forces and new technology finished the job by creating the intensive agribusiness monocultures we see today. At the start of that process, around 90 per cent of the population lived and worked in the countryside. Today our rural population is less than 20 per cent and very few of those are farming.

In a similar way, Africa's greatest landscapes – with all their cultural and spiritual connotations, and where extraordinary wildlife diversity and many millions of people co-exist – are likely to be dismantled. The rest of the world, which perceives African wildlife only in terms of the great game reserves, is unlikely to take much notice. Since the mid-2000s, a wave of agricultural enclosure has swept through Africa. Who are the protagonists and what are the drivers? The first thing to understand is that this has happened before both in colonial and post-colonial times. In South Africa the 1913 Natives Land Act appropriated 87 per cent of the land for the white colonists while European settlers came to own 49 per cent of the land in Southern Rhodesia (now Zimbabwe). In Sudan the massive Gezira irrigation scheme was established and remains one of the largest cotton production areas in the world. In Tanzania in the 1980s and 1990s large areas of grazing land were taken from the Masai to develop mechanised barley farming for breweries. In Kenya, 60 per cent of the tea plantations went under contract farming, whereby growers were increasingly controlled by outside companies.

But the scale of agricultural development over the past decade is unprecedented. The World Bank estimates that in the two-year period of 2008–09 foreign nations and corporations purchased almost 80 million hectares of land – approximately the area of Pakistan. Reports of people being dispossessed for modern farming come from Ethiopia, Ghana, Mali, Mozambique, Tanzania and Liberia, where *one-third of the nation's land* has been sold to foreign investors. The scale of individual operations is also significant. In 2011, Oxfam reported that 20,000 people had been evicted from just one commercial plantation in Uganda.

These land grabs are often assigned to the Chinese. But although the Chinese have become a massive presence in Africa, especially in relation to mining, and they certainly do import soy, cotton, sugar, palm oil and rubber, China is largely self-sufficient in food since its own agricultural revolution in the 1980s, and farming is not its main focus in Africa. More significant players include Brazil, India and also the Gulf States, which have no farmland of their own and are in easy reach of shipping access to Africa across the Indian Ocean. But the most important protagonists in the Great African Land Grab are probably Western Europe and North America. A recent study found that Europe and North America accounted respectively for 40 per cent and 13 per cent of land acquired in Africa between 2005 and 2011, with Britain the most acquisitive of all.

What is more, the new landowners are in many cases exactly the same people who preside over the ruins of the British landscape: the banks and pension funds. After three decades, when food prices were relatively low and agriculture as an issue in the developing world was largely off the agenda, many businesses decided that there were good financial returns to be made from intensive modern farming.

Intensive large- scale monocultures are sweeping into Africa. This immense plantation of irrigated sugarcane is in Vicinity Odienné, Côte d'Ivoire.

A fast-expanding and increasingly urbanised world guarantees an ever-increasing demand for food. The price of maize and wheat which are easily grown in Africa doubled between 2003 and 2008. For the moment African land remains at least seven times cheaper than land in the developed world, while in the UK farmland prices have outperformed stock markets in recent years, creating strong returns for British farmland investments. Swift purchase of African land will almost certainly result in a very valuable asset.

But it is not just food. The destruction of so many beautiful and diverse African landscapes is also driven by European environmental policy and carried out in the name of sustainability. *Jatropha curcas* is a poisonous shrub of the spurge family. It has large floppy leaves and grows wild as a weed of dusty wastelands in Mexico. From a distance it looks like a large aberrant cabbage. This depressing plant shot to stardom in 2007, when the multinational corporation Goldman Sachs announced that it was the new wonder crop for biofuel production.

Data from the Land Matrix suggest that biofuels account for 66 per cent of the land acquired in Africa between 2000 and 2011. Along with *Jatropha* the two most popular biofuel crops in Africa are sugarcane and palm oil. Very little wildlife lives in a sugarcane plantation except for the rats and the snakes which prey on them. It is also an extremely thirsty tropical grass and so dams must be built and scarce water resources tapped. The evils of palm oil are discussed in the first chapter of this book and, with the new biofuel rush, its ubiquitous monoculture is set to wreak a similar damage to the rainforests of West and Central Africa as palm plantations have already achieved in South East Asia. All this is so that European countries can tick the boxes required to fulfil their environmental targets without making any sacrifices themselves. Even worse is the fact that this policy makes Africa more vulnerable to climate change, the very problem which it claims to address. High-input agribusiness will be far less responsive to the droughts and floods of our worsening climate than the shifting low-input cultivation or nomadic pastoralism which they replace. The Great African Land Grab is an extreme example of attempting to replace a moderate balanced system of land use with an all-consuming monoculture. As we have learned all over the world, this approach will be ultimately unsustainable.

The enthusiasm for land acquisition in Africa is partly based on two false assumptions. The first is that Africa is full of empty wilderness. If you look down at Africa from a plane window or on Google Earth, it may at first appear unpopulated but the satellite imagery does not pick up the way that the land benefits the armies of shifting cultivators or nomadic herdsmen. The second fallacy is the impression given by a typical legal land search that much African land is state owned. This ignores the unwritten customary systems which have upheld existing populations for generations but are seldom recognised as legal ownership. Traditional land tenure lies at the heart of African society and is fundamental to the power structures of communities based on the extended family.

Ironically many new African agribusiness schemes have led to abandoned farmland in Africa because they have thrown off the local people and then failed in terms of practical farming. Many projects are badly thought out as investors scramble to get in on the latest boom. *Jatropha* itself is a relatively untried crop and its mass cultivation has echoes of the notorious East African ground nut scheme in 1946, when 3 million acres were ordered to be cleared by the British Government as an instant solution to the world's chronic shortage of fats. The whole crop failed and the project was abandoned. In 2011, failed *Jatropha* plantations in Tanzania left villagers landless, jobless and in despair for the future.

Another false assumption is that the developments will create many new jobs. Typically when an investment project arrives the local people have long been making a reasonable living from farming, herding, foraging and off-farm occupations. It can be seen all over the world that intensive mechanised farming reduces jobs and the people who gain from these projects are not the local farmers. In most African farming systems, small-scale farming sustains many more people on the land than a large plantation, as well as being more productive per acre because of the intensity of cultivation. The winners are businesspeople, government officials, customary chiefs and the investors from overseas companies or the urban African middle class. The greatest loser is the landscape.

Of course, it is easy to sentimentalise the poverty of rural Africa as it is to romanticise the pre-enclosure landscapes of Europe. It has to be a good principle to improve agriculture so that basic foodstuffs such as tomatoes are no longer imported to many African countries and that African farmers can afford to buy their own tractors and fertilisers. Well-conducted schemes work with local people to improve their conditions and maintain a balance between commercial farming, and also benefits to smallholders. The heart of the problem arises when there is no follow-up and governments and private developers ignore the environmental recommendations for short-term gain so that, as with minerals, the benefits from the land bypass local people.

Africa has a way of giving us surprises, however. Between 2011 and 2015, the wave of land deals in Africa has slowed. What is more, in response to environmental concerns, governments such as Tanzania have introduced ceilings on the land areas that investors can lease. The past twenty years have seen the huge increase of a professional middle class in Africa, a boost given to democracy and transparency by the now-universal mobile phones and unprecedented economic growth in many countries. In addition, as many African women become more educated, they are having fewer children and so the population is stabilising. It could be that, after a terrible half-century following independence, Africa is emerging stronger.

But the latest challenge to Africa's traditional farmed landscapes is immense and it is not of Africa's making, nor in its power to address: the global challenge of climate change.

CHAPTER 8

Hurricanes and hydropower

Energy and climate change

At Miami Beach the aquamarine ocean nibbles at the white sand. The lifeguard stations are picked out in purple, caramel and lime like candy boxes on stilts. Their art deco inventiveness is matched by the floating meringue confections of the cruise ships on the horizon and by the city at their back. Sleek cars cruise like sharks past the neon and chrome diners. The warm wind off the sea ruffles the palms on the boulevards and the fur of a Pekinese tucked under the arm of a muscle-bound rollerblader, weaving his way down the sidewalk. There is salsa, merengue music and the music of the Falla; tabasco sauce and key lime pie. Andalusia meets the Caribbean, with the USA almost an incidental extra at the party. It is one of the world's worst accidents waiting to happen.

Viewed from the air, you can see that Miami, constructed on spits, islands and lagoons, outrivals Venice as a modern metropolis rising from the waves. Walking back from the shore, the unpaved back alleys and parking lots are nothing more than dune. This is a city built on sand. Out in the suburbs, the skyscrapers of downtown Miami and the playground of Miami Beach give way to a grid plan of one-storey bungalows, extending over mile upon mile of dead-level reclaimed coast. At the back of the beach there is no proper sea wall, not even one as high as your knee. Along the coast at Palm Beach, Donald Trump's palatial Mar-a-Lago club sits right on the beach, exposed to all the storms and rising seas that climate change can throw at it. If you continue flying south-east, the turquoise Caribbean extends below you, the almost unnatural travel-brochure blue indicating an immense outlying rock platform, only just submerged by a shallow sea, from which emerge the scattered islands of the Bahamas. Here in 1492 Christopher Columbus made his first footfall in the New World. Native Indians came out to his boat offering parrots and skeins of cotton, though what Columbus was after was pepper.

Columbus's landfall was not just an accident of history. It was also one of geology. The eastern edge of the Bahamas platform extends so far and drops away so steeply into the Atlantic that it was first thought to be the remains of a volcano. In fact it is made entirely of coral, the foundations of which began to grow 150 million years ago, when America and Africa faced each other across a narrow shallow strait. Infinitely slowly the continents eased apart and equally patiently the coral polyps kept up. The reefs, which now project into the ocean cresting a 4-kilometre-high coral wall, lay across Columbus' path as the first obvious obstacle to any sailor venturing westwards on the trade winds. Now the accelerating collision between historic and geological timescales threatens to overwhelm the low-lying islands of the Bahamas altogether.

Oil originates from plankton and bacteria, which drifted slowly down to settle in the seabed and create carbon-rich ooze. In the Gulf of Mexico and the northern Caribbean, the main oil seams were laid down over a minimum period of 50 million years at the end of the Jurassic period and the start of the Cretaceous. The creation of coal, which is the compost of the Carboniferous forests, can be more precisely dated to a time span of 65 million years. We have now been burning coal on a large scale for 300 years and oil for a century. But if the discrepancy between the aeons taken to create fossil fuels and the speed of their consumption should give pause for thought, even more alarming is the sudden release of all that long-sequestered carbon. If you look at a graph showing average global carbon dioxide concentration in the atmosphere, there is a sudden jump over the past three centuries of the Industrial Revolution following a fairly constant pattern for the previous 4,000 years. In fact, the rise is so steep that scientists generally show it as a second graph. It is clear that we must do everything we can to contain this trend, and yet again a moderate approach to land use and a balanced approach to engineering have a positive part to play. This chapter looks at climate change in terms of agriculture and shows how intensive monocultures worsen its effects compared to more integrated systems, which may reduce the effects of global warming. It also shows how hydropower can be a positive benefit, provided it is not engineered wholesale and end to end through every mountain valley.

Hurricanes – and Hard Bargain

The scientific debate over climate change has shifted from *whether* change is taking place to *how* the problem will manifest itself in the future. There is consensus that the world is getting warmer and that there will be more climatic extremes, such as droughts, floods and increasingly severe storms. Hurricanes have always happened in the northern Caribbean. Indeed, Columbus seems to have weathered a small one. But in the last few years they have been getting worse. In 1999, Hurricane Floyd battered the Carolina coast and caused the mass evacuation of Miami. In the event the city escaped but the islands on the edge of the Bahamas platform were devastated. I was sent out to assess the damage.

Hard Bargain is a fishing village on Mores Island in the Bahamas. It consists of a row of salt-blistered homes, rusty oil drums and graves. They all face the sea, like the old ladies looking out from the thin shade of their tiny verandahs. There is nothing else to face. No tourists come to the remote coral sands of Hard Bargain.

This house on the island of Abaco in the Bahamas was destroyed by Hurricane Floyd in 1999. I was sent out to do the damage assessment.

It is a world which pre-dates the idea of going to the beach for fun. This sea-scoured uncompromising place, which feels like a tropical Hebrides, is as pristine and as poor as the Caribbean gets. Just across the water on the main island of New Providence is Lyford Cay, where the electric entrance gates slide open to allow a select few into the second homes of the stars. The golf course is groomed. Hibiscus is exquisitely arranged on dining tables, where a regular topic of conversation is the eyesore of the current extension to the nearby power station, supplying the island's electricity. At dusk, chilled Chardonnay is poured and candles are lit. They frame to perfection the breathtaking prospect of the opalescent ocean, melting to a shimmering horizon, beyond which lies Hard Bargain, where they have no electricity at all.

Hurricane Floyd fell upon the island of Abaco in the northern Bahamas on 14 September 1999 with winds estimated at 140 miles per hour. Like all hurricanes it had formed far out in the Atlantic as a body of air in which the atmospheric pressure is lower than that surrounding it. It moved westwards, rotating round its own centre as the falling air pressure caused wind speeds to increase beneath a spiral of cloud around 100 miles in diameter. This inexorable but steady advance is the saving grace of hurricanes, as it allows satellite monitoring to give warning for evacuation or, in a place like Abaco, a day for purchase of provisions and battening down. In the early hours of the morning, the lights went out. Families sought shelter in the pitch-dark in schools and churches, crowding up the stairs for fear of rising water. By daybreak, trees were bending in horizontal rain and a screaming wind. Pieces of flying debris lodged like arrows in walls and tree trunks. The timber jetties twisted and buckled. The big trees fell and the roofs began to come off. One house I saw had its front wall neatly removed like a doll's house, the sofa still facing the now spectacular ocean view.

In the afternoon, the wind dropped to an unnatural calm. People went out to take a look. There was even a trickle of birdsong. But this is the most dangerous moment in any hurricane. It is the eye of the storm, the vacuum which creates the terrifying tidal surges. In a couple of hours the southern wall of the storm came in from the other direction, accelerating through the gears of rising wind speed, the rain pulverised to a fine mist. Over the ocean, atmospheric pressure varies and so does the surface of the sea, which is depressed by high pressure and rises beneath low pressure. Beneath the eye of a hurricane, sea level rises to an exceptional degree. If this combines with following waves whipped up by the wind and the momentum of a gradual approach over a shallow coastal shelf, the ocean moves inland. The resulting wave is typically five feet high but may reach twenty feet or more. One old man on Abaco told me how he stood in his house holding his grandchildren as high as he could while the wave passed under his chin. His home was on a little hill. I stood on the brick rubble which was all that survived of his neighbour's beach house. Another householder told me how he had found a beached turtle floundering in the weedy slime deposited on his carpet. A gigantic wave split the island of Elbow Cay in two. In the newly created sandy strait, which was christened 'the Wrist', former residents staked out bamboo canes to mark their vanished homes, asking us with the sublime power of hope over experience whether they could be rebuilt.

In the village of Hard Bargain the water supply and twenty-five homes were destroyed. But the most terrible thing I saw on Abaco and its satellite islands was at a place called 'the Mud'. This is the settlement of the Haitian community, refugees who since the days of Papa Doc in the 1960s have been entering the Bahamas, often by open boat. Many drown. Some stay. Others are repatriated and a few achieve the ultimate goal of making it across to the United States. They are largely driven by poverty to flee their overgrazed eroded rock of an island where average annual income is £320, the infant mortality rate is one of the highest in the world and where they are hopelessly unprepared for earthquakes such as occurred in January 2010. The coral cays of Florida and the Bahamas are America's equivalent of Britain's asylum alley at the Straits of Dover. In the Bahamas, where a second generation of Haitians has been granted work permits since 1980, they do the work that many locals would despise, but they are also often the drug dealers and the prostitutes, while the fast-expanding number of illegal Haitians is seen as a threat by many other Bahamians.

The Mud consists of around 800 shacks in a partially filled-in harbour below sea level. Its residents are used to being flooded even in normal storms and, shortly before Floyd arrived, the settlement had been devastated by fire. As the hurricane hit, the Haitians fled to higher ground where refuge was offered them by the Catholic fathers but, even in the teeth of the rising storm, their path was blocked by other locals with a yellow digger anxious to prevent them squatting permanently on their land. Soon the Mud went under the sea, which filled the houses with a high tide of sewage and flotsam, including coffins from the adjacent graveyard.

As we counted the cost in the following days, those fishermen who had not lost their boats hauled in record catches, especially of lobster, which had escaped from the thousands of metal lobster traps carefully positioned around the seabed. But it was bad news for the fishermen of Hard Bargain, who, like all the fishermen of Abaco, depend on the lobster export business and would take years to recover and reset their traps.

But after the storm on Abaco nature seemed as resilient as ever. The wild sea grape trees, stripped of their leaves, began to sprout again fresh and green among the smashed buildings. Mockingbirds worked the ruins for a feast of disturbed insects. In the tumbled citrus orchards the bobwhite quails called in the long grass. Bahama parrots, the same species whose flocks, wrote Columbus, 'obscured the sun', were seen ranging over the stricken settlements for food. They have long evolved the sensible habit of nesting in burrows on this exposed island. Even the tiny warblers, which had somehow weathered their annual migration across the Gulf of Mexico, clung lightly to twigs of the uprooted garden shrubs. In the sea the branching corals were broken, but the reefs, which have survived so many storms, remained.

In the end nature will always survive the ravages of humanity and it will be humans who will be the victims of the natural world which they abuse. The storm of climate change, which we have unleashed upon ourselves largely through unrestrained consumption of fossil fuels but also through intensive agriculture, is now taken for granted on the school syllabus, in universities and in public life, if not by President Trump. Back in 2014, President Obama warned world leaders at the New York Climate Summit that we have now burned through two-thirds of our 'carbon budget', which is the maximum amount of greenhouse gas that can be emitted cumulatively before global temperature rises more than two degrees centigrade, which would create 'climate mayhem'. The problem with these statistics is that they always seem to affect someone else at some distant time in the future, but it took my visit to Abaco to really drive the lesson home to me. Never was there a clearer case for the central message of this book: we may nibble away at the planet, but we cannot afford to swallow the lot.

And the hurricanes have continued to grow in their intensity. In August 2005, when Hurricane Katrina hit New Orleans, hundreds of thousands of people in Louisiana, Mississippi and Alabama were displaced from their homes and there was more than $1,000 billion in damage. In a massive replay of Hurricane Floyd, the poorest communities were by far the hardest hit and 1,464 people died. In New Orleans corpses floated through the city. In 2010, Hurricane Tomas killed fourteen people in St Lucia, and in 2018, Hurricane Florence pounded the Carolinas. There will be worse to come.

City of pearls

Every age has its defining moments – and places. The desert city of Dubai, an Asian Las Vegas created by oil and shopping on the shores of the Persian Gulf, must surely sum up the aspirations and the perils of our dawning millennium. It is a developer's dream and for many tourists the ultimate luxury destination. But, for killjoy environmentalists like me, it has the irresistible fascination which a doctor sometimes finds in a really sick patient.

Backed by the great solitude of the Empty Quarter and, now that its oil is almost exhausted, underpinned by no local natural resources whatsoever except for the occasional date and some fast-dwindling fish stocks, Dubai's cloud-capped postmodern palaces rise like a baseless mirage in the milky light. Fantastic spears of reflective glass, they appear to be fashioned out of turquoise and maroon tinfoil. It is said that the tallest tower under construction will be a mile high. 'If I told you the exact height, I would then have to kill you', joked the developer with the kind of swagger which is the hallmark of this place.

Yet the Dubai dream often celebrates nature and the simple life without a hint of self- parody. Twice a day the traffic queues for two hours each way past a tower block on which images of wildlife embellish the massively printed legend: 'DISCOVER NATURE, SPACE, HARMONY, TRANQUILLITY'. Dubai's iconic Burj Al Arab hotel, which has come to symbolise the whole city and is said to be already sinking back into the sea, is modelled on the shape of a dhow. For centuries these simple sailing boats, with their crescent-shaped sails, plied the trade winds and survived attempts by the customs officials to outlaw them in favour of more easily regulated steamships. It was only the rise of the oil economy in the 1960s which created Dubai and finally destroyed the dhows' domination of Indian Ocean trade.

And then there are the gardens. If Dubai is the modern Babylon, its hotels and business parks, landscaped inside and out, must be the most expensive Gardens of Babylon the world has ever seen. One new residential area includes 'six themed communities inspired by garden living: Zen, Mediterranean, Contemporary, Cactus, Mogul and Mesoamerican'. In hotel foyers, manicured rainforests rear up over porphyry pools and polished marble floors which are highlighted with gold mosaic.

Outside the hot air hits you as if you had suddenly been thrown into a tumble dryer. Nonetheless the tropical vegetation and the pump-driven water features spill out of the buildings into this hostile environment. The sickly date palms, coated in chalky dust, look as if they were made of grey-green steel like the infrastructure upon which they depend. The hibiscus is constantly watered even in the heat of the day. Unlike its role models, Singapore and Hong Kong, Dubai has no rain, so all this water has had to be distilled from the sea through the breathtakingly expensive and totally unsustainable process of oil-powered desalination.

Christmas decorations at the indoor Snow Park in Dubai. Oil is used twice over: first to obtain the water from the sea by desalination, and then to freeze it for artificial snow.

But Dubai's most extravagant garden is the 'Snow Park' – complete with a grotto of ice sculptures. This is the largest indoor ski centre in the world, built in one of the hottest places on the planet. So high is the covered ski run that from outside it towers above the surrounding shopping malls. Inside, the men in their Arab robes and the women in their black burkas belt themselves into fleecy anoraks and set off up the foggy ski slope. Every element of this landscape depends upon oil or gas: the refrigeration, the glowing artificial yule logs, the plastic pine trees which sprout among plastic rocks, and of course the doubly unsustainable snow, which was desalinated water before it was frozen. In Dubai's latest landscapes there is no doubt about what is being worshipped. On a marble pedestal among the palm fronds of the hotel foyers or in the Snow Park, displayed on the roof of the plastic Swiss chalet, there is always centre stage a glittering new car.

On the edge of the city, where the only sounds are the waves of a warm sea and the piping of waders along the blazing sands, you can find a clue to Dubai's past and possibly to its future. Oyster shells decorate the tideline and in the shallow light-filled waters you can still dive for pearls. Before oil was discovered in 1966, pearls were the main export of the Emirates, then known as the Trucial States. In those days they were so short of fuel that they even resorted to burning date stones.

Realising that the oil would not last forever, the shrewd ruling dynasty of the Al Maktoums developed Dubai as a tax haven and as a centre for trade, banking and tourism. In the heyday of globalisation the construction boom has continued to feed on itself, and now the world's largest artificial islands, planned in the shape of palms and supporting hotels and apartments, are being built up to 17 kilometres out to sea. When you stand on the adjacent coastal construction site, the new breakwater is so huge that it disappears into the distance. You have to take a long journey round it by speedboat to establish where it is. The most ambitious is 'The World', a complex of 300 islands in the shape of the continents. The environmental assessment followed commencement of construction but many of the 'countries', still unbuilt, had already been sold. In London, new development is constrained by anticipated sea-level rise due to global warming optimistically calculated as a steady rise to one metre over the next century. In Dubai there are no such calculations and no sea defences. In 2006, the new main power station that I worked on was being planned right on the beach.

Uncertainty about the long-term stability of the construction is mirrored by unease about the economic future. 'DON'T FALL BEHIND' exhorts one anxious billboard. But the rest of the world is becoming less dependent on the Gulf States for its energy needs, and in 2016, as the price of oil dipped, expensive cars abandoned by expatriates fleeing the country rather than face debtors' prison became a familiar sight in the airport car park.

Meanwhile nature as always seizes a temporary toehold. Bee-eaters and sandgrouse flourish on the irrigated golf courses and fish have colonised the new breakwaters. Despite the much advertised success of artificial reefs on all that imported rock, the establishment of high-quality coral habitat seems unlikely. Coral polyps need a cool, nutrient-poor sea. The constant dredging for construction, high level of nutrients draining from the big city despite effective sewage works, and the warmer water resulting from developments, especially power stations, may prevent many corals from flourishing.

It is a matter of debate whether rising seas or falling profits will be the first to melt those desalinated Arabian snows and destabilise this pre-eminent symbol of unsustainable lifestyle. In 1975, I snorkelled over the remains of a submerged classical city in southern Turkey. The tentacles of sea anemones wafted among the fluted columns and crabs slipped between the lips of a marble gorgon's head. Give it time and one day divers may also search again for oysters among the ruined shopping malls of Dubai and swim through the 'Lost City Residential Development' and the atrium of the 'Atlantis Hotel'.

Trouble in Eden

Not only rising seas but also the tides of war. Our dependence on petroleum fuel is so great that we have increasingly fought over its production and consumption, especially in the countries where there are major oil reserves. The most graphic symbol of the connection between oil and climate change was the sight of the skies of Kuwait alight with the flames of over 600 oil wells ignited by retreating Iraqi forces in 1991. Since then the murderous Islamic State ISIS captured eleven oilfields in Iraq and Syria in 2014, the oil from which has probably been smuggled out to all of us in the international market through the Turkish port at Ceyhan. Recent conflicts in which oil has been a key factor include Russian military intervention in Ukraine, since Russia's interest in Ukraine is partly as a corridor for its oil and gas exports. Other modern oil wars have been the Iran–Iraq War of 1980–88, the Gulf War of 1990–991 and the Iraq War of 2003–11.

Saddam Hussein's invasion of Kuwait in 1990 was motivated by his desire to seize Kuwait's oil and, although the USA and UK based their rationale for the subsequent Iraq War on the believed presence of weapons of mass destruction, oil was surely the ultimate prize. It certainly seemed like that to me in 2012, when I found myself working for Shell on the Majnoon oilfield, an oil reserve which, while being only the sixth largest in the Euphrates delta of southern Iraq, completely dwarfs all the supplies ever known from Britain's North Sea, with estimated recoverable reserves of 13 billion barrels.

It was there that I found out that the Garden of Eden actually exists. It is marked on the map near Qurna in southern Iraq. Pointed out as the site of Paradise, it consists of a visitors' car park with a dying date palm. But as my Iraqi friends point out it is now truly a Paradise Lost. To the east beneath the white-hot heavens there extends the border between Iran and Iraq imposed on the Euphrates delta by the British in 1928, an obstacle to the holistic management of the marshes and a field of battle ever since. The Iran–Iraq wars of 1980–88 smothered this place with 20cm depth of shrapnel. As a result no metal detector can discern the landmines beneath these rusting fields. As their detonators corrode, the anti-personnel mines and the even more terrifying anti-tank mines go off with a stomach-churning crump in the stillness of no man's land.

With major reduction of the original water body, the local climate has deteriorated. Where once there was a natural wetland, there is instead a steel desert and a sky of lead. Mixed with the metal crust are the bones of some of the 500,000 soldiers killed in the war, including 100,000 untrained young Iranians who, as the 'human wave' threw themselves over the border equipped only with plastic keys, their personal passports to Paradise supplied by the Ayatollah as a reward for martyrdom. This place is now a haven for wildlife but never visited by men except by the occasional scavenger for scrap copper. As the Roman historian Tacitus wrote of another battlefield, 'They create a desert and they call it peace.'

Half a century ago this was a real paradise of reed and water where the Marsh Arabs still used reed to construct cavernous buildings unchanged since the days of the Old Testament. In the 1950s the travel writer Wilfred Thesiger elevated their timeless poverty to a celebration of the simple life. To Thesiger the marshes were his ideal Eden, unspoiled by the comforts of modern civilisation which he held in contempt. In the same decade, British engineers proposed diverting the Euphrates to exploit some of the 'wasted' marsh waters for irrigation and relieve what they saw as naked destitution.

In 1991, the Shia Marsh Arabs rose in revolt against Saddam Hussein. They were brutally repressed and thousands fled to Iran. Saddam set about completing the British drainage plans. He was helped by the fact that the headwaters of the Euphrates had already been partially siphoned off by the Turkish Atatürk dam, which the allies had considered further diverting in the First Gulf War to starve Saddam out. Now ongoing irrigation within Iraq continues to deplete the waters of the delta, beneath which lie the ultimate prize of war: oilfields unrivalled in the world for their immense size and the quality of their hydrocarbon. With the US invasion of 2003, the Marsh Arabs began to return. So confident was the coalition of the outbreak of peace that in the wake of the troops the British Department for International Development (DFID) brought in a team of tourism experts who, with plenty of blue and white paint, proceeded to brighten up Basra as a hotel destination.

The Marsh Arabs would provide the latest tourist attraction for jaded Western palates. But increasing anarchy was soon to dispel any dreams of a holiday paradise.

In the early spring of 2006 I found myself a guest of the Prince of Wales at St James's Palace, attending a reception for leaders of the Marsh Arab community. The invitation requested 'lounge suit or tribal dress'. In fact a third category was in evidence: the leathered and well-armed bodyguards of the tribal chiefs. I spoke to a minister from the Interim Iraq Government, a tall man with stubble and tired eyes. He was hobbling on crutches. I didn't dare ask whether it was an assassination attempt. We talked about the delta, where revenge killings were rife, unemployment was chronic and only the youngest and oldest survived, as a whole generation had been wiped out in the wars. 'As for the Marsh Arabs', said the minister, 'whatever the West wants to think, they do not live in an enchanted garden. All they really want are cars and satellite dishes like the rest of us.' Following the bombing of the Samarra Shrine, Iraq was descending into civil war and in Baghdad there was not enough water even to fight the fires. 'Wish us luck', said the minister's wife as her husband limped past the palace sentries into the gathering dusk. 'We will need it.'

But the minister's worldly predictions were to prove not entirely true. The Majnoon oilfield on which I worked is partly dried reed bed full of the ordnance of war, but also includes the Hawizeh Nature Reserve, the surviving core of the old Mesopotamian Marshes. In 2002–06, these were reflooded with spectacular ecological results. This was not the project of some worthy NGO or well-meaning international environmentalist. The restoration was carried out by the locals and the Marsh Arabs themselves, people who would be entirely baffled by Western questions about the cultural and ecological value of their famous homeland but who set about with a will to break the banks and bring back the fish, reeds and water buffalo on which they had always depended. Since then, Shell began oil extraction at Majnoon in 2013 but has

Marsh Arabs at al-Hawizeh on the Iraq–Iran border in 2001. Their survival has been threatened by upstream dams, massive drainage works and war.

been very careful to preserve the wetlands and protect the interests of the local communities.

In 2009 the reflooding received a major setback when the Iranians constructed a high bank along their border, thereby cutting off a lot of water to the centre of the delta. So it was with little optimism that we set about our survey of the marshes in the summer of 2012. What we found there, however, were large traditional communities still living on wild fish and water buffalo and still using reed for buildings whose design was recognisable from the clay tablets of Nineveh. Cynics may say that this is because they have no other options, but we definitely did not discover a stampede for Baghdad. On the green reflooded marshes which had once seemed burned and dried beyond recovery we found flocks of duck, pelican and sacred ibis, while in the scrub and shrapnel of the dried reed beds there were foxes, hares, hedgehogs and, along with the obligatory serpent, our camera traps even photographed a wolf, thought extinct here for generations. The Garden of Eden was not dead yet. But its powers of recovery continue to be tested. In 2018, the Turkish government filled the giant Ilisu Dam on the River Tigris just north of the Iraqi border. The consequence was an unprecedented drop in downstream water levels in the delta made worse by drought and salinity.

Farming fuels the flames of climate change

Global warming is affected profoundly by one of the central preoccupations of this book: agriculture. Intensive monocultures are a major part of the problem but many forms of farming can also be part of the solution. Farming influences climate change by directly emitting greenhouse gases, notably through the diesel required to drive its machinery, through the methane naturally produced in the dung and urine of cattle and sheep and also by the use of fertiliser. Synthetic nitrogen fertiliser uses fossil energy in its production and then also releases nitrous oxide, which has become the third most important greenhouse gas after carbon dioxide and methane. This has a global warming potential almost 300 times greater than the equal mass of carbon dioxide and also contributes to stratospheric ozone depletion. Another problem linked to agricultural exports is 'food miles', the energy cost of trucks and planes used to transport food to the shop or imported fertiliser to the farmer's field. Out of season fruit, however virtuously organic, carries an extra premium in such environmental costs.

Perhaps the most important way in which agriculture worsens global warming is land use change, which it is estimated produced a seventh of the world's total carbon dioxide emissions in 2017. Felling and burning rainforest for palm oil, as we saw in Indonesia, is doubly damaging. The intact forests absorb carbon dioxide through their leaves, storing it in their woody structure and the soils in which they grow, and are thus 'carbon sinks'. The forests' destruction by fire not only releases huge quantities of carbon dioxide into the atmosphere, but also stops them from actively removing carbon dioxide from the air. In this way forest clearance for agriculture massively accelerates climate change.

Peatlands are also carbon sinks and so the destruction of peat swamp forests in Sumatra for palm oil and other crops is especially bad for global warming, since both the trees and the peat are all storing carbon. In the Cambridgeshire Fens most peatlands were drained long ago but they are still being farmed, and even in that small corner of England the cultivated peat emits carbon dioxide into the atmosphere equivalent to 0.3 per cent of the UK's annual industrial emissions, or that of a small city.

So what are we to do about it? The setting aside of 10 per cent of the land for wildlife on standard monocultures, as we saw in the Indonesian palm oil estates or the English cereal farms, automatically preserves at least some important areas as carbon sinks. Even better, where it can be achieved, is the agroforestry such as the shea nut groves of West Africa, or the chocolate forests of Trinidad where the cocoa farmers make a living beneath the trees while the carbon remains locked up in their surrounding forest.

Eliminating all synthetic nitrogen fertiliser in agriculture worldwide isn't exactly an option and would mean that we would have less land to spare for habitat corridors or nature reserves. But we could certainly use less fertiliser and use it more efficiently. The fertiliser industry has been working on reducing emissions during the manufacture of nitrogen fertiliser and farmers can now adjust fertiliser applications according to the need of the crop. They can also be more efficient at the farm scale through the use of cover crops to capture soil nitrogen and use variable-rate fertiliser applications, resulting in higher yields. Carbon dioxide emissions are also reduced by zero till, which avoids opening the soil up by heavy ploughing. This reduced soil disturbance also encourages earthworms and soil fungi, which in turn improve soil structure and the capacity of the soil to absorb water during heavy rainfall. Eating less meat would also help, since feeding animals swallows huge amounts of land to grow food for them.

There is one popular strategy relating to agriculture and climate change that I do not support in all cases. Cultivating new crops for biofuel at first seemed an elegant solution since the plants absorb carbon dioxide as they grow, thereby remaining carbon neutral and can then be used to fuel cars or run power stations instead of fossil fuels. However, in no time this bright idea has become entangled with unintended consequences. As worthy environmental grants quickly became available, the protagonists of agribusiness and the sellers of fertiliser saw their chance to profit from yet another intensive monoculture. Indeed, for a period of years the over-production of cereals in America was disguised by marketing them as biofuels. We have seen how the rush to cash in on biofuels by rich investors prompted the Great African Land Grab, whereby habitats and communities are being systematically cleared to benefit investors from overseas. As the thirsty plantations of sugarcane worsen climate change in Africa, the first victims will be the local people if they haven't already been thrown off their land to make way for the plantations.

But we need look no further than the lush fields of England to see the negative consequences of a classic biofuel crop, maize. Known to many as corn on the cob, this giant grass was the most important crop in the New World when Columbus arrived, and he took seed back to Spain with him. It was the key staple of the Maya people who worshipped a maize god and had many ceremonies connected with its growing and harvesting. Some archaeologists believe that soil degradation and prolonged drought resulting from too much forest clearance for their maize monoculture may have contributed to the sudden and still mysterious collapse of the Mayan civilisation in the ninth century. In recent years plant breeders have made significant improvements to maize and it has become one of the most rapidly expanding crops in the UK, trebling in acreage between 1990 and 2000. You can see it everywhere blocking off the views from footpaths and with its widely spaced stalks leaving large areas of soil exposed to erosion throughout the growing season. But the worst thing about maize is its late November harvesting season, which leaves the cleared fields exposed to the winter rain until a new crop is sown in April. The resulting massive runoff is compounded by compaction of already wet soil at harvest and frequent ploughing by farmers up and down the hillsides rather than along the contour.

In maize growing areas the chocolate-coloured rivers of molten mud are eloquent testimony to its destructiveness at flood times. More than half of British maize is grown for animal feed but significant quantities (29,000 hectares in 2014) are grown as a biofuel for the production of biogas in anaerobic digesters. For this it receives a double grant, as a standard farm crop under the Common Agricultural Policy (CAP), and for its supposed environmental virtue as a biofuel under the Renewable Heat Incentive subsidies. To plant such a damaging crop in the name of the environment is a travesty.

Nonetheless there are some sensible biofuels, such as domestic waste. The most obvious one in the context of the English landscape is the wood that comes out of farm hedges and woodland. At the Game & Wildlife Conservation Trust's Allerton Project in Leicestershire, the dense hedges and little woodlands which also act as carbon sinks and wildlife reserves provide woodchip and logs which heat the farmhouse and offices in winter. They make up less than 10 per cent of the productive cereal farm but by careful harvesting there is always enough wood left to recover and provide more fuel for another year. In fact, many flowers and birds of English woodland depend on partial clearing, or coppicing, which was traditionally carried out on a four- to fifteen-year cycle depending on the nature of the wood.

When at school in Canterbury in the 1960s I used to cycle out to one of the Kent's largest woodlands known as the Blean. The best places in Blean Woods were the coppiced clearings. As you walked into them you were hit by the heady perfume of bluebells, kicked into an exuberant flowering by their sudden access to the light. The sun blazed on the lime- green wood spurge and the sizzling nests of wood ants. In the brambly thickets which within a few seasons succeeded this flowery prelude, the nightingales nested and sang all night. The heath fritillary butterfly, of which Britain's largest colony survived in Blean, fluttered round the open glades. This is known as the 'woodman's follower', because its caterpillars feed on a small plant called cow-wheat, which only flourishes in the sunny patches. Plant and butterfly migrate from clearing to clearing until it is time to begin the cycle again.

When the demand for hop poles evaporated and paper producers switched to recycled material, the market for coppice collapsed. The woods began to grow ever darker, the unmanaged thickets falling against each. But there are other ways of keeping the bluebells. One of the best hopes for continued coppicing is local wood-fuelled heating systems, to serve light industrial or housing estates. Large power stations would demand more timber than was available, but small units supplying all the energy needs of a 250-acre development can be neatly tailored to the supply. A biomass programme to harvest timber for energy supply is one of the sustainable aspects of the expansion of Ashford, which lies just down the road from the Blean Woods.

Another important use for fuelwood in the UK is the increasingly popular market in woodburning stoves. There was a 20 per cent rise in woodburners between 2015 and 2016 and around 175,000 are installed annually. They have been blamed for increased air pollution in London, which is a Clean Air Zone where they should not be used. But that still leaves plenty of small towns and villages which are also nearer the woodland sources, and by burning well-seasoned hardwood many of us can make a small but direct contribution to the war against climate change.

However, few things demonstrate the gulf between the developed and the developing world more profoundly than that most basic commodity of fuel wood.

Mountains of concrete

It was in the mountains of Central Asia that I realised how much we take energy for granted in the West, and that even those living in the remotest places require modern engineering technology for their energy needs.

'Mr Jeremy,' said my guide as we approached the control post at the border between Tajikistan and Afghanistan, 'put on Tajik hat and PLEASE TRY not to talk. Then perhaps you will look like Russian Tajik.' The guards nervously fingered their Kalashnikovs and, beyond the minefields and the watchtowers, we could see the mighty River Pyanj, traditionally known as the Oxus, an iron grey waste of gravel and freezing water ten miles wide. A more formidable frontier than any army post, this river and its tributaries sink cranes, break bridges, make and unmake islands and slice back valley sides, turning settlements to barren cliffs in a single flood. As the evening light cleared, the snowy Pamirs materialised to ring the horizon. The only colour in this stony solitude was the sudden rash of scarlet from the silky wild tulips, the most intense red of any flower. I thought I had never seen nature at once more beautiful or more terrible.

In the brief and perfect Tajik spring the mountains do sum up the good life. From the distance a village seems to lie on the flank of the hills like a flock of sheep. The clay garden walls germinate a capping of turf embroidered with tiny cranesbills. Quilts and carpets dry on the line and the old men in white woven skullcaps sit among the chickens in their green yards beneath the blossom of

A boy selling wild crown imperials beside the roadside in Tajikistan. He took me up the mountain to see them the following day.

almond, apple and apricot. Then for a week or two the wild almond trees burst into flower all up the valleys like a mountain echo of the domestic orchards. Wedding veil white and icing sugar pink, the plumes of rosy smoke seem to glow with their own light against the black rocks and rise ever higher to where the ravens float down from the implacable snows.

As a gardener and botanist my greatest thrill is to find a familiar garden flower in the wild. The flower that I had always dreamed of finding was the crown imperial. There is no bloom more glamorous both for its mountain homelands in Central Asia and for its romantic history in our culture ever since it reached

Europe along the Silk Route. Shakespeare, who must have seen it as a new Renaissance marvel, describes the crown imperial in his catalogue of flowers in *The Winter's Tale*. The name he used has stuck and indeed it is like a crown: a circlet of spiky golden bells round a pineapple topknot of green leaf. Imagine my excitement to be working in springtime in Tajikistan, where they were known to occur. But where were they? There were tulips and irises aplenty, but no crown imperials. Then, returning from my final site visit, a young man stepped up to our vehicle. He was selling wild flowers by the roadside and through the window he thrust under my astonished nose a magnificent bouquet of crown imperials. I had one day before I left the country. I worked all night to finish my report and met him early next morning to hunt for the elusive flowers.

It turned out to be the toughest hike of my life. For three hours we toiled up the bare crags of a treeless leafless valley, silent except for the chink of a rock nuthatch like two stones chipping together. My boots were cut to shreds and several times I nearly went into free fall down the screes. The river dropped far below and the snow peaks drew closer. At length some familiar leaves straggled across the path. They were wild grape vines, one of the earliest plants to be domesticated in history. Alexander's men may have crowned their brows with leaves from these ones when they passed this way. Eventually we reached wild almond woods, wet below the snowline, and suddenly there they were, the stately crown imperials, lighting the dappled shade like golden torches and facing across the valley to the glacial snows.

Now, ten years later, I doubt if that extraordinary wood is still there. Even fairly recently it would have extended much further down the valley. It is clear that those flowers only survive within the protective microclimate of their woodland. Beyond the trees the blazing sunlight comes down like a knife burning off everything but stones and scree. The terrain and distance over which my guide loped so insouciantly just to sell roadside flowers tells you about his poverty and the extent of woodland clearance driven by a desperate need for fuel. In Tajikistan, as with many mountain regions, the lack of reliable electricity causes ever more relentless clearance for fuelwood which in turn destroys habitats and further worsens poverty. Winter temperatures are minus 5 degrees Celsius in the day and minus 10 at night. Many villages only have power for two hours a day and often none at all. For cooking and warmth they rely on woodburning stoves, which would be no problem if there was any wood. The desperate search for fuelwood dominates daily life. Even in the capital city you will see people trudging home past the Opera House with branches taken from plane trees in the boulevards.

Clean energy from hydropower schemes offers an obvious alternative to fuelwood, since by heaven-sent coincidence hydropower schemes are designed to exploit the falling water of steep-descending streams which occur in the fast denuding mountains where electricity is most needed. Hydropower can be a by-product of typical large dams but it can also be produced by smaller-scale engineering known as 'Run of River' systems. To understand how these work, picture a traditional watermill. This generally consists of a small dam impounding a mill-pool at the upper end of the system from which a new channel known as the 'mill leat' is dug parallel to the existing river. The water level in the leat is maintained at the same high level as the millpond until it reaches the waterwheel and adjacent mill house where it is allowed to drop back down to the original river level. The force of the water falling over this engineered cascade drives the waterwheel round and so produces the energy to grind the miller's corn. In a modern small hydropower scheme, a water pipe leading from the dam and often buried in the hillside is the equivalent of the mill leat and a powerhouse takes the place of the water wheel to generate electricity. Run-of-river hydropower schemes are generally located in mountainous districts where steep, fast-flowing streams are the most efficient for harnessing power.

The benefits of such simple systems are many. Their water is released at the bottom of each scheme to flow off downstream. They provide constant clean energy in a world where excess carbon dioxide is threatening the climates of the world, not least in the mountains where these schemes are proposed and where the glaciers are starting to melt. This energy can be exported far afield through power lines and even sold to other countries. In India, 40 per cent of households lack reliable electricity, while 60 per cent of the rural population of Nepal has no electricity at all. In Pakistan, there are constant power shortages, and Bhutan depends on hydropower exported to India as its single biggest revenue earner. In the Indian Himalayas where I worked on hydropower in 2009, as in the Pamirs of Tajikistan, people scour the hillsides for firewood to keep themselves warm. The mountain slopes, which previously supported forest, are soon entirely cleared and reduced to iron-grey wastes of gravel punctuated by occasional dust clouds as yet another landslide takes off down the valley. No wonder the alternative energy provided by hydropower schemes seems like the right solution.

The dilemma – there is always at least one – arises as so often with engineering in the *way* these projects are carried out. Many larger hydropower schemes export all their energy to the big downstream cities which finance them. This is not a problem if the scheme is done well, but on badly designed schemes, where the protagonist has no interest in the locality, the immediate stretches of river can be starved of water, which is siphoned off for many kilometers down the adjacent pipe. To make matters worse, on many schemes an 'adit' is required at regular intervals along the pipeline. This is a tunnel bored into the mountainside at right angles to the pipe in order to facilitate construction and maintenance. This in turn requires an environmentally destructive access road. Imagine a steep and otherwise unspoiled valley in the Himalayas. High up along the valley there is generally one mountain road travelling along the contour. Perversely, the pipeline almost always seems to be built into the mountainside on the opposite side of the valley. To reach it the new road has to snake down to the valley bottom, cross the river and then climb all the way up again to the adit high on the other side. This creates a massive scar down either side of the valley and hugely increases erosion. As the valley sides start to slip and slide out of control the engineers have to come back to stabilise them. As a result, the wild precipices with their nimble goats, ferns and cataracts are encased in a corset of stone, steel and concrete like some massively engineered motorway embankment and alongside the roads the new pylons march off down the valley carrying away the power.

Hydropower in the Indian Himalayas. Severe erosion of mountain slopes is caused by new roads linked to the scheme.

What this means in terms of landscape loss was brought home to me in the valley of the Dhauli Ganga, which is one of the headwaters of the Ganges in the Indian Himalayas due for development. On one side the breathtaking walls of mountain fall sheer to the river. On the other they are clothed with majestic cedars. Delicate primulas peep from the crevices and the tracks of snow leopard are occasionally seen. Apart from one winding track there is nothing to compromise the pristine quality of this place. There is an absolute stillness in the cold mineral air and high above you float the sacred peak of Nanda Devi and the great glaciers of Tibet.

To make matters worse, the new roads create access for the local people desperate for firewood and without the benefit of any electricity generated by the scheme. Thus, vegetation removal and resulting erosion creeps ever higher up the mountain. Imagine this whole process repeating itself in a relentless sequence of roads, dams and powerhouses, as not one scheme but a whole procession of them backing up along the valley. In this way the world's great mountain wildernesses are being systematically tamed. The northern side of the Himalayas has been thoroughly dammed by the Chinese and the southern side is going the same way very fast. This is hastened by partial water privatisation in India, Nepal and Pakistan, whereby each section of valley is offered to private companies who can invest in building a scheme and then sell the lucrative electricity. Not surprisingly, there is a queue for every available stretch of river. The international banks, which over the years have painfully learned a high standard of environmental responsibility, are marginalised in this stampede of private enterprise. In this way it is the *cumulative* impact of hydropower which has created the greatest crisis our mountain wildernesses have ever seen. End to end, the high valleys of the Alps, the Pyrenees, the Balkans, the Caucasus, the Andes, the Pamirs and the Himalayas are being comprehensively cemented.

Yet properly managed, run-of-river hydropower schemes surely provide an elegant way of generating energy. The first thing is to make sure that the release flows from the dams are always sufficient to maintain adequate water in the adjacent river, especially for migratory fish, while siphoning off some of the electricity for the local people seems only fair and can help reduce the pressure for fuelwood. Then there need to be controls to limit the number of schemes and assess their cumulative impact rather than picking them off one by one in terms of environmental assessment.

With the right political will, solutions to some of the most intractable energy problems can be found. Four years after our visit to the Indian Himalayas, India's Supreme Court in 2013 halted further hydro schemes on the Dhauli Ganga and its adjacent upper catchment until there is more understanding of the cumulative impacts of the engineering on the environment. So it just may be that the last and best of those high valleys will not be encased in a straitjacket of concrete. Meanwhile, where I worked in Tajikistan in 2007, the entire community, led by the local mayor, is now planting a new forest of poplar and willow which should help hold back the floods from the River Pyanj and, felled on a regular rotation, will swiftly regrow and keep them supplied with reliable fuel. That's what I call a sustainable harvest.

CHAPTER 9

Creative resolutions

Love and understanding

I began this book with the revolution in river engineering, which began my own life's journey as an environmentalist. I have described how British river engineers have learned to widen their brief and design schemes not just to reduce flood flows but to work along with nature. Instead of felling trees and concreting riverbanks, they began to plant new trees and to retain the wetland margins. As they grew more confident they used the engineering projects as an opportunity to restore adjacent wetlands and to put the bends back in long-straightened rivers. Since then I have found that these creative principles need not be confined to rivers but can be applied to all forms of engineering.

Highways and bypasses

When I started working in the British water industry, the conflicts over rivers were accelerated by a 1975 government white paper, 'Food from our own Resources', which promoted massive drainage schemes working to the single brief of increased food production. On leaving the industry in 1989 and starting work as a consultant for the UK Highways Agency, I walked straight into another battle-

Treetop protesters at the Newbury bypass, Berkshire, in 1995.

ground, a road-building controversy being accelerated by another government white paper, 'Roads for Prosperity'. Road schemes were to be pushed through regardless of the cost and with few environmental controls. Once again, both the engineers and the politicians were going for broke.

In 1995, the proposal for the building of a major new bypass for Newbury in Berkshire became the climax of a nationwide road debate as angry protesters, engineers and police clashed. What will always stay with me is the contrast between these scenes of conflict and the extraordinary tranquillity of springtime Berkshire. Wrens were scuttling among the bonfire heaps and primroses were budding beside the bulldozers as the whole landscape was being torn up by the roots. While the main agenda may have been the urgent need to redirect national transport policy, the landscape was the field of battle. The Newbury bypass was pushed through without even an environmental assessment, on the technicality that the scheme pre-dated any such requirement (the project had been on the books for years). The result was more than the government or the engineers had bargained for. Large numbers of protesters moved in and set up camp on the site. They built tree houses in the trees that were marked for felling and from these platforms emptied buckets of excrement on the construction engineers' heads. The civil unrest dominated news headlines for months and the bill just for policing the project came to £26 million. After Newbury, John Major's government called a halt to all major road-building for a period of years.

Shortly before Newbury was the equally contentious bypass scheme at Winchester, where the potential route was blocked by nature reserves, outstanding landscapes, ancient monuments and, just as uncompromising, a golf course and a Masonic Lodge. The rest of the motorway was built up to each boundary of this environmental impasse, leaving a succession of bottlenecks. However, the most interesting aspect of the Winchester bypass was not the controversial cutting, which went through an SSSI (Site of Special Scientific Interest), but the positive mitigations resulting from the scheme. The grey medieval buildings of the ancient city of Winchester stand beside green water meadows of willows and trout streams, which in turn give way to the flowery eminence of St Catherine's Hill, crowned by an Iron Age fort. This marvellous continuum had long been severed by an earlier bypass, which was to be replaced by the new motorway on the further side of the hill. As part of the project, the opportunity was taken to entirely remove the existing road. The tarmac was broken up and flower-rich turf was established both along the old route and on nearby wheat fields. Under the supervision of scientists, who mimicked the chalk grassland of the adjacent nature reserve, the downland flowers of rock rose and fairy flax were rolled out like an expensive

Wilton carpet. Now it is possible to walk out from the cathedral across the meadows and over the hill hearing nothing but the skylarks until you reach the new bypass ploughing its way through the next crest at Twyford Down. Like foresters and farmers, road engineers are now learning to restore the landscapes they have previously done so much to destroy. This principle is increasingly accepted as part of the road-building process and is often required as environmental mitigation.

To see what is arguably the most creative resolution of the conflicts between landscape and major transport infrastructure in Britain you need to visit the leafy commuter belt of Surrey. The Devil's Punch Bowl is a natural basin carved out of the Surrey Hills. The Portsmouth Road, more familiar now as the A3, has always snaked round the rim of this spectacular landmark and for much of the twentieth century it was a continuous wall of traffic severing the two halves of the common, impassable to ramblers and polluting the heathy banks. As with Winchester, the environmental protection afforded to the adjacent landscape ensured that the road could not be widened. Consequently, more often than not, the Devil's Punch Bowl was the scene of the longest traffic queue in southern England. In contrast to Winchester, where the open cutting still leaves an unhappy compromise, a 1.8km tunnel successfully passed Public Inquiry in 2005 and was opened in 2011. Once the tunnel was built, the tarmac of the old A3 was broken up, the scar of the previous road filled over with earth and the old road corridor established with natural heathland as if it had never existed. Horse riders and walkers roam free. Adders sun themselves amid the heather and the empty heath is loud once more with birdsong. On Gibbet Hill, near where Tennyson once described the breathtaking prospect across England, the silenced trucks glide through the tunnel somewhere far beneath your feet.

You came, and looked and loved the view
Long known and loved by me,

Green Sussex fading into blue
With one grey glimpse of sea.

Now, after so many years of pollution and severance, the traffic engineers themselves have banished the traffic and peace has been restored.

Creative compromises

It has taken all my working life on road and river projects to see such creative compromises achieved by teamwork between engineers and environmentalists. As it is for the engineering, so it should be for the land use. But it will be a much harder and longer job.

We have looked at the monocultures of palm oil in Indonesia, cereals in Britain, prawn farming in the Caribbean and cotton in Asia and seen that it is possible to set aside a proportion of land for nature conservation and other uses. In this way a whole set of mitigations can moderate the great plantations without seriously compromising their basic productivity. What is more, we have seen that totally intensive monocultures are ultimately self-destructive, since problems such as floods, unmanageable weeds, salinity and the finite nature of such resources as oil, water and fish stocks are part of a natural law of limitation which makes the monocultures impractical in their own terms. Just as industrialisation was condemned as alienating in the factory age of the nineteenth century, the industrialised landscape of our own times is profoundly dehumanising.

The positive way in which certification can be used as a marketing tool for sustainably produced products is encouraging. There may nonetheless be a limit to how far certification will completely solve all these problems. There are still many producers and consumers who are failing to buy into eco-labelling and there is the eternal issue of *What does it mean, and How do you know?* But we have to make a start and it is remarkable how quickly some of the certification schemes have begun to be accepted. The Forest Stewardship Council (FSC) has only existed since 1994; the Marine Stewardship Council (MSC) since 1997 and the Roundtable on Sustainable Palm Oil (RSPO) since 2004. Certification is one of the few tools we have, together with education, to overcome the current post-colonial expropriation whereby developed countries such as Britain simply push the problem further away to maintain their comfortable lifestyles by exploiting peat from the Baltic States, fish from the Indian Ocean and South Atlantic, and worst of all offset their carbon credits by ruining the landscape of Africa for biofuels.

While sympathetically modified monocultures provide one model for sustainable agriculture, agroforestry provides a second. This is our oldest model for working the land and the only one we had before technology and money blew apart the ancient symbiosis between humanity and nature. Landscapes like the cocoa forests of the Caribbean, the bamboo and rice wetlands of Bangladesh and the shea nut groves and shambas of Africa should be nurtured wherever they occur, and their products should receive the maximum benefit of certification. Even in modern Britain, such approaches as coppiced woodland and apple orchards, provided they are carefully done, seem to me to approximate to this second model of agroforestry.

Synthetic food

There is, however, another potentially revolutionary strategy, which might just remove the need to cover vast areas of the world in sterile monocultures. This would be to simply bypass farming altogether and grow food in a laboratory. Largely unobserved and unheralded, this new technology, if it really takes off, will be the greatest land use revolution in history since the dawn of agriculture in Mesopotamia in 8000 BCE. An early meat substitute developed in the UK, Quorn is made by fermenting a filamentous soil fungus in large continuously oxygenated water tanks. The market for

Quorn has steadily expanded since its launch in 1985, but as a radical alternative to farmed food there have been some questions about its impact on health, palatability and the fact that it is usually mixed with eggs or potatoes as a binder.

For decades there has also been discussion in the press about the 'frankenburger', and now artificially synthesised burgers are arriving in American and European restaurants and supermarkets. Scientists take a few cells from a chicken, cow or tuna and feed them into a bioreactor, which looks like a vat in a brewery. Once in the bioreactor, they reproduce. The exponential logic of cell division means that in a few days the vats are full. One tonne quickly

The future of burgers? These are the ingredients of the meat-simulating Beyond Burger (sunflower not included).

becomes two tonnes. A much cheaper alternative to reproducing animal cells is now developing protein from genetically engineered yeast cells, also in a factory. Plant crops, dairy products and even wine can also be synthesised in these ways. The land consumed for this basic brewing process will be equivalent to the footprint of a factory building rather than the many hundreds of square miles of agriculture. This is a huge breakthrough in terms of land use compared to traditional farming (or other novel techniques for food production, such as cultivating algae, which requires extensive open tanks so that the algae can photosynthesise the sun's energy just as grass does).

Synthetic food is not to everyone's taste, served up on a plate. But what if a sludge of synthesised cereals is simply fed to cows? They won't complain. At a stroke the square miles of oilseed rape and maize grown to feed them would become redundant. And what about synthesising palm oil, the scourge of the rainforest or cotton, the creator of saline deserts, and above all the possible opportunity of reducing world hunger? Most gratifyingly this new technology promises to dent the eternal cry of food security – that we can't do without agribusiness because, without it we would all starve to death. It is a parallel to the worldwide success – and unstoppable progress – of renewable energy as an alternative to fossil fuels.

So, what is the likely availability and timescale for this astonishing revolution? Synthetic meat is regularly licensed in the US unless it can be shown to be a health risk, and the UK government could easily follow this model. In July 2016 the Impossible Burger, based on yeast, made its debut in a New York restaurant. Developed in California's Silicon Valley, it is now sweeping across the USA, where by the summer of 2018 it was served up in over 1,300 restaurants. In August 2018, Tesco introduced the Beyond Burger to 400 of its larger outlets. These burgers are reasonably cheap, only around twice the cost of a traditional one, and surprisingly tasty. Indeed, vegetarians can find them offputtingly like meat. But if the carnivores take synthetic meat on board, there will be a big question hanging over the future of all those square miles of cereal crops grown for animal feed.

As for the wider application of novel technologies such as the synthesising of animal feed or palm oil, their timescale and impact are hard to predict. Along with the opportunities there remain huge potential problems. It is very likely that the production of artificial food (along with genetic modification) will strengthen existing trends towards industrialisation of production, which boosts large corporate profits. So we are presented with more of the same, and without careful planning and intervention the smaller sympathetic farms may be the first casualties.

In addition, this new technology may save a lot of land, but it still uses a great deal of energy. Growing food in a laboratory bypasses the basic system whereby sunlight trapped by plants provides the life system of the planet. Therefore the energy for the organic carbons and amino acids, which will be the basic source inputs for this new food, will have to come from elsewhere and a typical artificial food factory will be heavily lit night and day. If the fields of agribusiness are replaced by fields of solar panels to provide the required electricity, that would hardly be an improvement. However, there are increasingly more acceptable forms of clean energy, such as offshore wind farms, solar panels attached to roofs or recycled waste. In addition the energy involved in this process may pale into insignificance compared to that from industrialised agriculture, which includes methane from cattle and transport of food to the cities, easily resolved by siting the new food factories close to urban centres. The brave new world of synthetic food offers a very exciting gleam of hope in terms of land use.

Land sharing v land sparing

As we face a massively increased demand for food, ecologists have begun to debate ways of balancing food production and wildlife protection and have come up with two competing solutions known as 'Land sharing' and 'Land sparing.' Land sharing is the wildlife-friendly farming we have discussed which boosts habitats and species on farmland but may decrease agricultural yields. Land sparing concentrates intensive agriculture and so increases yields while setting aside undisturbed areas as major nature reserves.

On the face of it, the land sparing solution has much to recommend it. A totally organic world, using no chemicals at all, would spread resources so thinly that every last forest would have to be felled in order to feed us. So it must be a good idea to maximise crop yields within those cultivated fields of a modern monoculture that are not set aside for hedges or forest corridors. Precision agriculture, the careful use of chemicals and plant breeding all help us to grow enough food so that we can afford to retain other parts of the farmland for wildlife habitats. In addition, very large blocks of rainforest and other undisturbed habitats are likely to support more species than the relatively diluted habitat of well-managed farmland. The science of land sparing appears incontrovertible: it guarantees the maximum number of species on the planet and is effective in combating climate change.

However, the outcome depends on which variable we want to optimise. If we want to preserve the maximum number of species, we will have to create the largest wilderness reserves possible and on a finite planet the price we will have to pay for that is a far greater area of intensive monoculture. This is where the neatly measurable science collides with the more intangible values of human happiness and what exactly we want from the landscapes we live in. Like rewilding, which it in some ways resembles, land sparing does not embrace the cultural and aesthetic aspects of the landscape. It also seems to me that there does not have to be a stark choice between the two alternative blanket solutions of sparing and sharing. Many places I know have both nature reserves and sympathetically managed farmland.

Land sparing also seems politically unrealistic, especially in the developing world. I worry that, as a generally recommended model for land use, it may give the green light to all the farmers and developers who cannot wait to rush into yet more intensive monocultures while someone else will take care of the biodiversity side of things on some distant nature reserves. If so, the developers would only be too delighted to be let off the hook. The protagonists of land sparing say that the intensive agriculture they propose would have to be sustainable. But the devil is in the detail and it is not always clear how this sustainability would be defined, let alone defended. The real power over our wild places, especially in the developing world, lies in the hands of those who hold the chainsaws. Of course major nature reserves should and do exist and they seem to be especially well protected in North America (despite Donald Trump's attacks). But in the tropics I have repeatedly witnessed so-called 'protected' places being cleared for development and their wildlife poached out in the political context of indifference and corruption coming right down from the top. Even in Britain our Sites of Special Scientific Interest (SSSIs) have suffered from steady erosion over the past decades despite their statutory protection.

A sense of ownership

In political reality, where there is seldom the safety net of an all-powerful planning system or a benign government to safeguard flowers and birds against the demands of development, we have to take all the opportunities we can to protect landscapes. These opportunities are often haphazard, relatively small scale and arise out of the enthusiasms of a particular individual or group.

In 1996, I was working for the Yorkshire Water Authority to provide the environmental assessment for a major water pipeline transferring water from the River Tees to the Yorkshire Ouse. A public meeting was held with local landowners and I asked if anyone owned land in the valley where we could create new wetland as mitigation for the major engineering scheme. At first

An ancient castle is reflected in the waters of a newly restored mere. Pepper Arden Bottoms, North Yorkshire.

there was an echoing silence, but then out from the back of the throng stepped a thoughtful Yorkshire farmer called Bill Horton. The next day he took me out to see his land, which comprised a green basin of fields ringed by low hills. It was known by the magnificent name of Pepper Arden Bottoms.

Pepper Arden Bottoms didn't look promising, with barbed wire fences, intensive grazing and not a drop of water to be seen. But then Mr Horton explained his idea. Many years before, the basin had been pump-drained. The pump didn't work very well and, if we could buy him an equivalent area of farmland on the adjacent hill, then he could afford to re-flood the valley bottom and into the bargain would be delighted to look after the new wetland. As we walked across from his farmhouse and descended into the hollow below, my jaw dropped and my mouth fell open. There on the far side of the little valley, hoar-grey in the misty Yorkshire light, was a battlemented medieval castle and alone in the fields beside it stood a little fifteenth-century church.

Yorkshire Water declined to buy out Mr Horton but the Carstairs Countryside Trust stepped into the breach and raised finance for the project. Even then the grant aid bodies could not see the conservation potential of the proposal because there was not a rare bird in sight and no records from the pre-drainage days. It was only when experts from Hull University took samples of the peat deposits in the bottom of the hollow that interest grew. This was because they found continuous buried deposits of peat going back to the last interstadial of the Ice Age when mammoths and woolly rhinoceros roamed the earth. In 1999, the land was purchased and the pump turned off. Immediately, a large lake filled the entire basin and very soon the birds arrived: cranes, spoonbills, clouds of duck, hundreds of snipe and the herons and cormorants working together to corral the newly arrived fish into the shallows. Every winter a stately flock of black-tailed godwits visit from their breeding grounds in Iceland. They wade and circle around the silver mere, which reflects to perfection the mossy battlements of the ancient keep.

The enduring timescale of the landscape is what makes nature conservation so rewarding. But it never fails to amaze me how small steps can bear fruit far into the future. The English landscape garden of Stowe in Buckinghamshire, with its lakes, statues and unexpected vistas, is one of the finest designed landscapes in the world. Gradually evolved through the eighteenth century by successive dukes of Buckingham it has since been perfected by the touch of nature. Lichened temples reflect in lakes where lily pads flap lazily in a summer breeze amidst the *crrrk* of moorhens and the scent of mint and meadowsweet. But in 1921 disaster struck. The last and most decadent duke went bankrupt and the estate was parcelled up for sale. The main part was purchased by a school. But the Grand Avenue, which proceeds for a mile and a half through triumphal arches over magnificent bridges and between elegant pavilions to the palatial climax of the great house, was targeted by a local builder who intended to build a procession of bungalows on either side. In this crisis the Welsh architect Clough Williams-Ellis bought the narrow roadside strips of land to block access. The line was held. It took nearly a century for Williams-Ellis's vision of full landscape restoration to come about, but in 2011 the National Trust reacquired the last parcel of farmland that had been sold ninety years before and thus was able to reunite the grand approach that the original designers intended. Conservation is often a blind relay race in which the baton is handed on to later generations.

Love and understanding

The peregrine nesting on its lonely sea cliff is a fine sight, but what warms my heart most of all is when I see it soar out from its eyrie in a cathedral tower. The beauty of the wild bird and the magnificence of the building seem to intensify each other. There is always a need for true wilderness and there is a case for rewilding in many places. We are also beginning to learn that if we undermine nature it will be to our peril. But it is important to state what a positive joy it is to work closely with nature in the production of the commodities that we need. I believe that the marriage between humanity and nature has created some of the best places in the world. The mossed cottage trees of an orchard, the cocoa tree, spangled and crusted with ferns and orchids, and the million little village gardens of Africa with their weaver birds, chameleons and dancing butterflies, seem to have a rightness in which culture and nature are perfectly combined. This is because behind each of these landscapes stand people, people who have shaped them, who depend upon them and who also love them.

Along with the wonderful places I have travelled to during my working career, like so many of us I take great pleasure in exploring landscapes and gardens. Each time, I find myself asking a question: Is it looked after with both 'love' *and* 'understanding'? This principle can apply to anything from teashops to a garden or a nature reserve. No matter how much understanding has gone into a place, if it lacks love it will never totally succeed or take off into the first rank. I know some land agents, who genuinely love the land they manage. But only a few. Many are just in it for the money, like the pension fund managers and businesses that own so much of the modern English countryside. On the other hand, I have met countless numbers of farmers and many landowners who really do love their land. This love, which in the dry language of a report would be described as a sense of ownership, is surely the redeeming factor that may save the landscapes which can be managed in partnership with nature all over the world.

Our own dislocation between the commodities we consume and the way they are produced is a major reason for the absence of both love and understanding. In the years to come we will need both qualities. We may nibble away at the cocoa forests but we cannot afford to swallow the lot. And, as our population continues to grow and our standard of living around the planet continues to rise, we are faced with a daunting increase in the world's demand for food. Good practice and technology will help; sun, wind and waves may

Rila Monastery clings to a forested mountainside in Bulgaria.

solve the energy crisis. But we still only have one planet with finite available fresh water and limited land to farm. We face a long-term collision between our consumerist desire for endless growth and the certainty that, if nature is ignored, we will be the losers.

But for now I return to my notebook, which records a small hydropower project undertaken in 2011 in the Balkans, where such schemes have increased by 300 per cent between 2015 and 2017. However, this scheme was carefully carried out and, like so many examples in this book, demonstrates how to harness nature without destroying it.

Bulgaria diary, June 2011

Rila Holy Cloister. A fortress of God perched high in Bulgarian beech forests, built and extended over 1,000 years. A great court contains a church and belltower – a single stone bowl set high in the mightier bowl of the Balkan Mountains. I step through an arch frescoed with cherubim and hung with a crown of elk antlers from the forest. Arcades and balconies encircle an arena paved with river boulders. The smooth grey stones shaped by the foaming River Rilska, and further polished by the tread of generations, fan out and tilt beneath my feet like dolphin backs.

Each year a million visitors reach this citadel, the size of a small town, which is home to just nine monks. But the bishop, who twinkles a canny smile behind his gold-rimmed specs and patriarchal beard, wields real power, since he owns the mountain. The church possesses 70 per cent of the Rila National Park and has absolute power of veto over all development-- far more than any planner or government official and surely the envy of any National Park director from Yellowstone to the Peak District. No wonder the Park boss is a crony of His Holiness. They sit together over cakes and coffee, and I could swear that when the bishop whipped a mobile from his cassock it played the strains of monastic plainchant. What is more, he knows how to use his phone to real effect. When a colleague of mine whom he was feasting at the monastery showed concern about missing his flight home, the bishop simply rang Sofia Airport and the international flight was delayed. The power of the Orthodox Church in the Balkans should not be underestimated, despite or perhaps because of 500 years of Ottoman rule and a century of Soviet communism.

Few are keen to challenge the hydropower project the monastery proposes which I am investigating for the funding bank. Bulgaria, like all of Europe, lies under the shadow of an energy crisis. The monastery lights often flicker out. The EU insists that 20 per cent of the country's energy should be clean and sustainable. However, at the time of my visit, Bulgaria was facing the threat of dependence on Russian gas. This is not a bad scheme, although it has had its critics. Environmental activists brought a court case against the monastery demanding a proper assessment, and in a roundabout Byzantine kind of way that is now what it has received from me. Sufficient flow should now be released down the river to ensure that the trout and the black and gold dragonflies are not starved of their silvery waters. We will be using the sparkling streams but using them carefully. The pipe should be laid away from the riverside meadows which, with their wild pinks, bellflowers and gladiolus, would be the pride of any English herbaceous border. The weeds of Eastern Europe are the prized flowers of the west. I found one agricultural report disparaging this delectable flora. 'This stuff,' it complained, 'makes very poor hay though with work it will just about do for adequate silage'. The local farmers find my enthusiasm baffling and indeed my arrival from the bureaucracy of Brussels seems like a collision of worlds.

The fathers feed me with their justly famous beans and bread and put me in a simple cell with warnings that the gates are shut at night. By day the sun-baked court flutters with a congregation of house martins and echoes to the bubbling of ferny fountains brimmed from the sweetest springs in Bulgaria. At dusk the bronze Byzantine bell tolls ten o'clock and from the mountain slopes cool air slips down, replenishing the empty court like holy water in a basin. The oak and iron gates creak shut. The bolts shoot home. Cats peep like gargoyles and suddenly the darkening space is filled with screaming, whirling swifts. The perils of the night may seem shut out, but looming round our battlements, the cliffs ascend, fang-like, fantastical through beech then fir, running with wolves and bears, up to the bald hermitical peaks where imperial eagles soar.

Beyond the circle of the crags a wider world of tower blocks and airports – all of modern life – dissolves into an unimaginable dream, though only an hour's drive away. On every painted wall the monastery church proclaims apocalypse and, if our fragile cities do succumb to all the prophecies of food and water shortage, these earlier prophets will stonily outstare our glass-capped towers. Sufficient with its honey, beans and bread, Rila presents us with a challenge but also a reassuring vision of the uncertain future. If we continue our unchecked consumption, nature will overwhelm us in a return to the Dark Ages. But the monks have a lesson for our far more complex modern lives. In so many ways, we too can harvest our resources moderately and so preserve a world of use and beauty.

Next morning at their early prayers, the fathers celebrate the place they love and understand so well. The farmers are making hay in the flower-filled meadows. The first tourists arrive and pay for their tickets, while up in the cool forests the charcoal burners are busy in their little woodland clearings. The house martins are twittering and fussing round the courtyard eaves. Warm coffee steams in the modern monastic kitchen. The gates swing open and I step out into the simple sunshine of a beautiful day.

Selected sources

References are given broadly according to the order in which these sources appear in the book.

Chapter 1

E.J.H. Corner, *The Marquis: A Tale of Syonan-to* (Heinemann Asia, 1981).

R.E. Holttum, *A Revised Flora of Malaya*, Volume 1, *Orchids of Malaya* (Government Printing Office, Singapore, 1953).

John K. Corner, *My Father in His Suitcase* (Landmark Books, 2013).

C.M. Turnbull, *A History of Singapore 1918–1988* (Oxford University Press, 1977).

Alfred Russel Wallace, *The Malay Archipelago* (Macmillan, 1896).

Tony Whitten, *The Ecology of Sumatra* (Periplus, 2000).

Tony Whitten, *The Ecology of Kalimantan* (Periplus, 2012).

Neil Nightingale, *New Guinea. An Island Apart* (BBC Books, 1992).

Nigel Dudley, et al., *Bad Harvest? The Timber Trade and the Degradation of the World's Forests* (Earthscan Publications, 1995).

Roundtable on Sustainable Palm Oil (RSPO, 2015).

Chester Zoo Palm Oil Challenge www.chesterzoo.org/support-us/palm-oil; www.fsc-uk.org/en-uk/newsroom/id/307

SPOTT ESG Transparency Assessments www.sustainablepalmoil.org

Forest Stewardship Council (FSC) www.fsc-uk.org

Felicity Lawrence, *Not on the Label: What Really Goes into the Food on Your Plate* (Penguin Books, 2004).

Tony Juniper, *Rainforest. Dispatches from Earth's Most Vital Frontlines* (Profile Books, 2018).

Chapter 2

W.H. Auden, *Collected Poems* (Faber and Faber, 1976).

Adam Nicolson, *Sissinghurst: an Unfinished History* (HarperCollins, 2008).

Vita Sackville-West, *The Land* (William Heinemann, 1926).

Christopher Lloyd, *The Well-Tempered Garden* (Collins, 1970).

Joan Thirsk, *Alternative Agriculture, A History: From the Black Death to the Present Day* (OUP, 1997).

F.A. Roach, *Cultivated Fruits of Britain. Their Origin and History* (Blackwell, 1985).

James Russell, *The Naked Guide to Cider* (Tangent Books, 2012).

George Monbiot, *Feral, Rewilding the land, Sea and Human Life* (Penguin, 2014).

Philip Merricks, 'Lapwings, Farming and Environmental Stewardship' (British Wildlife, October, 2010).

Isabella Tree, *Wilding: The return of Nature to a British farm* (Picador, 2018).

Chapter 3

Catherine Caulfield, *Thorne Moors* (The Sumach Press, 1991).

Thorne and Hatfield Moors Papers, Volumes 6,7, 8 and 9 (Thorne and Hatfield Moors Conservation Forum, P.O. Box 879, Thorne, Doncaster, DN8), and at www.thmcf.org/home.html

David Miles, *The Tale of the Axe: How the Neolithic Revolution Transformed Britain* (Thames and Hudson, 2016).

Graham Harvey, *The Killing of the Countryside* (Vintage, 1998).

Jeremy Purseglove, *Taming the Flood: Rivers, Wetlands and the Centuries-Old Battle against Flooding* (William Collins, 2017).

James C. Scott, *Against the Grain: A Deep History of the Earliest States* (Yale University Press, 2017).

Emile Zola, *The Earth* (Penguin Books, 1980).

C. Stoate, A. Leake, P. Jarvis and J. Szczur, *Fields for the Future: The Allerton Project – A Winning Blueprint for Farming, Wildlife and the Environment* (Game & Wildlife Conservation Trust, Fordingbridge), and at www.gwct.org.uk/allerton/

M. Harper and M. Sly, *Hope Farm – Farming for Food, Profit and Wildlife* (RSPB, 2012), and at www.farmbusinesssurvey.co.uk/benchmarking/

Mark Cocker, *Our Place: Can We Save Britain's Wildlife Before it is Too Late?* (Jonathan Cape, 2018).

Chapter 4

John C. Kricher, *A Neotropical Companion* (Princeton University Press, 1989).

Richard ffrench, *A Guide to the Birds of Trinidad & Tobago* (C. Helm, 1991).

Sophie D. Coe and Michael D. Coe, *A True History of Chocolate* (Thames and Hudson, 1993).

B. Head, *The Food of the Gods: A Popular Account of Cocoa* (Routledge, 1903).

Anthony Trollope, *The West Indies and the Spanish Main* (1859).

Charles Clover, *The End of the Line: How Overfishing is Changing the World and What We Eat* (Ebury Press, 2004).

Marine Stewardship Council (MSC) www.msc.org

Aquaculture Stewardship Council (ASC) www.asc-aqua.org

Niaz Ahmed Khan and Sukanta Sen, *Indigenous Knowledge and Practices in Bangladesh* (Bangladesh Resource Centre for Indigenous Knowledge, Dhaka, 2000).

Jacqueline M. Piper, *Rice in South-East Asia: Cultures and Landscapes* (OUP 1993).

Polly Patulo, *Last Resorts:, The Cost of Tourism in the Caribbean* (Cassell, 1996).

J.W. Purseglove, *Tropical : Dicotyledons* (Longman, 1968).

J.W. Purseglove, *Tropical Crops:, Monocotyledons,*(Longman, 1972).

Henry Hobhouse, *Seeds of Change: Five Plants That Transformed Mankind* (Sidgwick and Jackson, 1985).

Chapter 5

T.J. Roberts, *The Birds of Pakistan* (OUP, 1991).

Fred Pearce, *The Dammed* (Bodley Head, 1992).

Peter H. Gleick, *The World's Water. The Biennial Report on Freshwater Resources,* Volume 8 (Island Press, 2014).

Tony Dorcey, *Large Dams: Learning from the Past, Looking at the Future* (IUCN and World Bank, 1997).

Rudyard Kipling, *Kim* (1901; Penguin Classics, 2012).

Ahmed Rashid, *Pakistan on the Brink* (Allen Lane, 2012).

Simon Reeve, *The New Jackals. Ramzi Yousef, Osama bin Laden and the Future of Terrorism* (André Deutsch, 1999).

Sven Beckert, *Empire of Cotton: A New History of Global Capitalism* (Penguin Books, 2014).

Chapter 6

Richard Dowden, *Africa: Altered States, Ordinary Miracles* (Portobello, 2008).

Richard Leakey, *Wildlife Wars:. My Battle to Save Kenya's Elephants* (Macmillan, 2001).

Ken Saro-Wiwa, *A Month and a Day: A Detention Diary* (Penguin Books, 1995).

Matthew Hart, *Diamond: The History of a Cold-Blooded Love Affair* (Fourth Estate, 2002).

Duncan Clarke, *Africa: The Struggle for Africa's Oil Prize* (Profile Books, 2010).

Chris Goodall, *The Switch – How solar, storage and new tech means cheap power for all* (Profile Books, 2016).

Chapter 7

Jonathan Kingdon, *Island Africa: The Evolution of Africa's Rare Animals and Plants* (William Collins, 1990).

Lorenzo Cotula, *The Great African Land Grab? Agricultural Investments and the Global Food System* (Zed Books, 2013).

Lorenzo Cotula and Thierry Berger, *Trends in Global Land Use Investment: Implications for Legal Empowerment* (IIED, 2017).

Fidelis Kaihura and Michael Stocking, *Agricultural Biodiversity in Smallholder Farms in East Africa* (United Nations University Press, 2003).

Fantu Cheru and Renu Modi, *Agricultural Development and Food Security in Africa* (Zed Books, 2013).

Robert I. Rotberg, *China into Africa: Trade, Aid and Influence* (Brookings Institution Press, 2008).

Chapter 8

Franke Heard-Bey, *From Trucial States to United Arab Emirates* (Motivate Publishing, 2004).

Al Gore, *An Inconvenient Truth: The Crisis of Global Warming* (Bloomsbury, 2007).

John R. Maiolo et al., *Facing Our Future. Hurricane Floyd and Recovery in the Coastal Plain* (Coastal Carolina Press, 2001).

Global Carbon Project www.globalcarbonproject.org

Naomi Klein, *This Changes Everything: Capitalism Versus the Climate* (Simon and Schuster, 2015).

Marc Reisner, *Cadillac Desert: The American West and its Disappearing Water* (Penguin Books, 1993).

Shripad Dharmadhikary, *Mountains of Concrete, Dam Building in the Himalayas* (International Rivers, 2008).

Chapter 9

Jeremy Purseglove, *Taming the Tarmac: Rivers, Wetlands and the Centuries-Old Battle Against Flooding* (Landscape Design, April 1999).

John Prescott, *A New Deal for Transport: Better for Everyone* (Department of Environment, Transport and the Regions, 1998).

Paul Arnold, 'Going under the Devil's Punch Bowl: The Story of the A3 Hindhead Tunnel, UK' (*Civil Engineering*, 165-4, 2012).

Gill Cassar et al., *Harnessing the Fourth Industrial Revolution for Life on Land* (World Economic Forum, January 2018).

'Would You Eat Slaughter-Free Meat?' www.bbc.com/news/world-us-canada-45865403

'The Impossible Burger' www.wired.com/story/the-impossible-burger

'High-Yield Farming Costs the Environment Less Than Previously Thought – and Could Help Spare Habitats' www.cam.ac.uk/research/news/high-yield-farming-costs-the-environment-less-than-previously-thought-and-could-help-spare-habitats

Clough Williams-Ellis, Architect Errant (Constable, 1971).

Clive Hamilton, *Growth Fetish* (Allen and Unwin, 2003).

J.E. Lovelock, *Gaia: A New Look at Life on Earth* (OUP, 1979).

Acknowledgements

This book has been gradually growing over so many years that some of the people who have helped me are now dead. The first germ of the book was a letter sent by me in November 1993 to my late godfather, Edward Thomas, the nephew of the poet, whose name he shared. I still have the copy he returned to me in which I say: 'I feel if I don't write to you straightaway about my adventures in Pakistan, they'll never get written down at all – so quickly does my memory fade and the present obliterate what seemed unforgettable only the week before'. So began a habit of recording my travels undertaken for my employer, the engineering consultancy Mott MacDonald, for whom I worked as an environmentalist between the years 1989 and 2014. By the time I retired, the raw material was all there and then began the task of turning it into a coherent book, which I would not have achieved without the skills and patience of my agent, Jessica Woollard, and my editor at Profile Books, Mark Ellingham.

I am grateful to the many individuals who gave me so much detailed information and morale-boosting support during the long journey, especially: Bill Adams, Mike and Anne Baird, Julian and Hazel Bland, Dick Beales, Peggy Bevan, Lisa Chaney, Dick Fenner, Tim Forman, William Foster, Martin Gayford, Chris Gerard, Keith Howells, Phil Jarvis, Phil Jones, Martyn Kenefick, Helen Kirk, Alastair Leake, Jo Morrison, Robert Moss, Philip Merricks, Adam Nicolson, Tom Powell, Pete Raine, Nick and Sarah Ray, Marielle Rowan, Priscilla Roxborough, John and Anne de Trafford, Graham White, Barbara Wibbelmann and Patrick Wildgust. Thanks also to Nikky Twyman (proofreading), Bill Johncocks (indexing) and Henry Iles (design).

In particular I am very grateful to Robert Macfarlane, who gave me practical and inspirational support at a time when I was considering giving up on the project, to my oldest friend Geoff Pawling, who has been a sounding board from beginning to end and above all to my partner, Sue Taylor, who has helped me in a thousand ways. All errors and omissions in the text are my responsibility and the views expressed are my own.

Photo Credits

Anne Baird (pp.11, 48); Peter C. Roworth (p.89); Andy Hay, rspb-images-com (p.103); Tim Hill (p.143); Richard Baker (p.247); Jeremy Purseglove (pp.8, 16, 23,25, 33, 37, 124, 199, 210, 229, 233).

All other photos © Getty Images: Visit Britain (p.53); Jason Hakes (p.57); Dan Kitwood/Getty Image News (p.63); Terry Whittaker/Nature Picture Library (p.67); Fox Photos (p.73); Hulton Archive (p.77); Picavet (p.83); Hulton Archive (p.94); Daniel Berehulak (p.99); Wayne Lynch/All Canada Photos (p.110); John Harper/Corbis Documentary (p.114); Judy Bellah/Lonely Planet Images (p.131); Wayne Lynch/All Canada Photos (p.133); David Cumming/Corbis Documentary (p.139); Mohammed Sawaf/AFP (p.151); Dean Conger/Corbis Documentary (p.157); Yann Arthus-Bertrand (p.162); Peeterv (p.171); Tom Stoddart/Getty Image News (p.176); Tom Stoddart/Hulton Archive (p.184); Macduff Everton/National Geographic (p.193); Eco Images (p.203); Dan Kitwood/Getty Image News (p.216); Karim Sahib/AFP (p.222); PYMCA (p.237); James P. Blair/National Geographic (p.251).

Author photo on cover: Marielle Rowan.

Index

Note: Italic *entries* are book or play titles, unless identified as poems: italic *page references* indicate illustrations.

Jeremy Purseglove was born in Uganda and grew up in Singapore, Trinidad and Kent. Working as an environmentalist in the water industry, he helped pioneer a new approach to reducing floods that also preserved the beauty of rivers. This culminated in a TV series and influential book, *Taming the Flood*, first published in 1986 and revised in 2017. In 1989 he joined an engineering consultancy, where he worked around the world with engineers to promote practical development while enhancing wetlands, forests and flower-rich meadows.